NORWEGIAN KNITTING DESIGNS— 90 YEARS LATER

A NEW LOOK AT THE CLASSIC COLLECTION OF SCANDINAVIAN MOTIFS AND PATTERNS

WENCHE ROALD
AND ANNICHEN SIBBERN BØHN

PHOTOGRAPHY: SARA JOHANNESSEN

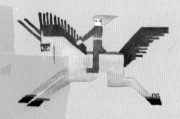

TRAFALGAR SQUARE
North Pomfret, Vermont

First published in the United States of America
in 2020 by
Trafalgar Square Books
North Pomfret, Vermont 05053

Originally published in Norwegian as *Inspirerende Norske Strikkemønstre*.

Copyright © 2019 Wenche Roald and Font Forlag
English translation © 2020 Trafalgar Square Books

ISBN: 978-1-57076-989-4
Library of Congress Control Number: 2020932883

Interior graphic design: Lilo Design | Liselotta Dick
Photography: Sara Johannessen
Paper: Arctic Volume White
Translation into English: Carol Huebscher Rhoades and Robin Orm Hansen

Printed in Hong Kong
10 9 8 7 6 5 4 3 2 1

TABLE OF CONTENTS

FOREWORD

In the 1920s, **ANNICHEN SIBBERN BØHN** carried out the enormous project of collecting knitted patterns from all over Norway. One result was her book, *Norske strikkemønstre*, first published in 1929 and translated into English as *Norwegian Knitting Designs* (1952). It has been a source of inspiration ever since. Countless garments knitted from the motifs in her book have warmed generations of children and adults. What a lovely thought!

I don't remember when I first became aware of her book, but afterward I often popped into used bookstores I happened upon, hoping to find a copy. When I did finally find one, I was thrilled. My copy is both stained and loosened from its binding, but nothing has diminished my joy at finally becoming the owner of this treasure.

Then, suddenly, I was given the opportunity to become part of this collection, a project that will breathe new life into Annichen Sibbern Bøhn's little book and bring it back into the public eye. It's almost too good to be true, and I feel blessed! Producing this book is one of the most exciting projects I've ever worked on as a designer. My challenge and my goal is to inspire a wider use of Annichen's classic. Some of the patterns here are almost identical to those in the original book—with a few small tweaks. Others are much more different, serving as examples of ways to adapt the traditional motifs and create something new. In the hope that all knitters will find something to tempt them, I've arranged a varied selection of patterns based on different yarn qualities and knitting tensions. Many designs are also shown in different color combinations to illustrate how color choice can influence a look. This book shows only some of the doors Annichen opens for us with her fine little book.

Remember, the only boundaries here are set by your imagination! Use the charts for all they're worth: combine different bands, motifs, and cable patterns. Turn them upside down, sideways, or mirror-image. Pick small or large elements from the same chart or different charts, and rearrange them in new patterns. Use sock patterns as ideas for mittens, or use a mitten pattern as an idea for socks. Take a band of patterning from a jacket design and knit it on a hat. Use the thumb chart for an adult mitten for baby mittens or egg cozies. Knit a baby blanket with the pattern from a jacket body.

Enlarge or reduce the patterns by using different yarns and needle sizes. Changing, adjusting, and developing old patterns is absolutely allowed and sometimes even necessary. This is how our knitting traditions are protected and evolve.

Early knitting patterns often had sparse directions and could be rather imprecise. Knitting was important, and many people—both men and women—were accomplished knitters. Not everyone was an expert, but they all knitted as well as they could, and generally their work was pretty good—not always perfect, but does it have to be?

Look through old photo archives, at museum collections, and in drawers and closets, and you'll soon see that many variations started with the same motifs or instructions. They could have been the result of, among other things, abbreviated directions or perhaps no directions at all; varying degrees of skill and access to materials; and, not least, creativity. Although people often had to knit to have warm clothing, I choose to believe that inspiration and the pleasure of creation were also strong motivators.

I'm both humbled and proud to have been given the opportunity to produce this book. I hope it brings happiness and insight, and is useful to many. It's important that we carry our wonderful knitting heritage into the future—and uplifting, too, to think of later generations doing the same. It warms a knitter's heart.

Best wishes for your knitting!

Wenche Roald

Et lite strikkekurs i husmortimen

1., 8. og 15. juni ved Annichen Sibbern Bøhm.

Fig. 1

Fig. 2

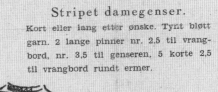

Fanakofte og lue.

Strikket av norsk husflidsgarn eller lignende. 5 korte pinner nr. 2,5.

Stripet damegenser.

Kort eller lang etter ønske. Tynt bløtt garn. 2 lange pinner nr. 2.5 til vrangbord, nr. 3,5 til genseren, 5 korte 2,5 til vrangbord rundt ermer.

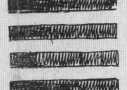

Fig. 3

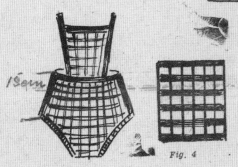

Fig. 4

Badedrakt til 5-6 år.

Tykkelse på garnet som strømpegarn, helst godt tvunnet. 2 lange pinner nr. 2,5.

Jeg skal forklare strikningen av disse forskjellige ting dere ser her. Det er greiest at dere har nøstet garnet, og at det er noenlunde som beskrevet både garnet og pinnene. Ha også blokk og blyant så dere kan notere ned for å huske.

Dere som ikke har strikket mønster før — kan legge opp på 4 korte pinner 15 m. på hver pinne og strikk rundt av det garnet — som koften og luen skal lages

av — en vrangbord på 2 cm, og så 2 cm rett — så tar vi fatt på en liten prøve her første gang. Legg også opp 31 m. på 1 rett pinne og strikk perlestrikning (1 rett og 1 vrang maske annen hver gang og neste pinne — kommer den rette over den vrange). Strikk slik 2 cm — så skal jeg forklare badedraktstrikningen.

Velkommen til første strikketime torsdag 1. juni.

Annichen Sibbern Bøhn offered knitting classes on "The Housewife's Hour" radio program, and sketches of her garments were published in the weekly Programbladet [The Program Guide].

NORSK FRA UTLANDET

CANADA: 16,84 m - 17815 kc/s og 19,58 m - 15320 kc/s. Hver dag kl. 20.20—20.40.

Søndag: La oss reise. Mandag: Uka som gikk. Tirsdag: Land og folk. Onsdag: Postkassa. Torsdag: Det utvandrede Norge. Fredag: Løst og fast. Lørdag: Med øks og plog. Lytternes ønskeprogrammer.

ENGLAND: 464, 232, 49,67, 31,01 og 25,68 m.
Hverdager kl. 12—12.15: Nyheter og Lloyds liste over norske skipsposisjoner. Søndager: Nyheter og engelskundervisning. Alle dager kl. 18.30—19 (232 m og kortbølgene): Nyheter. Søndag: «Postkassa». Mandag: Kronikk om R. C. Churchills bok «Disagreements: A Polemic on Culture in English Democracy». Tirsdag: «På kryss og tvers i Cornwall». Inntrykk fra en reise på og utenom allfarveien. Onsdag: Engelsk pr. radio. Torsdag: «Britiske institusjoner». Et arbeidskontor. Fredag: «Loven i arbeid». Rettssaken i anledning av forsøket på å nasjonalisere bankene i Australia. Lørdag: «Uka i lydbilde».

ITALIA: 11810 kc/s - 25,40 m. — 9630 kc/s - 31.15 m. Søndag og torsdag kl. 19.20—19.40.

SOVJET-SAMVELDET: 290 m, 375 m og 31,6 m. Hver dag kl. 18.45—19: Presseoversikt og nyheter. Hver dag kl. 19.30—20: Nyheter. Søndag: Foredrag om de folkedemokratiske landene. Mandag: Glimt fra Sovjet-Samveldet. Tirsdag: Program for sjøfolk. Onsdag: Ungdomsprogram og sport. Torsdag: Økonomiske kommentarer. Fredag: Foredrag om sovjet-kulturen. Lørdag: Postkasse. Kl. 21—21.15: Søndag: Konsert. Torsdag: Foredrag om Sovjet-Samveldet. Andre dager: Utenrikspolitiske kommentarer.

TSJEKKOSLOVAKIA: 6010 kc/s 49,9 m Hver dag kl. 21.45—22.

U S A: WRUL: 17755 kc/s 16,9 m og 15350 kc/s - 19,6 m.
Torsdag kl. 21.00—21.30: Postkasse. Andakt. Fredag kl. 21.00—21.15: Hilsener fra sjøfolk

NESTE UKE HØRER DE

SØNDAG 4. JUNI:
9.15 Jordbruk. 10.55 Høgmesse i Kongsberg kirke. 13.30 Gudbrandsdals Sangerforbunds stevne på Otta. 14 Fotballkåseri. Ved Finn Berstad. 14.10 Landskamp i fotball Norge—Luxembourg. 15.05—15.45 Mannskvartetten Skalden, Sandefjord. Eline Nygaard, klaver, og Alf Sjøen, fiolin. 16.15 Musikk. 16.45 Reportasje fra Båtsfjord. 17.05 Stavangerensemblet. 17.40 Norske portretter: Ragnar Vogt. Foredrag av overlege Johan Scharffenberg. 18 Folkemusikk. Myllarguten i Bergen 1850. Arne Bjørndal spelar og fortel. 18.30 Heime hos oss. — Oppdal. Ved Ola J. Rise og Inge Krokann. 19.30 Kringkastingsorkestret og Engelhardt Jarlseth, tenor. 19.50 Resultatet av den nordiske hørespillkonkurransen. 20 Kringkastingsorkestret. 20.20 Familiekveld. Program på dagen for folkeedruskap. 21.05 Filharmoniske. Dir.: Albert Wolff. 22.45 Dansemusikk på grammofon.

MANDAG 5. JUNI:
13.30 Nordisk pressekongress. 17.05 Dansk musikk og lyrikk. 18 Guden som sviktet. 18.30 Trekkspill. 18.45 Økonomisk oversikt. 19.35 Bergensensemblet. 20.10 Foredrag: India i dag. 20.30 Gammel dansemusikk. 21 Utenrikskronikk. 21.20 Schumann: Sonate a-moll for fiolin og klaver. 21.45 Foreldrenes kvarter. 22.30 Dansemusikk.

PROGRAMBLADET

REDAKTØR: EDVIN STRAND
Redaksjonssekretær: Odd Refsdal

Utgitt av
Norsk Rikskringkasting

Redaksjonens telefon: 46 38 20
Ekspedisjon: Bladcentralen Munchsgate 5, Oslo - Telefon 33 24 70 - Postgirokonto 83 80.

i Oslo tegnes abonnement gjennom Bladcentralen, ellers i landet ved poststedene. Kr. 12,50 for året, kr. 6,25 for halvåret. Postgirokonto 83 80 bør benyttes

Salgsdag: Torsdag 25. mai.

Trykt i
Fabritius Rotationstrykkeri, Oslo

*Left and right: Nostalgia Cardigan
(instructions on page 167)
Center: Waves on Waves Sweater
(instructions on page 129)*

Annichen Sibbern Bøhn regularly wrote newspaper articles on handwork, and Norwegian Knitting Designs drew much favorable comment in the press.

ANNICHEN SIBBERN BØHN

If we are to honor one woman for giving classic knitting designs a reputation of being specifically Norwegian, and for making knitting and knitted garments especially popular in Norway, that woman must be Annichen Sibbern Bøhn.

Annichen Sibbern was born in Kristiania (now Oslo) in 1905, in a family committed to Norwegian folk art and self reliance. Educated at the State School for Handcraft and Industrial Arts from 1923 to 1926, she began working at the Norwegian Handcrafts Design Office in 1928 with her cousin Else Poulsson. She also worked at the Norwegian Folk Museum. In 1931, she married Supreme Court barrister Ole Bøhn and became Annichen Sibbern Bøhn. She died in 1978, leaving three children, some undying design instructions, and the idea of knitting as an essential part of Norwegian national culture.

NORWEGIAN KNITTING DESIGNS

In 1929, she published the book most associated with her name and work: *Norske strikkemønstre* (translated into English as *Norwegian Knitting Designs*). The copy included with this book is reproduced from the first edition, which knitwear designer Wenche Roald has used as the basis for her designs. The final edition was published in 1947. The first English translation appeared in 1952.

Annichen was only 24 years old when *Norske strikkemønstre* was first published. In her introduction, she wrote that she had set herself the task of collecting and re-working a number of patterns which, in her opinion, were the prettiest and most typical for the various districts of Norway. She began photographing garments herself and collected original patterns from different districts. Annichen traveled to Selbu, Hallingdal, Telemark, and Jæren, and studied collections at The Norwegian Folk Museum and other museums.

Norwegian Knitting Designs attracted much attention in the Norwegian press and was regarded as a "a wonderful book" and "fun and instructive." *Dagbladet* [The Daily] wrote that "[h]ere we find such precise drawings that every stitch is recorded, and anyone with any feeling at all for knitting will immediately want to get underway with their own compositions," and "[a]fter today, there will be no more talk of cheap German reproductions of Selbu mittens." Today, we can see that the book contributed something completely new. No one had ever coupled knitting patterns with their geographical origin before. There were books with patterns reminiscent of those Annichen presented, including *Strikkemønstre fra Oldemors Tid* [Knitting Patterns from Great-Grandmother's Time], which included eight-pointed stars, lines of dancing men and women, and other motifs we now consider Norwegian. But these were not presented as essentially Norwegian, nor as characteristic of specific regions or representing Norwegian style or color sense.

COMPLETELY NORWEGIAN INSPIRATION

Annichen put great weight on historical and folk traditions with the patterns and wrote in her preface: "The Norwegian farm woman and her knitting have been bound faithfully together through the ages …. Our national temperament and our imaginative sense of pattern and color soon demanded their place in knitting. It has in time developed into a distinctive craft, which is worth preserving and developing further by giving it entry into a thousand homes." This understanding of Norwegian knitting has developed apace since then, but when Annichen wrote those words, knitting traditions in Norway were not particularly well-defined or well-known, compared with those of many other countries.

Annichen published the book to steer a campaign for change. This came out clearly out in a 1930 interview with her and the artist Frøydis Haavardsholm (1896-1984) in *TidensTegn* [Sign of the Times] under the headline "Art, Knitting Women, and a Mill in Drammen." The subject of the conversation was that Annichen's iconic "Eskimo" pullover had become an industrial product, mass-produced in Christensen's Trikotage Fabrik in Drammen. Annichen and Frøydis discussed wanting to promote action for the coordination of art, handcrafts, and industry. They were, however, in agreement about "how sad it was to see the ugly things women and girls knit and how poorly all their efforts were rewarded monetarily." They were, in other words, concerned about both aesthetics and economy. The plan was that artists should band together to work with yarn and patterns, and thereby produce some "tip-top modern" knitwear. That would, in turn, create income-producing work for knitting women and provide Norwegian boys and girls with handsome Norwegian-made pullovers and mittens. Annichen herself would choose the colors and design patterns for both handwork and industrial production. "All too little effort is put into pattern and color choices for machine knitting," continued Annichen in the newspaper interview. "And we must remember that it is the pattern composer who dictates the stitches and not the opposite: the artist should create life in the patterns and harmony in the colors."

In a note found after her death and now in the ownership of her family, Annichen speaks of her desire to educate the people to good taste, thus: "Here is a large area of work that lies open: we must work in good patterns and colors for machine production as well—so that good taste won't falter but be improved little by little." It goes on: "What got me to take notice of knitting was that everything we had of good, homey patterns was about to fade away. We are on the verge of losing our sense of the richness we owned in the old patterns."

Her ideas about handsome practical arts and cooperation between art and industry based on Norwegian tradition and nice colors followed the trends of the period. In other materials and techniques such as wood and tapestry, these ideas were already well-established through the *Brukskunst* (practical arts) association in Norway, the Bauhaus school internationally, and other organizations.

THE HERITAGE OF SETESDAL AND FANA

The garments from which Annichen Sibbern Bøhn collected patterns were likely knitted in the 1800s as local variants of garments and patterns that had originally been imported. Most were anonymous, everyday items without special regional or national value. There were exceptions: In Setesdal and Fana, knitted sweaters had been part of the men's traditional dress from the mid-1800s, and starting at the close of the 1800s, Selbu had developed a livelihood based on the richness of their local patterns. Annichen's wish that a "thousand homes" become familiar with these patterns became a reality. We can say then that in addition to collecting tradition, Annichen contributed to creating it. In today's interest in sweater-jackets, we see the same comprehension of pattern origin that she emphasized. Through her knitting book, she helped to give knitting a new status as both old and Norwegian, and the patterns themselves as specific to different regions, an expression of national color and pattern sense.

In *Norwegian Knitting Designs*, there's a cardigan—the "lusekofte"—from Setesdal. The other garments are mittens, hats, socks, as well as an "old handbag." Many of the patterns are straightforward bands, to be used on various garments as desired. In the presentation of the patterns and instructions, the reader is urged to use the designs in the book "as you will." That's also why the book contains so many "assorted motifs."

THE "ESKIMO" (GREENLANDER) SWEATER

Annichen Sibbern Bøhn wasn't satisfied with just collecting knitting patterns and publishing books. She wrote newspaper articles, held workshops, and gave knitting classes on the radio's "Women's Hour," publishing accompanying drawings and notes in the weekly program guide. Her ambitious goal was to strike a blow for Norwegian knitting, at the same time creating a bond between art, handcraft, and industry. She worked to connect home knitters with buyers to stimulate the practice of handknitting as a source of extra income, in addition to creating imaginative patterns herself.

When we look at handknitting, one pattern dominates alongside variations on Setesdal sweaters such as the Marius and Cortina styles. There are endless variations of the "Eskimo" (Greenlander) sweater. This is a pullover with a round yoke and a wide band of pattern around the shoulders. It often has contrasting colors and zigzags, and has nearly dominated Iceland's knitting since the 1950s. Annichen Sibbern Bøhn was the first to transform the wide bead collars—or capes—on Greenlander Inuit dress clothing into a knitting pattern. She called it the "Eskimo" and is one of several women to be regarded as an inventor of this legendary design. Circular knitting needles have been in use since the 1880s, but were rediscovered and presented as new in Norway in 1925. They quickly became popular, because they were so suited to making the pattern-knitted sportswear fashionable at the time.

Interest in Greenland was strong in Annichen's youth. The 1930 film *Eskimo* was the first Norwegian talkie. The film's heroine was Inuit, and wore traditional festive costume with a wide beadwork collar. Inspired by that beadwork, Annichen created one of knitting's most important designs. She described it in a note probably written in the fall of 1930:

"I grabbed hold of the idea and composed a sweater for us with the same motif. A typical women's pullover with the dark band around the neckline and wrists that is so flattering, and a knit shoulder section like a wide collar, but otherwise quite simple. It was exactly the garment we should have, whether for sports or another use, summer or winter, in fine or heavy yarn."

Annichen launched the "Eskimo" sweater for both hand- and machine-knitting in 1930. "Here I have joyfully seized the idea of starting a collaboration with artists, and the very first product is already on the market. It was shown to the press yesterday—a very pretty sweater or pullover with the same pattern in different colors," read the announcement as it appeared in Oslo's *Tidens Tegn* [Sign of the Times].

A WILLFUL, IMAGINATIVE, AND MANY-SIDED WOMAN

Annichen was a willful and courageous woman. As a true child of her time, she was interested not only in all things Norwegian, but also nature, sports, and life in the open. She ski-jumped at Husebybakken near Oslo as a 15-year-old, and early in life published a book that would have great consequences for knitting in Norway. World War II also had its effect on her life. Re-use and salvage became important. Annichen held courses on the subject all around the country and published the book *Gammelt til nytt* [Old to New]. Both she and her husband Ole took part in underground work. In 1944, pregnant, she fled to Sweden in a load of hay. Her family followed, and her daughters relate that the only thing they took with them were their bunads, their traditional dresses. After the war, Annichen worked for refugees, and the family took in a couple who had survived a prison camp in Poland to live with them. In other words, Annichen combined principle and practicality in many areas.

Ingun Grimstad Klepp and Tone Skårdal Tobiasson

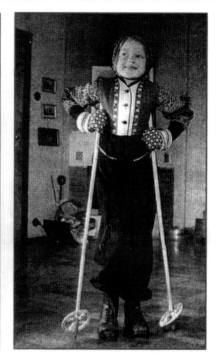

Annichen Sibbern Bøhn and her daughters. Photo: private collection.

ANNICHEN SIBBERN BØHN'S PUBLICATIONS

Norske strikkemønstre (Norwegian Knitting Designs), (1929, 1933, 1942, 1947; editions in English: 1952, 1965, 1966, and 1975).

Strikkeoppskrifter [Knitting Patterns] (1931).

Nye strikkeoppskrifter [New Knitting Patterns] (undated, 1943).

Strikkemønstre [Knitting Designs] (1930, 1932).

Småtøi: alt til våre barn I strikning og søm: alder 0-3 år [Little clothes: everything for our children in knitting and sewing: ages 0 to 3 years], (no date). Written with Ingrid Fleischer, illustrated by Annichen Sibbern Bøhn.

Gammelt till nytt [Old to New] (1941).

Knit Your Own Norwegian Sweaters: Complete instructions for 50 authentic sweaters, hats, mittens, gloves, caps, etc., published by the Dale Yarn Company (1974).

SOURCES:

Klepp, Ingun Grimstad and Tone Skårdal Tobiasson. *Norsk strikkehistorie* [A History of Norwegian Knitting], Haugesund: Vormedal, 2018.

Kringstad, Sidsel Bøhn and Annichen Bøhn Kassel. "Kvinnen bakom boken" [The Woman Behind the Book], *Kulturarven* 47 (pages 47-48) 2009.

Oxxal, Astrid. "Et norsk strikkemønster fra Grønland," *Kunst og Kultur*, Year 86, no. 3, pages 158-171. 2003.

Schreinder, Johanna. *Strikkemønstre fra oldermors tid* [Knitting from Great-Grandmother's Time]. Kristiania: Cappelen, 1910.

BEFORE YOU BEGIN KNITTING

READ THE PATTERN INSTRUCTIONS

We recommend that you always read through all instructions before you begin knitting. Consider this part of the planning stage. Find out what yarn and equipment you need. Be sure you understand the knitting terms, abbreviations, and techniques used in the instructions. Carefully review the overall process and any unusual steps.

YARN

All the yarns recommended in this book are produced at Hillesvåg Ullvarefabrikk. Most of the yarns used to knit the example pieces was spun from Norwegian wool, with the exceptions of the worsted-spun and cotton yarns. Using Norwegian wool added meaning to our work and reminded us that these patterns are built on rich Norwegian traditions. As a general rule, the yarn amounts listed in the patterns are rounded up to the nearest 50-gram amount, although Hillesvåg usually sells yarn in 100-gram skeins. The reason for this is to provide a better idea of how much yarn you'll need. It also makes it easier to use up leftovers from earlier projects.

Many of Hillesvåg's yarns can be substituted for each other. Nothing prevents you from substituting another Hillesvåg yarn for the recommended yarn, but if you do, remember to compare the recommended tension and the total length of a 100-gram ball (this information is usually listed on the label). There's no doubt that "wool is gold," but sometimes, when you want a lighter garment, you might choose to use cotton instead.

GAUGE: IT REALLY IS IMPORTANT!

The given measurements in the patterns require that the projects be worked at the correct gauge. Deviations from that gauge will have consequences.

For example, let's say you want to knit a sweater with a circumference of 39½ in / 100 cm. The recommended gauge is 22 stitches in 4 in / 10 cm. If your gauge is actually 23 stitches in 4 in / 10 cm, your sweater will turn out at 37½ in / 95.5 cm around instead of 39½ in / 100 cm—2 inches / almost 5 cm smaller. Similarly, a gauge of 21 stitches in 4 in / 10 cm instead of 22 will make the sweater almost 2 inches / 5 cm bigger. Practically speaking, seemingly small differences in gauge may mean almost a whole size larger or smaller. Just think about what the change in sizing would be if your gauge differed by more than one stitch per 4 in / 10 cm!

Knitting a gauge swatch might not be the first thing you want to focus on when you're eager to get started on a new knitting project, but it will definitely be worth your time to make sure you're knitting at the correct gauge. Adjust your gauge by changing to needles of a smaller or larger size. During the past few years, it's become easier to find quarter-increment metric needles (up to 3.75 mm) in Scandinavia and Europe, and to find metric sizes in the US. The greater availability of different sizes and smaller gradations between them makes it easier to fine-tune your gauge.

If it's particularly important that the row/length gauge also match, that will be mentioned in the pattern.

GAUGE IN SINGLE-COLOR STOCKINETTE AND COLOR-PATTERN KNITTING

Many knitters find themselves knitting more tightly in two-color pattern knitting than in single-color stockinette. If that's the case for you, we recommend going up a quarter or half size in millimeters, or a whole US size, for the color pattern sections. Also, take care that the floats on the wrong side are not pulled tight.

CAST-ON TENSION

Working garter stitch and other edgings can be tough going if the cast-on edge is too tight. When casting on, make sure the tension is neither too tight nor too loose, but rather just right. The ideal outcome is a match between the size of the cast-on stitches and those in later rows. Use needles of the same size as for the edging itself to cast on, and cast on the way you always do—but make sure there's a little space between each of the stitches, so they aren't jammed together too closely on the needle. It's the length of the yarn between the cast-on stitches that determines whether the cast-on will be too tight, just right, or too loose, not the size of the loops on the needle.

BIND-OFF TENSION

It's also irritating—not to mention uncomfortable—when bind-off stitches are too tight. If you often have trouble with this, one helpful tip is to use a crochet hook in your right hand instead of a knitting needle and "crochet-knit" the bind-off. (You don't need to know how to crochet to achieve this; just use the hook to catch the yarn and pull through.) After a little practice, it'll be easy to achieve an even bind-off that won't pull up too much. Use a hook of the same size or a slightly larger size than the knitting needle. (Many knitting needle gauges have US crochet hook and US and metric knitting needle sizes listed together.)

COLOR DOMINANCE IN STRANDED PATTERN KNITTING

Color dominance in stranded pattern knitting is a constantly debated topic among knitters. Much has been and will be said on the subject.

One thing that's certain is that the way you hold the yarns influences your results. The dominant color—usually the darker or background color—is the one that will be most prominent on the right side of the garment. If this isn't kept consistent throughout, the knitted fabric will be uneven. Below, find three methods for ensuring a smooth, clear color pattern. For simplicity's sake, we explain the methods as though you're working with only two colors.

Method 1: Hold both strands in your left hand, and "pick" the strands from your index or middle finger. Keep the dominant color (darker or background color) closest to your work (i.e., closer to your fingertip), and pick it from *beneath* the other. Hold the other strand (the pattern color) farther from the work (i.e., farther from your fingertip) and pick it *over* the nearer strand.

Method 2: Hold one strand over your left index finger, and "throw" the other strand with your right hand. The color held by your left hand will be dominant.

Method 3: "Throw" both yarns with your right hand; always pick up the strand you want to dominate from *under* and in *front* of the non-dominant strand—and the non-dominant from over and behind the dominant strand.

If you look on the back (wrong side) of the piece, you'll see one strand running below the other. The color of that strand will dominate on the front of the work. For smooth results and a clear pattern, it's important to be consistent in how each yarn is held and picked.

DECREASING WITHIN A COLOR PATTERN

When decreasing within a round—for raglan shaping, for example—work the decrease stitch with the color shown on the chart alongside the decrease. So, when decreasing on the right side of a decrease line, work the decrease with the color shown on the chart to the right of the two stitches to be joined. On the left side, work the decrease with the color on the chart to the left of the two stitches to be joined.

LONG FLOATS

It's impractical to have long floats on the wrong side of a knitted garment. Therefore, when a yarn strand must be carried over more than 3 or 4 stitches, secure it by knitting over (or under) that strand on the wrong side of the work. Be careful, though, not to do this at the exact same spot in every row, and make sure the caught float doesn't show between stitches on the right side—that will make the color pattern uneven.

HOW TO READ THE CHARTS

Unless otherwise specified, read the charts in this book from the bottom up. When knitting in the round, read from right to left. If working back and forth, read the chart from right to left on right side rows and from left to right on wrong side rows.

KNIT FROM THE BOTTOM UP, OR TOP DOWN?

Many sweater-jackets, cardigans, and pullovers are worked from the bottom up, while others are knitted top down. In Norway, we usually work from the bottom up. However, it has become more common over the past few years to work from the top down, usually for a yoke or raglan sweater. Knitting top down is not, as you might believe, a new method. We've found evidence that this method was used in earlier times as well. Annichen Sibbern Bøhn's "Eskimo" sweaters are a good example. Interestingly, on some older cardigans and pullovers, the body has been worked from the bottom up, and when beginning the sleeves, the knitter picked up stitches around the armhole and worked the sleeves from the top down.

Which method is better? The answer depends on who you're talking to: each method has its advantages and disadvantages, and everyone has their own preference.

TOP DOWN

Sometimes there's practical reasoning behind how you might choose to work or adjust a design: how much yarn you have, or how well the measurements are turning out. There are also practical reasons to knit from the top down. The parts of the garment where fit typically matters most are worked first, and can be tried on while the project's still in progress. As a rule, the sooner you can make adjustments to improve fit, the better off you'll be. Some knitters also prefer this method because they feel they can see the results that matter most sooner.

Some knitters dislike having to work charts "upside down," in colored patterns designed to be worked from the bottom up; for other knitters, that may make no difference at all.

BOTTOM UP

Knitting a garment from the bottom up is regarded by many as the "usual" method. Some will even go so far as to say it's the "correct" way. Luckily, though, there's no actual rule you need to follow—

choose the way that suits you. One of the advantages of choosing to work from the bottom up is that individual pieces are often knitted separately, either all the way up or in some cases up to the armhole for a raglan or round yoke; working one part at a time can be simpler than tackling an entire sweater at once. It's also easier and less cumbersome to knit a separate sleeve, as opposed to knitting a sleeve already "sitting" on the yoke (with or without the body).

In this book, both methods are represented among the various designs. You can always revise any pattern to be worked the other way, if you prefer!

It's also entirely possible to knit side-to-side; but as this method isn't used in this book, we won't discuss it here.

"CUT! CUT! CUT!" SCREAMED GRANNY

Cutting open a knitted garment can be a frightening step in the process, but there's no reason to be afraid. As with many other things, practice makes perfect. If you're uncomfortable with the idea, you can always practice on a couple of knitted swatches before you take scissors to your garment.

For simplicity's sake, so as not to review all your options every single time, the directions in this book will always recommend reinforcing your knitting with machine-stitching on both sides of the intended cut beforehand. This isn't strictly necessary, though, because there are other ways to secure stitches. You can, for example, crochet along both sides of the cut, or hand-stitch with either backstitch or a tight running stitch. If you knit with pure wool yarn (not superwash-treated) or pelsull, you can, as a rule, cut it open without sewing or crocheting first. In that case, it's best to have knitted a steek at least 6 stitches wide along the future cutting line. It's also best to carefully wash, or at least steam press, the garment before cutting it open. The cut edges can then be covered with tape or a knitted facing during the finishing process.

FINISHING AND WEAVING IN ENDS

The saying, "Haste makes waste," is definitely relevant when it comes to finishing a knitted garment. Being careful and taking your time in this last phase of your project may determine whether you'll be satisfied with the result.

Use a sharp tapestry needle to weave in ends, and a blunt tapestry needle when sewing pieces together. Sew on buttons with the same yarn and in the same color that was used for button bands or edgings.

WASH OR STEAM-PRESS THE FINISHED GARMENT?

A knitted garment isn't at its best until it's been washed, or, at a minimum, carefully steam pressed. Washing evens out the stitches, and the yarn "puffs up." Use wool-safe detergent or mild soap. A softener can be used on pure wool, but *not* on superwash-treated wool. It's always best, in our opinion, to wash a finished garment by hand, taking care that the wash water and the rinse water are the same temperature; do not scrub. You can use your washing machine's spin cycle to work out excess water. Then, gently spread the damp garment, smooth it out into its finished shape, and leave flat until completely dry.

If you decide to steam press instead, work very carefully—especially over ribbed or seed stitch edges, which can lose their shape entirely if pressed flat.

Wool garments, knit in pure rather than superwash wool, don't need to be washed often. If the garment has a few flecks of dirt, they can be wiped away with a damp cloth or a little "local" washing. Otherwise, the garment can be freshened up with a good airing.

USE YOUR OWN COLORS

We each have our own taste and style. When making your own garments, they can easily be fitted and redesigned to show off your personal taste. Changing one or more colors in a pattern is perhaps the simplest way to change the overall look. Do you find it hard to judge whether a color combination looks good? Or maybe you don't want to take the chance of getting all that yarn and knitting a whole sweater in colors totally different from the ones we used .... If that's you, try knitting a sample swatch first. Or kill two birds with one stone: knit a small garment—a pair of wrist warmers or a hat—in the colors you're considering, so you can see how they look in a finished piece and end up with something wearable in the bargain.

BUTTONS

We used pewter buttons for most of the designs in this book. Pewter buttons are elegant and rich in tradition, but feel free to use other kinds of buttons. It's a matter of taste. When choosing pewter buttons, keep in mind that some are heavier than others. I recommend lighter buttons, particularly for children's garments. Each pattern lists the buttons that were used for the garments in the photos.

ABBREVIATIONS AND TERMS

ABBREVIATIONS USED IN THIS BOOK

approx.	approximately	rem	remain(s)(ing)
beg	begin(ning)	rep	repeat(s)
BO	bind off (= UK cast off)	rnd(s)	round(s)
ca.	circa, about, approximately	RS	right side
cm	centimeter(s)	sc	single crochet (= UK double crochet)
CO	cast on	sl	slip
dec	decrease(s)	ssk	(sl 1 knitwise) 2 times, insert left needle left to right through the 2 sts and knit together through back loops = left-leaning decrease
DK	double knitting (yarn)		
DS	German double-stitch (see below)		
dpn	double-pointed needles		
est	as established, that is, continue in pattern	ssp	(sl 1 purlwise) 2 times, insert left needle left to right through these 2 sts and purl together through back loops = left-leaning purl decrease
in	inch(es)		
inc	increase(s)		
k	knit (as contrasted to purl)	steek	5 to 7 additional sts knitted in a vertical line, intended to be cut open later, and sewn down as a hem or covered with a facing
k2tog	knit 2 together = right-leaning decrease		
k3tog	knit 3 together		
m	meter(s)		
M1L	make 1 left = with left needle tip, from front to back, pick up strand between 2 sts and knit into back loop = left-leaning increase	st(s)	stitch(es)
		tbl	through back loop(s)
		wyb	with yarn held behind work (as if to knit)
		wyf	with yarn held in front of work (as if to purl)
M1R	make 1 right = with left needle, from back to front, pick up strand between 2 sts and knit into front loop = right-leaning increase	WS	wrong side
		wyb	with yarn held in back
		wyf	with yarn held in front
p	purl	yd	yard(s) (measurement)
p2tog	purl 2 together	yo	yarn over. Throw yarn over needle as if to knit, but don't.
pm	place marker		

Stitch holder: Stitches that are to be set aside for a while can be slipped onto a stitch holder—which can be, for example, a strand of scrap yarn, a double-pointed needle, a safety pin, or a locking metal stitch holder.

ABBREVIATIONS, CROCHET

ch   chain stitch
sc   single crochet (= UK double crochet)
sl st   slip stitch

SPECIAL TECHNIQUES

CABLES

C3B   cable 3 back (leans right): Slip the next 2 sts from left needle onto a cable needle and hold *behind* work, knit next st on left needle, k2 from cable needle.

C3F   cable 3 *front* (leans left): Slip the next 1 st from left needle to a cable needle and hold in front of work, knit next 2 sts on left needle, k1 from cable needle.

C4B   cable 4 back (leans right): Slip the next 2 sts from the left needle onto a cable needle and hold *behind* work, knit next 2 sts on left needle, k2 from cable needle.

C4F   cable 4 front (leans left): Slip the next 2 sts from the left needle onto a cable needle and hold in *front* of work, knit next 2 sts on left needle, k2 from cable needle.

SEED STITCH

Knitted back and forth
Use a stitch count of 2 + 1. Worked the same way on both RS and WS.
Pattern Row: K1, *p1, k1* to end of row. Repeat this row.

Knitted in the round (with an odd number of stitches)
Pattern Row: *K1, p1* until 1 st remains, end with k1.
On the next and all following rnds, work purl over knit and knit over purl. Because you are working with an odd number of stitches, the pattern will shift naturally from round to round.

Tip for a firmer seed stitch
Seed stitch has a tendency to "shift out" a little and to become too loose. If you work all the knit stitches through the back loop, on both right and wrong sides (if worked back and forth), the seed stitching will be firmer, and the overall look will be about the same.

DS = DOUBLE STITCH FOR GERMAN SHORT ROWS

Short rows are used to knit shorter rows within a row or round—for example, to make the back of a neckline higher than the front. This method makes it possible to turn and go back and forth within a row or round without leaving a hole at the turning points.

The method is the same on both sides of the fabric: work up to and including the stitch where you'll turn. Turn the work around (to WS). With yarn in front, slip the first stitch as if to purl. Pull the yarn up, over, and then behind the needle, so the stitch turns over to the back of the needle and forms two "stitch legs." The stitch will look like a double stitch but counts only as one. Pull firmly but not excessively when laying the stitch over. Now continue in pattern. When you later come to this "double stitch," work both legs together as one stitch.

Fig. 29. Mønsterskjema til hosstående fig. 30.
Mønstrets maskeantall 4.

THE DESIGNS
AND THEIR
INSTRUCTIONS

CLOVER MEADOW PULLOVER

Chart from *Norwegian Knitting Designs*: figure 56, page 52, "Nordenfjelske."

The motif "Nordenfjelske" (part of Norway, north of the Dovre Mountains) adds a decorative detail to this comfy, simple, and rustic raglan pullover. It's a fairly quick and easy knitting project, worked in a bulky yarn with large needles and only a bit of color patterning. In other words, it's a manageable project even for a knitter who's less experienced with stranded colorwork. You decide whether or not you want the split lower edge à la gansey.

SKILL LEVEL
Experienced

SIZES
Women's XS (S, M, L, XL, XXL)

FINISHED MEASUREMENTS
Chest: 33¾ (37¼, 40½, 43¾, 47¼, 50½) in / 85.5 (94.5, 103, 111.5, 120, 128.5) cm
Total Length: 25½ (26, 26¾, 27½, 28¼, 29¼) in / 65 (66, 68, 70, 72, 74) cm
Sleeve Length to Underarm: 17¼ (17¾, 18¼, 19, 19¼, 20) in / 44 (45, 46, 48, 49, 51) cm

YARN
CYCA #5 (bulky) Hifa Troll (100% wool, 125 yd/114 m / 100 g)
Alternate Yarn: CYCA #5 (bulky) Hifa Blåne Pelsullgarn (100% wool, 125 yd/114 m / 100 g)

YARN AMOUNTS
Color 1: approx. 550 (600, 650, 750, 800, 900) g
Color 2: approx. 50 (50, 50, 50, 50, 100) g

COLORS SHOWN
Gray Heather Version
Color 1: Gray Heather 02703; Color 2: Charcoal Gray 02733

Dark Gray Version
Color 1: Dark Gray 02742; Color 2: Black 02708

Light Blue-Turquoise Heather Version
Color 1: Light Blue-Turquoise Heather 027060; **Color 2:** Dark Brown Heather 02707

SUGGESTED NEEDLE SIZES
US 8 / 5 mm: 24 or 32 in / 60 or 80 cm circulars and set of 5 dpn
US 9 / 5.5 mm: 16 and 32 in / 40 and 80 cm circulars and set of 5 dpn
Optional for neck band: crochet hook US 7 or H-8 / 4.5 or 5 mm

GAUGE
14 sts x 22 rounds in stockinette on larger gauge needles = 4 x 4 in / 10 x 10 cm.
Knit a test swatch and adjust needle size to obtain correct gauge if necessary.

SPECIAL TECHNIQUES
Broken k1, p1 ribbing, worked back and forth, for slit-sided lower edge
Multiple of (2) + 1 sts
Row 1 (WS): Sl 1 purlwise wyf, (p1, k1) to last st, p1.
Row 2 (RS): Sl 1, knit to end of row.
Repeat Rows 1-2.

Broken k1, p1 ribbing without split, worked in the round
Multiple of (2) + 1 sts
Rnd 1: (K1, p1) to end of rnd.
Rnd 2: Knit around.
Repeat Rnds 1-2.

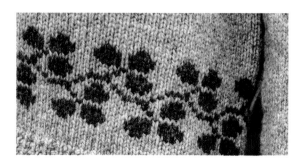

INSTRUCTIONS

This pullover is worked from the bottom up. After the optional split edging, the body is knitted in the round to the armholes. The sleeves are each knitted in the round, also to the armholes. The sleeves and body are then placed on the same circular needle and knitted around with raglan shaping. The neck band can either be knitted or crocheted. The sweater can be worked with or without side splits on the lower edge.

BODY

Ribbed Lower Edge With Split

The ribbed edge is worked in two pieces. With Color 1 and smaller gauge circular needle, CO 61 (67, 73, 79, 85, 91) sts. Work broken k1, p1 ribbing back and forth (see previous page). Work in ribbing for 1½ in / 4 cm on front piece and 2½ in / 6 cm on back piece. End each piece with a WS row. Change to larger gauge circular needle and place both pieces on it to begin working around. Knit 1 rnd, k2tog to join the last st of one piece with the first st of the other on both sides = 2 sts decreased = 120 (132, 144, 156, 168, 180) sts. Pm at each side st with 60 (66, 72, 78, 84, 90) sts each for front and back.

Ribbed Lower Edge Without Split

With Color 1 and smaller gauge circular needle, CO 120 (132, 144, 156, 168, 180) sts. Join to work in the round, being careful not to twist cast-on rnd. Work broken k1, p1 ribbing in the round (see previous page) for 1½ (1½, 1½, 1½, 2, 2) in / 4 (4, 4, 4, 5, 5) cm. Change to larger gauge circular needle and knit 1 rnd. Pm at each side with 60 (66, 72, 78, 84, 90) sts each for front and back.

K 5 rnds and then work pattern following chart on p. 31. The pattern is repeated 10 (11, 12, 13, 14, 15) times around. After completing color pattern, continue in Color 1 until body above ribbing measures 15¾ (15¾, 16¼, 16¼, 16¼, 16¼) in / 40 (40, 41, 41, 41, 41) cm. (These measurements must be taken above the ribbing because there were two choices for the ribbing and lower edge, each with different measurements.)

On the last rnd, BO 7 sts for each underarm, centered at each side as follows: Knit until 4 sts rem before side marker, BO 7 sts, knit to last 4 sts of rnd, BO 7 sts. Set body aside while you knit the sleeves.

SLEEVES

With Color 1 and smaller gauge dpn, CO 30 (34, 34, 36, 38, 38) sts. Divide sts over 4 dpn and join to work in the round. Work broken k1, p1 ribbing in the round (see previous page) for 1½ (1½, 1½, 1½, 2, 2) in / 4 (4, 4, 4, 5, 5) cm. Change to larger gauge dpn and pm for beg of rnd. Work around even until sleeve measures 2½ in / 6 cm.

Inc Rnd: M1, knit until 1 st before marker, M1, k1.

Continue in Color 1, working inc rnd every 2¼ (2¼, 2, 2, 2, 1¾) in / 5.5 (5.5, 5, 5, 5, 4.5) cm, a total of 7 (7, 8, 8, 9, 10) times = 44 (48, 50, 52, 56, 58) sts. Continue in Color 1 until sleeve is about 17¼ (17¾, 18¼, 19, 19¼, 20) in / 44 (45, 46, 48, 49, 51) cm long or desired length.

On the last rnd, BO 7 sts centered on underarm as follows: BO 3 sts, knit until 4 sts before marker, BO the last 4 sts. 37 (41, 43, 45, 49, 51) sts rem.

Set this sleeve aside, and make another sleeve just like it.

YOKE

Place the body and sleeves on larger gauge circular needle in this sequence: back, left sleeve, front, right sleeve = 180 (200, 216, 232, 252, 268) sts total. Pm at each intersection between sleeve and body. Begin rnd at back, between the back and the right sleeve. Knit 2 (3, 2, 3, 2, 2) rnds.

Raglan Dec Rnd: *K2, k2tog, knit until 4 sts before next marker, ssk, k2*. Work dec from * 4 times = 8 sts decreased.

Knit 3 rnds. Repeat the raglan dec every 4th rnd, a total of 3 (2, 2, 3, 3, 4) times. Now work raglan decs every other rnd a total of 7 (10, 11, 11, 13, 14) times. End with a dec rnd (= do not knit a rnd after the last decrease rnd) = 100 (104, 112, 120, 124, 124) sts rem. Total raglan dec rnds: 10 (12, 13, 14, 16, 18).

On the next rnd, BO the center 11 (11, 11, 11, 13, 13) sts on front for neckline and complete rnd. Cut yarn, leaving a tail of 4-5 in / 10 cm.

Slip sts back from right to left needle until you reach the front neck edge. Attach yarn at right side of neck and work back and forth in stockinette (knit on RS, purl on WS).

Note: Before beginning neck, read carefully through the next section, as several actions take place at the same time. References to raglan decs refer to the number of raglan decs counted on the *back*.

BO at neck edge at the beg of every row 2,2,1,1 (2,2,1,1; 2,2,1,1,1; 2,2,1,1,1; 2,2,1,1,1; 2,2,1,1,1) times, while, *at the same time*, continuing the raglan decs on every other row. On the front, work the raglan decs as long as there are stitches to dec.

Sizes XS and S: Continue as est until there are a total of 15 (17, -, -, -, -) raglan dec rows. The raglan shaping is now finished; do not cut yarn.

Size M: Continue until there are a total of - (-, 19, -, -, -) raglan dec rows, and, *at the same time*, when 7 sts rem on each sleeve, stop decreasing on the sleeves; do not cut yarn.

Sizes L–XXL: Continue until there are a total of - (-, -, 18, 19, 20) raglan decrease rows. Now dec for front and back on both right and wrong sides (but not on the sleeves) a total of - (-, -, 2, 3, 4) times and, *at the same time*, when 7 sts rem on each sleeve, stop decreasing on the sleeves. Do not cut yarn.

To dec *on the WS before the marker* (to the right of the marker): p to 4 sts before marker, p2tog, p2. Do not cut yarn.

To dec *on the WS after the marker* (= to the left of the marker): P2, ssp. Continue as est until there are - (-, -, 20, 22, 24) raglan dec rows. Do not cut yarn.

NECK BAND
Choose a knitted or crocheted neck band.

Knitted Neck Band
Change to smaller gauge circular. Beg on right side at front neck where the yarn is waiting. In addition to the rem sts, pick up and knit sts along the front neck edge for a total of 60-62 (64-66, 66-68, 74-76, 78-80, 82-84) sts. The stitch count must be a multiple of 2. Work broken ribbed edge (alternate k1, p1 rnds with k rnds) around for 1 in / 2.5 cm. BO in ribbing.

☐ Color 1
■ Color 2
☐ 1 repeat

Crocheted Neck Band
BO all rem neck sts. Using crochet hook US size 7 or H-8 / 4.5 or 5 mm and Color 1, work around neck in single crochet. Work approx. 60 (64, 66, 74, 78, 82) sc.

ASSEMBLY
Sew underarms. Weave in all ends neatly on WS.

ASTRID CARDIGAN

Chart from *Norwegian Knitting Designs*: figure 62, page 56.

The motif used here was simply called "BORDER" in *Norwegian Knitting Designs*. It's geometric and quite striking—and of course the nice thing about knitting is that you can make your own adjustments in pattern and shaping, if you like. We changed the pattern a little for a simpler and more open look, which also resulted in shorter floats. A narrow band of patterning above and below frames the main motif. If you want to use the original motif from *Norwegian Knitting Designs*, you could substitute it for the center section in Chart C.

SKILL LEVEL
Experienced

SIZES
Women's XS (S, M, L, XL, XXL)

FINISHED MEASUREMENTS
Chest: 34¾ (36¾, 40, 42, 45, 48½) in / 88 (93, 101.5, 106.5, 114.5, 123) cm
Waist (with shaping): 32 (34, 37½, 39½, 42½, 45¾) in / 81.5 (86.5, 95, 100, 108, 116.5) cm
Total Length: 22½ (22¾, 24, 24½, 25¼, 25½) in / 57 (58, 61, 62, 64, 65) cm
Sleeve Length: 17¾ (17¾, 18¼, 18½, 19, 19¼) in / 45 (45, 46, 47, 48, 49) cm

YARN
CYCA #2 (sport, baby) Hifa Ask (100% wool, 344 yd/315 m / 100 g)

YARN AMOUNTS
Color 1: approx. 250 (300, 300, 350, 350, 400) g
Color 2: approx. 150 (150, 150, 200, 200, 200) g
Color 3: approx. 50 (50, 50, 50, 100, 100) g

Note: If you are making the sweater without "lice," you'll need
Color 1: approx. 25 (25, 25, 30, 30, 30) g more.
Color 2: approx. 25 (25, 30, 30, 30, 30) g less.

COLORS SHOWN
Steel Gray Heather Version
Color 1: Steel Gray Heather 346550
Color 2: Natural White 316057
Color 3: Dark Gray 316051

Light Brown Heather Version
Color 1: Light Brown Heather 316058
Color 2: Semi-bleached White 316047
Color 3: Light Gray-Blue 316129

SUGGESTED NEEDLE SIZES
US 2.5 / 3 mm: 24 and 32 in / 60 and 80 cm circulars and set of 5 dpn
US 4 / 3.5 mm: 16, 24, and 32 in / 40, 60, and 80 cm circulars and set of 5 dpn, or needle size needed to obtain correct gauge in stockinette.

GAUGE
24 sts in pattern on larger gauge needles = 4 x 4 in / 10 x 10 cm.
Adjust needle size to obtain correct gauge if necessary.

NOTIONS
8 buttons and (optional) tape or ribbon to cover cut edges

BUTTONS USED
Heather Steel Gray Version
GJENDE ¾ in / 20 mm, K362925 from Hjelmtvedt

Heather Light Brown Version
NUMEDAL ⅝ in / 18 mm, K312983 from Hjelmtvedt

A VARIATION ON THE CARDIGAN
The Light Brown Heather version shown in the photo was knitted without lice and with smaller needles for a tighter gauge. It was knitted on needles US 1.5 / 2.5 mm with a gauge of 28 sts x 43 rnds = 4 x 4 in / 10 x 10 cm.

If you want to duplicate it, you must adjust the number of sts to attain the correct measurements widthwise. For example, to obtain the measurements listed for size M (approx. 39 in / 99 cm chest), you'd ignore the stitch count given, and instead work as many stitches as it takes to achieve the correct measurements. You'll also need more yarn for this variation, if you knit more tightly. Only try this if you're comfortable making these kinds of adjustments on the fly!

INSTRUCTIONS

This sweater is knitted in the round from the bottom up. It can be worked either straight up and down or with a lightly shaped waist. You can also decide whether to knit it with or without lice on the body and sleeves—the top part above the pattern band has no lice in either version. The body and sleeves are worked first, and are separate up to the underarm. The pieces are then placed on the same circular needle The yoke begins with some raglan decreases; when the yoke is worked, the decreases are shown on the chart. After the chart, the last part is knitted in one color and with decreases.

Stitches are picked up and knitted for button bands along the front edges. The cut edges are folded in and sewn down on the wrong side. Optionally, the edges can be covered by tape, ribbon, or a knitted facing. The neck band is knitted last.

Read through the entire pattern before you start to knit. Sometimes instructions a few lines after what you consider a problem will clarify that problem and make the whole process "come together."

BODY

With smaller gauge 24 in / 60 cm circular needle and Color 2, CO 187 (199, 213, 225, 245, 263) sts. Work the lower edge back and forth:

Row 1 (WS): K1 (edge st), (p1, k1) to end of row.
Row 2 (RS): K1 (edge st), k1 then (p1, k1) to end of row.

Rep these two rows until ribbed edge measures 2 (2, 2, 2, 2½, 2½) in / 5 (5, 5, 5, 6, 6) cm. End with a WS row.

Change to larger gauge circular needle. Knit 1 row, increasing 20 (20, 26, 26, 26, 28) sts evenly spaced around. CO 5 new sts at the end of the row. These 5 sts form the steek, along with the 2 edge sts of the lower edge = 7 steek sts total. The body now has 205 (217, 237, 249, 269, 289) sts total. The steek sts are not worked in pattern and are not included in stitch counts. Pm on each side of the steek. On rounds with more than 1 color, alternate colors in vertical stripes within the steek.

The sts are divided as follows: right front = 51 (54, 59, 62, 67, 72) sts, next st (right side "seam" st), pm, back = 101 (107, 117, 123, 133, 143) sts, next st = left side "seam" st pm here, left front = 51 (54, 59, 62, 67, 72) sts.

Work in pattern following Chart A. Begin at the arrow, repeat the sts within the red frame, and end as indicated. The chart is worked once in length.

Work the rest of the body following Chart B (lice) or in stockinette with Color 1 if you want the version without lice. For the version with lice, begin at lower right side of chart (at the arrow), and repeat section within red frame. Work until piece measures 4¼ (4¼, 4¾, 4¾, 4¾ 4¾) in / 11 (11, 12, 12, 12, 12) cm. Beg optional waist shaping. If you want straight sides, skip "Shaping Waist."

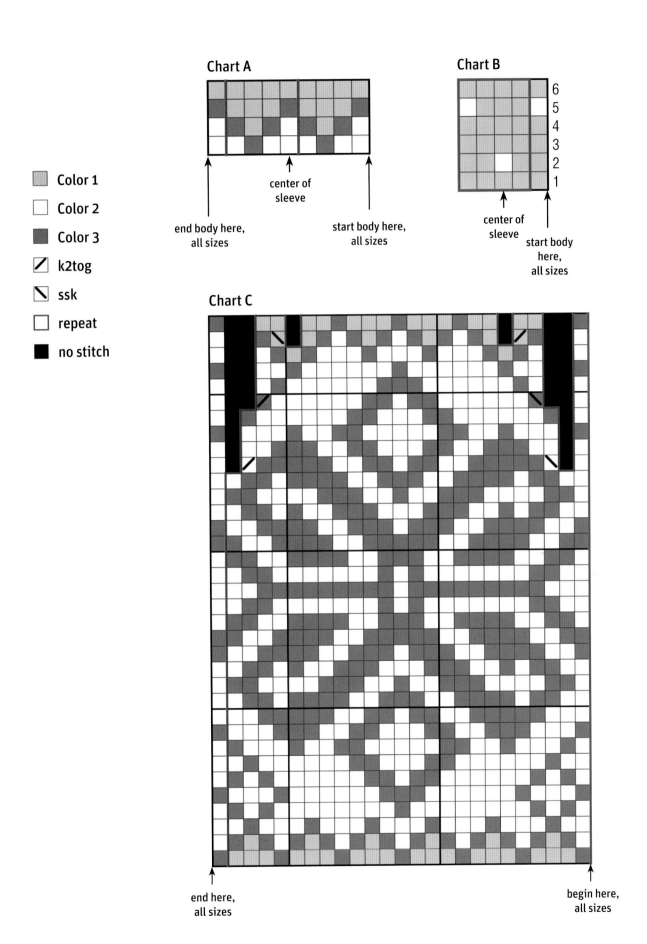

Chart A

center of
sleeve

end body here,
all sizes

start body here,
all sizes

Chart B

6
5
4
3
2
1

center of
sleeve

start body
here,
all sizes

Color 1

Color 2

Color 3

k2tog

ssk

repeat

no stitch

Chart C

end here,
all sizes

begin here,
all sizes

Shaping Waist

Decrease Rnd: *Knit until 2 sts before side marker, ssk, k1 (side "seam" st—knit in the color which fits best into the rest of the pattern), k2tog*; rep from * to * once more = 4 sts decreased. Repeat the dec rnd approx. every 1¼ (1¼, 1¼, 1¼, 1½, 1½) in / 3 (3, 3, 3, 3.5, 3.5) cm for a total of 4 dec rnds = 189 (201, 221, 233, 253, 273) sts rem.

Work 1½ in / 4 cm without decreasing.

Increase Rnd: *Knit to side marker, M1, k1 (side seam st and, if working lice, knit with the color that fits best into the pattern), M1, rep from * 1 more time = 4 sts increased. Repeat the inc rnd approx. every 1¼ (1¼, 1¼, 1¼, 1½, 1½) in / 3 (3, 3, 3, 3.5, 3.5) cm for a total of 4 inc rnds = 205 (217, 237, 249, 269, 289) sts.

Body, continued: Work until body measures approx. 14¼ (14¼, 15, 15, 15¾, 15¾) in / 36 (36, 38, 38, 40, 40) cm. If working lice, end on Row 4 (6, 4, 1, 6, 3) of chart. *At the same time*, on the same round, begin armholes: k 44 (47, 52, 55, 58, 63), BO 15 (15, 15, 15, 19, 19) sts, k 87 (93, 103, 109, 115, 125) sts, BO 15 (15, 15, 15, 19, 19) sts, k to end of rnd. Set body aside and knit sleeves.

SLEEVES

With smaller gauge dpn and Color 2, CO 46 (46, 48, 50, 52, 54) sts. Divide sts onto 4 dpn and join. Knit around in k1, p1 ribbing until cuff measures 2 (2, 2, 2, 2½, 2½) in / 5 (5, 5, 5, 6, 6) cm. Change to larger gauge dpn. Knit 1 rnd; *at the same time*, inc 8 (10, 10, 12, 12, 12) sts evenly spaced. 54 (56, 58, 62, 64, 66) sts.

Now work in pattern following Chart A. The last st of the rnd marks the center of underarm and is purled on all rnds: in Color 2 for the first 2 rnds, and then in Color 1. The center of rem sts of rnd is the center of sleeve—count back from the sleeve center on the chart to determine where to start the pattern. The pattern should be symmetrical on each side of the marking p st.

Chart A is worked once in length. Work the rest of the sleeve from Chart B, or (without lice) in stockinette with Color 1. If you do want lice, count back from center st of sleeve to determine where the charted pattern begins. Work 2 rnds in pattern. Now begin inc to shape sleeve at underarm on each side of marker st.

Inc Rnd: M1, work in pattern to marker st, M1, p1 (2 sts increased). If working lice pattern, work the new sts into pattern as they appear. Work the inc rnd every 1½ (1¼, 1, 1, ¾, ¾-1) in / 3.5 (3, 2.5, 2.5, 2, 2-2.5) cm, 11 (13, 15, 16, 16, 18) times = 76 (82, 88, 94, 96, 102) sts. Change to short circular needle when sts no longer fit comfortably around dpn.

Work until sleeve is 17¾ (17¾, 18¼, 18½, 19, 19¼) in / 45 (45, 46, 47, 48, 49) cm long. If working lice, end on same row of the chart as for body = Row 4 (6, 4, 1, 6, 3). *At the same time*, on the same rnd, BO 15 (15, 15, 15, 19, 19) sts centered on underarm: BO 7 (7, 7, 7, 9, 9) sts; k until 8 (8, 8, 8, 10, 10) sts rem. BO rem 61 (67, 73, 79, 77, 83) sts.

Set sleeve aside and make a second sleeve the same way.

YOKE

Place the pieces onto larger gauge circular as follows: right front, right sleeve, back, left sleeve, left front = 297 (321, 353, 377, 385, 417) sts total. Pm at each intersection of body and sleeves.

If working lice, continue in pattern from where the lice ended on the individual pieces, but, work the last 2 sts before and the first 2 sts after each marker with Color 1. Knit 1 rnd.

On the first part of the yoke, the raglan decs are worked at the same time as the pattern. Read both sections before proceeding.

Dec Rnd: *Knit in pattern (for lice) until 3 sts before marker. With Color 1, work: ssk, k2, k2tog*; rep from * a total of 4 times. 8 sts decreased.

Work the dec rnd every rnd 4 (0, 0, 0, 0, 0) times. Now rep dec rnd every other rnd 3 (7, 8, 5, 7, 7) times. Rep dec rnd every 3rd rnd 0 (0, 0, 3, 2, 3) times.

A total of 241 (265, 289, 313, 313, 337) sts rem and the pattern has reached the end of a whole repeat in length.

Work 1 rnd with Color 1 and, *at the same time*, remove markers at raglan dec lines. Start pattern on Chart C. Begin the rnd at (right) arrow, work rep within red frame, and end as shown (at left arrow). Dec as shown on chart. After completing Chart C, 181 (199, 217, 235, 235, 253) sts rem.

The rest of the yoke is worked in stockinette with Color 1. Dec rnds continue with stockinette sections in between. First, work 1 rnd stockinette.

The next rnd is a dec rnd: *K7, k2 tog*; rep from * to * end with k1; end with k1. 20 (22, 24, 26, 26, 28) sts decreased = 161 (177, 193, 209, 209, 225) sts rem.

K 3 rnds.

Next rnd is a dec rnd, eliminating 32 sts:
XS: (K3, k2tog) until 1 st rem in rnd, end with k1.
S: (K3, k2tog, k4, k2tog) until 1 st rem in rnd, end with k1.
M: (K4, k2tog) until 1 st rem in rnd; k1.
L: (K4, k2tog, k5, k2tog) until 1 st rem in rnd; k1.
XL: (K4, k2tog, k5, k2tog) until 1 st rem in rnd; k1.
XXL: (K5, k2tog) until 1 st rem in rnd; k1.

Total st count: 129 (145, 161, 177, 177, 193) sts. Knit 3 rnds stockinette.

Next rnd is a dec rnd, eliminating 16 (24, 32, 32, 32, 32) sts:
XS: (K6, k2tog) until 1 st rem in rnd; end with k1. 16 sts decreased.
S: (K4, k2tog) until 1 st rem in rnd; end with k1. 24 sts decreased.
M: (K3, k2tog) until 1 st rem in rnd; end with k1. 32 sts decreased.
L: (K3, k2tog, k4, k2tog) until 1 st rem in rnd; end with k1. 32 sts decreased.
XL: (K3, k2tog, k4, k2tog) until 1 st rem in rnd; end with k1. 32 sts decreased.
XXL: (K4, k2tog) until 1 st rem in rnd; end with k1. 32 sts decreased.

Total st count: 113 (121, 129, 145, 145, 161) sts.

K 3 rnds.

Next rnd is a dec rnd, eliminating 16 (16, 17, 29, 24, 32) sts:

XS: (K5, k2tog) until 1 st rem in rnd; end with k1. 16 sts decreased.

S: (K5, k2tog, k6, k2tog) until 1 st rem in rnd; end with k 1. 16 sts decreased.

M: K3, k2tog, (k5, k2tog, k6, k2tog) until 4 st rem in rnd; end with k 4. 17 sts decreased.

L: K1, k2tog, (k3, k2tog) until 2 sts rem in rnd; end by k2 = 29 sts decreased.

XL: (K4, k2tog) until 1 st rem in rnd; end by k1 = 24 sts decreased.

XXL: (K3, k2tog) until 1 st rem in rnd; end by k1 = 32 sts decreased.

Total st count: 97 (105, 112, 116, 121, 129) sts.

Back of Neck

The back of the neck is raised with a few German short rows (see page 23). Work as follows:
Knit until 20 (20, 20, 20, 22, 23) sts rem in rnd, turn and DS; p until 20 (20, 20, 20, 22, 23) sts before beginning of rnd; turn and DS. *K until 8 (8, 8, 9, 9, 10) sts before gap at previous turn, DS and purl back until 8 (8, 8, 9, 9, 10) sts before gap at previous turn; turn and DS. Rep from * once more. Knit around and, when you come to a double st, work as a single st. BO steek sts. Knit 1 more rnd and work the last double sts as before. Leave the sts on the needle for the neck, or slip them onto a holder.

FINISHING

At center front, machine-stitch (small stitches) on each side of the center steek st. Cut steek open between lines of stitching.

BUTTON BANDS

Now, with Color 2, smaller gauge circular needle, and RS toward you, pick up and knit an *odd number* of sts along each front edge in the space between steek and sts of body. On right front, begin at lower edge of ribbing, and, on left front, begin at top of neck. Pick up about 3 sts for every 4 rows along edge of body (i.e., skip every 4th row). Pick up 2 sts for every 4 rows along ribbing.

The button bands are worked in ribbing as for lower edge of body. Follow the instructions for either with or without buttonholes. You can work buttonholes on either side of the front.

Band Without Buttonholes

Work a total of 10 rows of ribbing back and forth. BO in ribbing.

Band With Buttonholes

Work 4 rows in ribbing. On the next row (WS), make 7 buttonholes. **Note:** The 8th buttonhole is worked later at the center of the neck band. Place the lowest buttonhole about ⅝ in / 1.5 cm from lower edge. Position rem buttonholes equally spaced between them. Make each buttonhole as follows: BO 3 sts. On next row (RS), CO 3 new sts over each gap on previous row. Continue in ribbing until you've worked a total of 10 rows. BO in ribbing.

NECK BAND

The neck band is worked in ribbing as on the lower edge of body.

With smaller gauge circular and Color 2, slip held sts onto needle.

With RS facing, begin above right button band: pick up and knit 7 sts along edge of neckline. Continue knitting into the neck edge, but at the same time dec 8 (8, 8, 7, 8, 10) sts evenly spaced across. Pick up and k 7 sts along top of left button band. 103, 111, 118, 123, 127, 133) sts. Work 4 rows back and forth in ribbing. On the next (WS) row, make the last buttonhole: work in ribbing until 7 sts rem, BO next 3 sts, work in ribbing to end of row. On the next row, also in ribbing, CO 3 sts over the gap. Continue even until you have worked a total of 10 rows of ribbing. BO in ribbing.

FINISHING

Weave in ends on WS. Sew underarms. Fold steek to inside of front edges. You can sew (whip stitch) the raw edge to the WS, cover it with a decorative tape, or knit a facing, whichever you prefer. If you use cotton tape, it's wise to preshrink it by washing or steam pressing it.

If you decide to knit a facing to cover the raw edges, work as follows: With smaller gauge needles and desired color, pick up and knit sts in the loops on the WS of the first row of the button bands. Pick up and knit 1 st for each st in the band, beginning just below neck band and down to shift from ribbing at lower edge of body—enough to cover the cut edges. Work 4 rows in stockinette, BO loosely and sew down facing on WS.

Sew on buttons and, if necessary, reinforce buttonholes.

FAVORITE PULLOVER FOR WOMEN

Chart from *Norwegian Knitting Designs*: figure 33, page 38.

The yoke panel on this pullover has been enormously popular, and shows up in numerous patterns. In this instance, it's accompanied by a zigzag border above and below, and is tinted with grays. The three versions shown are identical except for their main color. Choose a completely different main color if you prefer! A variant of the pattern band is used on the "Favorite Pullover for Men" on page 51, and it can be used for many other designs as well— on a hat, for example, or on the legs of a pair of socks.

SKILL LEVEL
Experienced

SIZES
Women's XS (S, M, L, XL, XXL)

FINISHED MEASUREMENTS
Chest: 33 (35, 38½, 40½, 43, 45¾) in / 84 (89, 98, 103, 109, 116) cm
Total Length: 22¾ (23¼, 24, 24½, 25¼, 25½) in / 58 (59, 61, 62, 64, 65) cm
Sleeve Length: 17¾ (17¾, 18, 18½, 19, 19) in / 45 (45, 46, 47, 48, 48) cm

YARN
CYCA #2 (sport, baby) Hifa Ask (100% wool, 344 yd / 315 m/100 g)

YARN AMOUNTS
Color 1: approx. 250 (300, 300, 350, 400, 400) g
Color 1 varies depending on version: Dark Terracotta Heather 346503; Violet Heather 346577; Maize Yellow Heather 346502
Colors 2–4 are the same for all three versions:
Color 2: Light Gray Heather 316054, approx. 50 (50, 100, 100, 100, 100) g
Color 3: Dark Gray Heather 316061, approx. 50 g for all sizes
Color 4: Charcoal 316056, approx. 50 g for all sizes

SUGGESTED NEEDLE SIZES
US 2.5 / 3 mm: 16, 24, and 32 in / 40, 60 and 80 cm circular needles and set of 5 dpn
US 4 / 3.5 mm: 24 and 32 in / 60 and 80 cm circular needles and set of 5 dpn

GAUGE
24 sts x 32 rnds in stockinette on smaller gauge needles = 4 x 4 in / 10 x 10 cm.
24 sts x 28-30 rnds in color pattern on larger gauge needles = 4 x 4 in / 10 x 10 cm.
Adjust needle size to obtain correct gauge if necessary.

INSTRUCTIONS

This pullover is knitted in the round from the top down. The sweater begins with the neck band and continues to the yoke. The sleeve stitches are placed on hold while the body is knitted; the sleeves are worked last.

YOKE

Neck Band

With Color 2 and 24 in / 60 cm smaller gauge circular needle, CO 102 (114, 120, 120, 129, 132) sts. Join, being careful not to twist cast-on row. Pm for beginning of rnd at center back. Work around in k2, p1 ribbing for 1-1¼ in / 2.5-3 cm. Change to stockinette and, on the first rnd, inc 0 (0, 0, 6, 3, 6) sts evenly spaced around = 102 (114, 120, 126, 132, 138) sts.

Back of Neck

The neckline is a little higher in back for a better fit across the shoulders. This is worked with short rows across the back of the neck and shoulders. (See "German Short Rows" on page 23.) Work as follows:

Row 1 (RS): K22 (25, 26, 28, 29, 31) sts, turn and DS.
Row 2 (WS): P43 (49, 51, 55, 57, 61) sts, turn and DS.
Row 3 (RS): Knit to previous turn, knit the DS as 1 st, k8 turn and DS.
Row 4 (WS): Purl to previous turn, purl the DS as 1 st, p8, turn and DS.

Rep Rows 3-4 once more. On the next (RS) row: Knit to beg of rnd (center back). There are now 6 more rows across back of the neckline = about ¾ in / 2 cm higher than the rest of the rnd.

Continue in stockinette around. K 2 rnds, but, on the first rnd, k the last DS as 1 st as you pass it.

SHAPING YOKE

Inc Rnd 1: *K3, M1; rep from * around. 34 (38, 40, 42, 44, 46) sts inc = 136 (152, 160, 168, 176, 184) sts total. Knit 4 rnds.

Inc Rnd 2: *K4, M1*; rep from * around. 34 (38, 40, 42, 44, 46) sts inc = 170 (190, 200, 210, 220, 230) sts total. Knit 4 rnds.

Inc Rnd 3: Inc 10 (8, 16, 24, 14, 22) sts evenly spaced around as follows:
XS: K8; (M1, k17) 9 times; M1, k9.
S: K12, M1, k23; (M1, k24) 5 times; M1, k23, M1, k12.
M: K6; (M1, k13) 4 times; (M1, k12) 7 times; (M1, k13) 4 times; M1, k6.
L: K4; (M1, k9) 9 times; (M1, k8) 5 times; (M1, k9) 9 times; M1, k4.
XL: K8; (M1, k15) 2 times; (M1, k16) 9 times; (M1, k15) 2 times; M1, k8.
XXL: K5; (M1, k11) 5 times; (M1, k10) 11 times; (M1, k11) 5 times; M1, k5.

After increasing: 180 (198, 216, 234, 234, 252) sts total.

Knit 2 rnds.

Now start the pattern on Chart A. Switch to larger gauge needle if you typically knit stranded colorwork more tightly. Work the rep 30 (33, 36, 39, 39, 42) times around. The repeat has 6 sts on the first 4 rows of the chart. The spaces with slashes mean "no stitch" and are skipped. **Note:** After incs on Row 5 of Chart A, each repeat has 8 sts. 240 (264, 288, 312, 312, 336) sts.

Work to end of Chart A and then cut Colors 2, 3, and 4. Change back to smaller gauge circular (if you changed to the larger gauge for the colorwork). Continue in stockinette with Color 1, knitting 2 rnds. Work the last yoke increase on the next rnd:

Inc Rnd: Inc 54 (54, 60, 60, 60, 60) sts evenly spaced around as follows:
XS: K2; (M1, k5) 12 times; (M1, k4) 29 times; (M1, k5) 12 times; M1, k2.
S: K2; (M1, k5) 24 times; (M1, k4) 5 times; (M1, k5) 24 times; M1, k2.
M: K2; (M1, k5) 24 times; (M1, k4) 11 times; (M1, k5) 24 times; M1, k2.
L and XL: K3; (M1, k5) 24 times; (M1, k6) 11 times; (M1, k5) 24 times; M1, k3.
XXL: K3; (M1, k5) 12 times; (M1, k6) 35 times; (M1, k5) 12 times; M1, k3.

After increasing: 294 (318, 348, 372, 372, 396) sts total.

Continue until work from bottom of center front neck band measures approx. 7½ (8, 8¼, 8¾, 9, 9½) in / 19 (20, 21, 22, 23, 24) cm = yoke is complete.

Color 1

Color 2

Color 3

Color 4

Inc 1 st

no stitch

Chart A

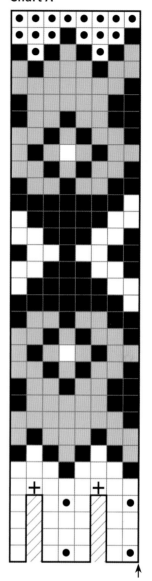

start here

Chart B

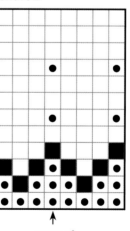

center of sleeve

DIVIDE SLEEVES AND BODY

The yoke is now finished. Divide the work into body and sleeve portions: K45 (48, 53, 56, 56, 60) sts (half the back), place next 58 (64, 69, 75, 75, 79) sts on a holder (right sleeve); CO 6 (6, 6, 6, 10, 10) sts for underarm, pm (right side "seam" and new beg of rnd); CO 6 (6, 6, 6, 10, 10) sts; k 89 (95, 105, 111, 111, 119) sts (front); place next 58 (64, 69, 75, 75, 79) sts on a holder (left sleeve); CO 12 (12, 12, 12, 20, 20) sts (left underarm); knit to new beg of rnd, removing marker at center back as you pass it. There should be 202 (214, 234, 246, 262, 278) body sts.

BODY

Knit in stockinette until body measures, from underarm, 13½ (13½, 13¾, 13¾, 14¼, 14 ¼) in / 34 (34, 35, 35, 36, 36) cm, or 2 in / 5 cm shorter than your desired total length.

Knit 1 rnd, decreasing 1 (1, 0, 0, 1, 2) sts = 201 (213, 234, 246, 261, 276) sts rem. Work around in k2, p1 ribbing for 2 in / 5 cm. BO in ribbing.

SLEEVES

Transfer sts for 1 sleeve onto smaller gauge short circular needles or dpn. With Color 1 and beg at the center of the new sts at underarm, pick up and k 6 (6, 6, 6, 10, 10), k 58 (64, 69, 75, 75, 79) sts around sleeve, pick up and k 7 (7, 6, 6, 10, 10) sts along underarm, pm for beg of rnd. 71 (77, 81, 87, 95, 99) sts. Work until sleeve measures 1½ (1½, 1½, 1¼, 1¼, ¾) in / 4 (4, 4, 3, 3, 2) cm.

Decrease Rnd: K2tog, k to 3 sts before marker, ssk, k1 = 2 sts decreased.

Work dec rnd approx. every 1¼ (1, 1, 1, ¾, ¾) in / 3 (2.5, 2.5, 2.5, 2, 2) cm, a total of 11 (13, 14, 16, 19, 20) times = 49 (51, 53, 55, 57, 59) sts rem. *At the same time*, when sleeve is 13¾ (13¾, 14¼, 14¼, 15, 15) in / 35 (35, 36, 36, 38, 38) cm long or 4 in / 10 cm shorter than desired length, work pattern on Chart B. Count back from center of sleeve to find the point on the chart to start the pattern. Complete Chart B, then continue with Color 2 until sleeve measures 15¾ (15¾, 16¼, 16½, 17, 17) in / 40 (40, 41, 42, 43, 43) cm or 2 in / 5 cm shorter than desired sleeve length. On the last rnd, dec 1 (0, 2, 1, 0, 2) sts = 48 (51, 51, 54, 57, 57) sts rem.

Work around in k2, p1 ribbing for 2 in / 5 cm. BO in ribbing.

FINISHING

Weave in all ends neatly on WS.

FAVORITE PULLOVER
FOR MEN

Chart from *Norwegian Knitting Designs*: figure 33, page 38.

As on the "Favorite Pullover for Women," I've used this popular band of pattern, "Figure 33," on page 38 of *Norwegian Knitting Designs*. The same pattern is shown on an "old stocking cap" on the page facing the chart. For this raglan sweater, we adjusted the design by repeating it twice on the yoke. It took some refiguring to align the motifs so they'd hang together naturally, but the pattern is still easily recognizable.

SKILL LEVEL
Experienced

SIZES
Men's XS (S, M, L, XL, XXL)

FINISHED MEASUREMENTS
Chest: 36¾ (39¾, 43¼, 45½, 48¼, 51¼) in / 93.5 (101, 110, 115.5, 122.5, 130) cm
Total Length: 25¾ (26¼, 27¼, 28, 29¼, 30) in / 65.5 (66.5, 69, 71.5, 74, 76) cm
Sleeve Length: 19¼ (19¾, 20, 20½, 21, 21) in / 49 (50, 51, 52, 53, 53) cm

YARN
CYCA #3 (DK, light worsted) Hifa Tinde pelsullgarn (100% Norwegian wool, 284 yd / 260 m / 100 g)
CYCA #2 (sport, baby) Hifa Sol lamullgarn (100% Norwegian lamb's wool, 317 yd/290 m / 100 g)

YARN AMOUNTS
Color 1 (Tinde): approx. 450 (450, 500, 550, 600, 650) g
Color 2 (Tinde): approx. 50 (50, 50, 50, 100, 100) g
Color 3 (Sol): approx. 50 g for all sizes

COLORS USED FOR THE VERSIONS SHOWN
Light Turquoise Version
Color 1: Tinde, Light Turquoise 652130
Color 2: Tinde, Navy Blue 652133
Color 3: Sol, Unbleached White 58400

Ochre Version
Color 1: Tinde, Ochre 652108
Color 2: Tinde, Black 652109
Color 3: Sol, Unbleached White 58400

SUGGESTED NEEDLE SIZES
US 2.5 / 3 mm: 24 and 32 in / 60 and 80 cm circulars and set of 5 dpn
US 4 / 3.5 mm: 16, 24 and 32 in / 40, 60 and 80 cm circulars and set of 5 dpn
US 6 / 4 mm: 32 in / 80 cm circular

GAUGE
22 sts x 28 rnds in stockinette on US 4 / 3.5 mm needles = 4 x 4 in / 10 x 10 cm.
22 sts x 26 rnds in color pattern on US 6 / 4 mm needles = 4 x 4 in / 10 x 10 cm.
Adjust needle size to obtain correct gauge if necessary.

INSTRUCTIONS

This traditional men's pullover has a raglan yoke and a nice crew neck. The sleeves and body are worked separately and then joined on one circular. The raglan yoke is knitted in the round and finished with a neck band.

BODY

With smallest gauge circular needle and Color 1, CO 196 (212, 232, 244, 260, 276) sts. Join to knit around, being careful not to twist cast-on row. Work k2, p2 ribbing for 2¾ in / 7 cm. Change to US 4 / 3.5 mm circular needle. K 1 rnd, increasing 10 sts evenly spaced around = 206 (222, 242, 254, 270, 286) sts.

Place side markers: the first marker is at beginning of rnd; also pm after 103 (111, 121, 127, 135, 143) sts. Continue until body measures 18¼ (18¼, 19, 19¼, 19¾, 20) in / 46 (46, 48, 49, 50, 51) cm. Removing markers as you come to them, on the next rnd, BO 12 (12, 12, 12, 14, 16) sts for underarm at each side: Work up to 6 (6, 6, 6, 7, 8) sts before side marker, BO 12 (12, 12, 12, 14, 16) sts; work up to 6 (6, 6, 6, 7, 8) sts before next marker, BO 12 (12, 12, 12, 14, 16) sts = 91 (99, 109, 115, 121, 127) sts rem.

Set body aside while you work sleeves.

SLEEVES

With smallest gauge dpn and Color 1, CO 48 (52, 52, 52, 56 56, 60) sts. Divide sts evenly onto 4 dpn and join to work in the round. Work around in k2, p2 ribbing for 2½ in / 6 cm. Change to US 4 / 3.5 mm dpn. K 1 rnd and inc 7 (5, 7, 5, 7, 7) sts evenly spaced around = 55 (57, 59, 61, 63, 67) sts. Pm at beg of rnd. Work around in stockinette. When sleeve measures 3¼ in / 8 cm, begin incs at beg of rnd.

Inc Rnd: M1, work until 1 st before marker, M1, k1 (= 2 sts increased).

Rep the inc rnd approx. every ¾ in / 2 cm until you've worked 18 (18, 18, 19, 21, 22) inc rnds = 91 (93, 95, 99, 105, 111) sts. Continue until sleeve is 19¼ (19¾, 20, 20½, 21, 21) in / 49 (50, 51, 52, 53, 53) cm long, or desired length to underarm.

On the next rnd, BO 12 (12, 12, 12, 14, 16) sts centered on underarm as follows: BO the first 6 (6, 6, 6, 7, 8) sts, knit until 6 (6, 6, 6, 7, 8) sts before marker, BO the last 6 (6, 6, 6, 7, 8) sts = 79 (81, 83, 87, 91, 95) sts rem.

Set first sleeve aside and knit a second sleeve just like it.

YOKE

Place body and sleeves onto one circular needle as follows: back, left sleeve, front, right sleeve = 340 (360, 384, 404, 424, 444) sts total. Pm at each intersection of sleeve and body. Beg of rnd is on the back, between the back and the right sleeve. Knit 1 rnd.

Start color pattern following chart. Check arrows at bottom of chart. Black arrows indicate starting point for front and back pieces for your size; red arrows are for the sleeves. The pattern should be centered on each section; make sure the stitch with the * at the top of the chart is centered on each section. (It should be, if you have the correct number of sts for each section and start where indicated.) Knit Row 1 in pattern. On next rnd, begin raglan decs, while continuing the charted pattern:

Dec Rnd: *K2tog, knit to 2 sts before next marker, ssk. Rep from * a total of 4 times: 8 sts dec. (See Tips for Decreasing in a Color Pattern, page 18, to understand which color to use for dec sts.)

Work dec rnd every other rnd 20 (21, 22, 23, 23, 24) times. Change to shorter circular needle when sts begin to pull tight on the needle. After completing chart, continue in Color 1 and stockinette. Complete all dec rnds, and end on a dec rnd = 180 (192, 208, 220, 240, 252) sts rem; front and back have 51 (57, 65, 69, 75, 79) sts apiece, and each sleeve has 39 (39, 39, 41, 45, 47) sts.

On next rnd, BO center 19 (21, 23, 25, 27, 29) sts for front of neck. K to end of rnd. Cut yarn. Slip the sts from the left to the right needle (without knitting them) up to front edge of neck. Now, starting on right side of neck, join Color 1 and *work back and forth* in stockinette. *While continuing* raglan decs, BO 2 (2, 1, 1, 1, 1) sts (for all sizes) at neck edge at the beg of every row. When you've worked a total of 28 (29, 30, 32, 34, 36) raglan dec rnds/rows, end with RS row = 77 (87, 101, 103, 105, 107) sts rem.

■ Color 1

■ Color 2

□ Color 3

start front/back here

XS   M   XXL   S   L   XL

start sleeve here   XL   XS   S   M   L
                     XXL

NECK BAND

With US 2.5 / 3 mm circular needle and Color 1, pick up and knit about 11 sts per 2 in / 5 cm along front neck edge, and knit rem sts of shoulders and back. On first rnd, adjust st count to a multiple of 4 = 128 (132, 132, 136, 140, 140) sts. Work around in k2, p2 ribbing for 3¼ in / 8 cm. BO in ribbing. Fold neck band inward and hem somewhat loosely on WS.

FINISHING

Sew seams at underarms. Weave in all ends on WS.

AUTUMN PULLOVER

Chart from *Norwegian Knitting Designs*: figure 54, page 51.

This high-necked, roomy pullover is perfect for snuggling up inside on cold fall evenings. It's trendy worn with either skirts or fitted pants. To fill a slightly wider area on the sleeves and the lower edge of the body, I've made a few small changes to the original color pattern from *Norwegian Knitting Designs*.

SKILL LEVEL
Experienced

SIZES
Women's XS (S, M, L, XL, XXL)

FINISHED MEASUREMENTS
Chest: 35½ (37¾, 40¼, 42½, 45, 47¼) in / 90 (96, 102, 108, 114, 120) cm
Total Length: 24½ (24¾, 25¼, 26, 26½, 27¼) in / 62 (63, 64.5, 66, 67, 69) cm
Sleeve Length: 17¾ (18, 18, 18¼, 18¼, 18½) in / 45 (45.5, 45.5, 46.5, 46.5, 47) cm

YARN
CYCA #4 (worsted, afghan, Aran) Hifa Embla (100% wool, 230 yd/210 m / 100 g)

YARN AMOUNTS
Color 1: Light Gray Heather 326054, approx. 200 (200, 200, 200, 200, 250) g
Color 2: Purple Heather 356577, approx. 400 (400, 450, 450, 500, 550) g

SUGGESTED NEEDLE SIZES
US 4 / 3.5 mm: 16 in and 32 in / 40 and 80 cm circulars and 5 dpn
US 6 / 4 mm: 16 in and 32 in / 40 and 80 cm circulars and 5 dpn

GAUGE
20 sts and 27 rnds in stockinette on smaller gauge needles = 4 x 4 in / 10 x 10 cm.
20 sts and 25 rnds in pattern on larger gauge needles = 4 x 4 in / 10 x 10 cm.
Adjust needle size to obtain correct gauge if necessary.

INSTRUCTIONS

This sweater is knitted in the round from the bottom up. It has straight sides, slanted shoulders, and set-in sleeves sewn on at the end.

BODY

With Color 1 and US 4 / 3.5 mm circular needle, CO 180 (192, 204, 216, 228, 240) sts. Join, being careful not to twist cast-on row. Work k1, p1 ribbing for 2 in / 5 cm. Change to US 6 / 4 mm circular needle and stockinette. On the first rnd, pm for each side "seam": 90 (96, 102, 108, 114, 120) sts each for back and front. When body measures 2½ in / 6 cm, begin charted pattern. The rep is worked 15 (16, 17, 18, 19, 20) times around. After completing charted rows, continue with Color 2 until body measures 16¼ (16½, 17, 17, 17¼, 17½) in / 41.5 (42, 43, 43, 43.5, 44) cm. On the last rnd, BO for underarms, removing markers as you come to them: BO 4 (5, 5, 6, 6, 7) sts. Knit until 5 (6, 6, 7, 7, 8) sts before side marker, BO 9 (11, 11, 13, 13, 15), knit to end of rnd.

Now work back and front separately, working back and forth.

FRONT

Work back and forth in stockinette. The first row is the WS. BO the first 5 (6, 6, 7, 7, 8) sts at the underarm, and purl to end of row = 81 (85, 91, 95, 101, 105) sts.

Shape Armholes:

At the beg of each of next 2 rows, BO 3 sts = 75 (79, 85, 89, 95, 99) sts.
At the beg of each of next 2 rows, BO 2 sts = 71 (75, 81, 85, 91, 95) sts.

Color 1

Color 2

center of
sleeve

start body here,
all sizes

BO 1 st at beg of next row 4 (4, 8, 10, 14, 14) times = 67 (71, 73, 75, 77, 81) sts rem.

Continue in stockinette, working outermost st at each side as an edge st knitted on all rows. When armhole measures 4¼ (4½, 4¾, 5, 5½, 6) in / 11 (11.5, 12, 13.5, 14, 15) cm, end with a WS row.

Shape front of neckline: K28 (29, 30, 30, 31, 32) sts, BO the next 11 (13, 13, 15, 15, 17) sts, k to end of row. Work each shoulder separately.

Work right shoulder first:

Right shoulder, front: Beg on WS. Purl 1 row. Now BO on neck edge at beg of knit rows only: 3 sts once, 2 sts once, 1 st 9 times = 14 (15, 16, 16, 17, 18) sts rem. *At the same time*, when armhole measures 7¼ (7½, 7¾, 8¼, 8½, 9) in / 18.5 (19, 19.5, 21, 21.5, 23) cm, shape shoulder: on next 2 WS rows, at beg (armhole side) of row, BO 5,5 (5,6; 6,6; 6,6; 6,6; 6,6) sts. On next row, BO remaining 4 (4, 4, 4, 5, 6) sts.

Left shoulder, front: Beg on RS at armhole edge. K 1 row. BO for neckline on WS 3 sts once, 2 sts once, 1 st 9 times = 14 (15, 16, 16, 17, 18) sts rem. *At the same time*, when armhole measures 7¼ (7½, 7¾, 8¼, 8½, 9) in / 18.5 (19, 19.5, 21, 21.5, 23) cm, shape shoulder. At beg (armhole side) of next 2 k rows, BO 5,5 (5,6; 6,6; 6,6; 6,6; 6,6) sts. BO remaining 4 (4, 4, 4, 5, 6) sts.

Armhole depth is now approx. 8 (8¼, 8½, 9, 9¼, 9¾) in / 20.5 (21, 21.5, 23, 23.5, 25) cm.

BACK

Begin on WS, on left side. P 1 row. Working back and forth in stockinette, shape armhole exactly as for armhole front: 67 (71, 73, 75, 77, 81) sts rem. Continue in stockinette with outermost st on each side knitted on every row as edge sts. When armhole measures 7 (7¼, 7½, 8, 8¼, 8¾) in / 18 (18.5, 19, 20.5, 21, 22.5) cm, end with a WS row.

Neck shaping: K16 (17, 18, 18, 19, 20). BO next 35 (37, 37, 39, 39, 41) sts, k to end of row. Now work each side separately, starting with left shoulder.

Left shoulder, back: Beg on WS. P 1 row. Shape neck on RS by binding off 1 st 2 times and, *at the same time*, shape shoulder as for right front shoulder. On next row, BO rem 4 (4, 4, 4, 5, 6) sts.

Right shoulder, back: Beg on RS, armhole side. K 1 row. Shape neck on WS by binding off 1 st 2 times and, *at the same time*, shape shoulder as for left front shoulder. On next row, BO rem 4 (4, 4, 5, 6) sts.

The armhole depth is now approx. 8 (8¼, 8½, 9, 9¼, 9¾) in / 20.5 (21, 21.5, 23, 23.5, 25) cm. Set body aside and work sleeves.

SLEEVES

With smaller gauge dpn and Color 1, CO 48 (48, 50, 50, 52, 54) sts. Divide onto dpn and join. Work around in k1, p1 ribbing for 2 in / 5 cm.

Change to larger gauge dpn. Knit ⅜ in / 1 cm. Sleeve now measures about 2½ in / 6 cm.

Begin charted pattern. The last st of rnd is a marking st and is not worked in pattern. Pm here. Work marking st in Color 1 when working color pattern. Center st of sleeve is opposite marking st, and is indicated on chart. Count back on your needles from the center st to find the charted st where you will begin your pattern. Work the pattern following the chart and, *at the same time*, begin inc to shape sleeve at underarm when sleeve measures 2¾ in / 7 cm.

Inc Rnd: M1, work in pattern to marker st, M1, k1. 2 inc sts.

Please read this section through before continuing: Continue in pattern. The chart is worked once vertically. Work new sts into pattern as they are added. Rep inc rnd every 2¼ (1¾, 1½, 1¼, 1¼, 1) in / 5.5 (4.5, 3.5, 3, 3, 2.5) cm, a total 7 (9, 11, 13, 14, 15) times = 62 (66, 72, 76, 80, 84) sts. After completing charted pattern, cut Color 1 and continue in stockinette with Color 2. Change to short circular needle when needles become crowded. After completing incs, work until sleeve measures 17¾ (18, 18, 18¼, 18¼, 18½) in / 45 (45.5, 45.5, 46.5, 46.5, 47) cm, or desired length.

On last rnd, BO center sts at underarm: BO 4 (5, 5, 6, 6, 7) sts and knit to end of rnd. The rest of the sleeve is worked back and forth. Turn. WS: BO the first 5 (6, 6, 7, 7, 8) sts and p to end of row = 53 (55, 61, 63, 67, 69) sts.

Shape Sleeve Cap
BO 0 (0, 2, 2, 2, 2) sts each at beginning of next 0 (0, 2, 2, 2, 2) rows = 53 (55, 57, 59, 63, 65) sts rem.

Dec Row (RS): K2, k2tog, k until 4 sts rem, ssk, k2 = 2 sts dec.

Next row (WS): K1, p until 1 st rem; end with k1.

Rep the last 2 rows a total of 17 (18, 18, 18, 19, 19) times = 19 (19, 21, 23, 25, 27) sts rem.

Now BO 2 sts at beginning of every row on the next 4 rows and then BO rem 11 (11, 13, 15, 17, 19) sts. Set first sleeve aside and knit the second one the same way.

ASSEMBLY
Sew or knit shoulders together.

COWL NECK
With RS facing, using short smaller gauge circular and Color 2, begin at right shoulder seam. Pick up and knit 39 (41, 41, 43, 43, 45) sts along back neck edge and 59 (61, 61, 63, 63, 65) sts along front neck edge = 98 (102, 102, 106, 106, 110) sts total. Work around in k1, p1 ribbing for about 4-4¼ in / 10-11 cm. Change to larger gauge circular and continue in k1, p1 ribbing until neck band measures 8¼-8¾ in / 21-22 cm. BO loosely in ribbing.

FINISHING
Sew in sleeves. Take care that center of each sleeve cap meets shoulder seam and that marker st at sleeve underarm matches center st of underarm on body.

Weave in all ends neatly on WS.

WINTER NIGHT PULLOVER

Chart from *Norwegian Knitting Designs*: figure 5, page 14; figure 31, page 36; and figure 41, page 43.

The Winter Night pullover combines the traditional and the modern for a timeless and classic garment. The pattern consists of large, handsome "eight-petaled roses," smaller stars, several pattern bands, and lice. The overall design makes me think of the stars in the night sky on a glistening, clear, cold winter night.

SKILL LEVEL
Experienced

SIZES
Men's XS (S, M, L, XL, XXL)

FINISHED MEASUREMENTS
Chest: 35½ (37¾, 41, 43¼, 46½, 49¾) in / 90 (96, 104, 110, 118, 126) cm
Total Length: 26½ (26¾, 27¼, 27½, 28¼, 28¾) in / 67 (68, 69, 70, 72, 73) cm
Sleeve Length: 19¼ (19¾, 20, 20½, 21, 21¼) in / 49 (50, 51, 52, 53, 54) cm

YARN
CYCA #4 (worsted, afghan, Aran) Hifa Embla (100% wool, 230 yd/210 m / 100 g)

YARN AMOUNTS AND COLORS
Color 1: Dark Gray Heather 326061, approx. 500 (500, 550, 600, 650, 700) g
Color 2: Unbleached White 326057, approx. 200-225 (250, 250, 250, 300, 300) g

SUGGESTED NEEDLE SIZES
US 4 / 3.5 mm: 24 and 32 in / 60 and 80 cm circulars and set of 5 dpn
US 6 / 4 mm: 16, 24, and 32 in / 40, 60 and 80 cm circulars and set of 5 dpn

GAUGE
20 sts x 27 rnds in lice on US 4 or 6 / 3.5 or 4 mm needles = 4 x 4 in / 10 x 10 cm.
20 sts x 25 rnds in pattern other than lice on US 4 or 6 / 3.5 or 4 mm needles = 4 x 4 in / 10 x 10 cm. Adjust needle size to obtain correct gauge if necessary.

INSTRUCTIONS

This sweater has a traditional cut with dropped shoulders and sewn-in sleeves. It is knitted from the bottom up with the body and sleeves worked separately. The body is cut open at the sides for the armholes and the sleeves later sewn on. The neck band is worked last.

Pay close attention to the gauge information. Follow the given measurements and adjust needle size as necessary. For sections with "tighter" patterns (not the parts with the lice), it may be necessary to go up in needle size to obtain the correct gauge.

BODY

With Color 1 and smaller gauge circular needle, CO 180 (192, 208, 220, 236, 252) sts. Join into a rnd, being careful not to twist cast-on row; pm for beginning of rnd. Work around in k1, p1 ribbing for 2 (2, 2, 2, 2½, 2½) in / 5 (5, 5, 5, 6, 6) cm.

Charts A1 and A2

If necessary to achieve gauge, switch to larger gauge circular needle. Begin Chart A1, repeating red-framed section around. Chart A1 (Rows 1-8) is worked once vertically. On the last rnd (marked with the arrow for "body"), adjust st count to a multiple of 6 sts, as follows:

Sizes XS, S, XXL: No change.
Sizes M and L: Inc 2 sts evenly spaced around.
Size XL: Dec 2 sts evenly spaced around.

Total for body: 180 (192, 210, 222, 234, 252) sts.

Continue to next section, Chart A2, which is repeated until body measures approx. 11¼ (11½, 12, 12½, 13¼, 13½) in / 28.5 (29.5, 30.5, 31.5, 33.5, 34.5) cm (or 15¼ in / 38.5 cm less than total length of body). End with a single color or lice rnd. *At the same time*, on last rnd, adjust stitch count to a multiple of 4 sts (where arrow indicates "body: adjust stitch count") as follows:

Sizes XS, S, XXL: No change.
Sizes M and L: Dec 2 sts evenly spaced around.
Size XL: Inc 2 sts evenly spaced around.

Chart A

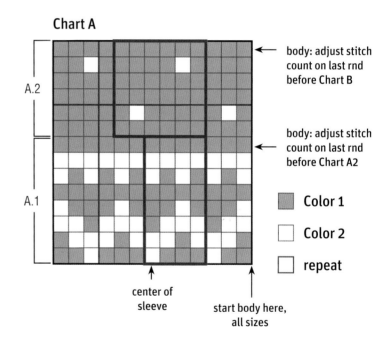

body: adjust stitch count on last rnd before Chart B

body: adjust stitch count on last rnd before Chart A2

- ▨ Color 1
- ☐ Color 2
- ☐ repeat

center of sleeve

start body here, all sizes

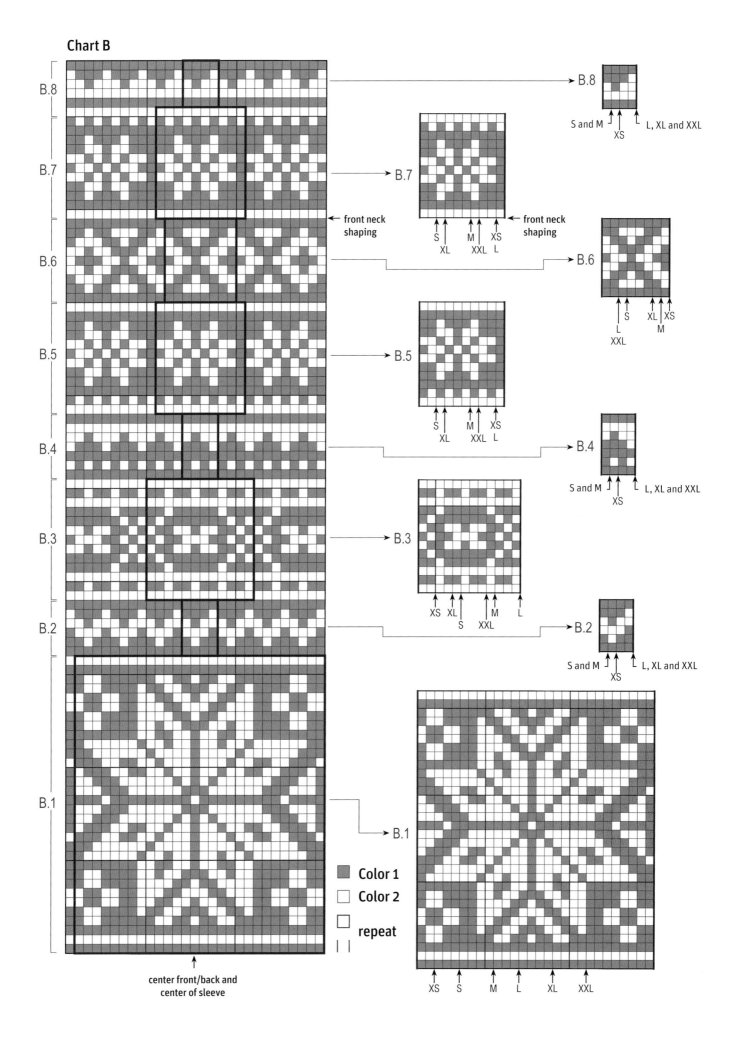

Chart B

B.8

B.7

B.6

B.5

B.4

B.3

B.2

B.1

← front neck shaping

front neck shaping →

B.8

S and M | XS | L, XL and XXL

B.7

S | XL | M | XXL | XS | L

B.6

L | XXL | S | XL | M | XS

B.5

S | XL | M | XXL | XS | L

B.4

S and M | XS | L, XL and XXL

B.3

XS | XL | S | XXL | M | L

B.2

S and M | XS | L, XL and XXL

B.1

XS | S | M | L | XL | XXL

center front/back and center of sleeve

■ Color 1
□ Color 2
▢ repeat
| |

You should now have 180 (192, 208, 220, 236, 252) sts total.

Charts B1-B8

Mark 1 st at each side: Place a contrasting loop of yarn around the 90th (96th, 104th, 110th, 118th, 126th) st and around last st of the rnd (the marker sts). The 2 marker sts are not included in the charted patterns and are consistently worked with Color 1 except in rnds where only Color 2 is used; then and only then, work marker sts with Color 2.

Chart B consists of 8 sections: B1 through B8. The large Chart B, at left, provides an overall picture of the pattern. Begin with Chart B1 and continue to B2, B3, etc. The charts are worked as follows: *Begin at arrow for your size, work repeat up to marker, work marker st, rep from * once. The pattern is symmetric on both sides of the marker.

Work up through Chart B6 (up to arrow on B7 for "front neck shaping," where body measures approx. 23¾ (24, 24½, 24¾, 25½, 26) in / 60 (61, 62, 63, 65, 66) cm, which is equivalent to 2¾ in / 7 cm less than total body length. If your vertical gauge doesn't match the directions or you want a different length, make the necessary adjustments, but start next section 2¾ in / 7 cm before you will reach total body length.

NECKLINE SHAPING AND REMAINING CHARTED PATTERN
Note: Please read entirely through this section (up to "SLEEVES") before continuing, because several steps take place at the same time.

Begin at "Neckline Shaping, Front" *while* continuing through Charts B7 and B8. When body measures 25½ (26, 26½, 26¾, 27½, 28) in / 65 (66, 67, 68, 70, 71) cm (= ¾ in / 2 cm less than total body length), begin "Back Neck Shaping."

Neckline Shaping, Front
Place center 15 (15, 17, 17, 19, 19) sts of front on a holder. Work rest of body back and forth and, *at the same time*, on each side of neck, at beg of each row, BO 2 sts 3 times and then 1 st 3 times.

Neckline Shaping, Back
Place center 29 (29, 31, 31, 33, 33) sts of back on a holder. Each side is now worked separately and back and forth. *At the same time*, on each side of back neck opening, BO 1 st 2 times at beg of next 2 rows = 4 sts bound off.

Complete charted rows. Body should measure approx. 26½ (26¾, 27¼, 27½, 28¼, 28¾) in / 67 (68, 69, 70, 72, 73) cm, with 114 (126, 138, 150, 162, 178) sts rem. If necessary, work a few single color rows or stripes to reach total length. On last row, BO the 2 marker sts. For each shoulder, 28 (31, 34, 37, 40, 44) sts rem. Place rem sts on a holder. Set body aside and knit sleeves.

SLEEVES
With smaller gauge dpn and Color 1, CO 48 (48, 50, 50, 52, 54) sts. Join and pm for beg of rnd. Work around in k1, p1 ribbing until sleeve measures 2 (2, 2, 2, 2½, 2½) in / 5 (5, 5, 5, 6, 6) cm. Change to larger gauge dpn or short circular needle (when sts fit around). K 1 rnd, increasing 4 (4, 4, 6, 6, 6) sts evenly spaced around = 52 (52, 54, 56, 58, 60) sts.

Begin working Chart A. The last st of rnd (just before marker) is the center of underarm and is *not* worked in pattern. Purl this st every rnd. Make sure center st of sleeve matches center st of pattern—count back from center of sleeve to determine starting point for pattern. The pattern should meet symmetrically at the marker st.

First, work Chart A1 (Rows 1-8, once). When sleeve is 2¾ in / 7 cm long, inc at center of underarm:

Inc Rnd: M1, k up to last st, M1, p1.

Inc this way every ¾ in / 2 cm, 14 (15, 16, 17, 18, 19) times total = 80 (82, 86, 90, 94, 98) sts.

Continue with Chart A2, Lice, *at the same time* continuing incs, until sleeve is about 14¼ (14½, 15, 15¼, 15¾, 16¼) in / 36 (37, 38, 39, 40, 41) cm long (or 5¼ in / 13 cm shorter than full length). End with a single-color rnd, right after a lice rnd. At this point, before last band of pattern, check that length is as desired. Measure the large star panel (Chart B1) on the sweater body to estimate remaining length.

Begin final band of pattern, Chart B1. The pattern is centered on the sleeve (see arrow below chart). Count out from center of sleeve to determine where to start on Chart B1. When B1 is completed, sleeve should measure about 19¼ (19¾, 20, 20½, 21, 21¼) in / 49 (50, 51, 52, 53, 54) cm. Cut Color 2. Knit 1 rnd. Make a facing as follows: Turn WS out and work ¾ in / 2 cm back and forth in stockinette (k on WS of sleeve). BO all sts loosely.

Make the second sleeve the same way.

ASSEMBLY

On the body, machine stitch tightly on both sides of the marker sts, from top to bottom, only to the same length as the width of the sleeve top—about 8 (8, 8½, 8¾, 9¼, 9½) in / 20 (20.5, 21.5, 22.5, 23.5, 24.5) cm. Ideally, measure directly from the sleeve top below the facing.

Carefully cut open armholes between seam lines.

Join shoulders with Kitchener st on RS or 3-needle BO on WS, carefully matching pattern front to back. Sew in sleeves about 1 st away from machine stitching. Lay sleeve facings over cut edges and hem on WS.

NECK BAND

With Color 1, move all held sts onto smaller gauge circular needle and k around, picking up and knitting sts at each side along neck shaping for a total of 104 (106, 108, 112, 114, 118) sts. Work around in k1, p1 ribbing for 1¼ in / 3 cm. BO in ribbing. Weave in all ends on WS.

SELBU PULLOVER

Chart from *Norwegian Knitting Designs*: figure 11, page 18, and figure 12, page 19.

A single Selbu mitten can have so many patterns and details that there are enough to fill a whole sweater and then some. Here, the motifs from the palm of a Selbu mitten have become the main pattern on a sweater's sleeves and body. The wave pattern from the mitten wrist serves as a frame. The patterns from the back of the hand are adapted and built out to a lovely, expansive design on the yoke. Despite an easy mixture of many patterns, the white neck band and lower edges of sleeves and body give the sweater a clean and delicate look. This is a delightful, practical, and timeless pullover!

SKILL LEVEL
Experienced

SIZES
Men's XS (S, M, L, XL, XXL)

FINISHED MEASUREMENTS
Chest: 35 (37¾, 40¼, 43¾, 46¼, 49¾) in / 89 (96, 102.5, 111, 117.5, 126) cm
Total Length: 26½ (26¾, 27¼, 27½, 28¼, 28¾) in / 67 (68, 69, 70, 72, 73) cm
Sleeve Length: 19¾ (20, 20½, 21, 21¼, 21¾) in / 50 (51, 52, 53, 54, 55) cm

YARN
CYCA #2 (sport, baby) Hifa Ask (100% wool, 344 yd/315 m / 100 g)

YARN AMOUNTS
Color 1: approx. 350 (400, 400, 450, 500, 550) g
Color 2: approx. 150 (200, 200, 200, 200, 250) g

COLORS SHOWN
Natural White/Charcoal Version
Color 1: Natural White 316057
Color 2: Charcoal 316056

Semi-bleached White/Rustic Blue Version
Color 1: Semi-bleached White 316047
Color 2: Rustic Blue 316082

SUGGESTED NEEDLE SIZES
US 2.5 / 3 mm: 24 and 32 in / 60 and 80 cm circulars and set of 5 dpn
US 4 / 3.5 mm: 16, 24, and 32 in / 40, 60, and 80 cm circulars and set of 5 dpn

GAUGE
24 sts x 32 rnds in single color stockinette on smaller gauge needles = 4 x 4 in / 10 x 10 cm.
24 sts x 28 rnds in pattern on larger gauge needles = 4 x 4 in / 10 x 10 cm.
Adjust needle sizes to obtain correct gauge if necessary.

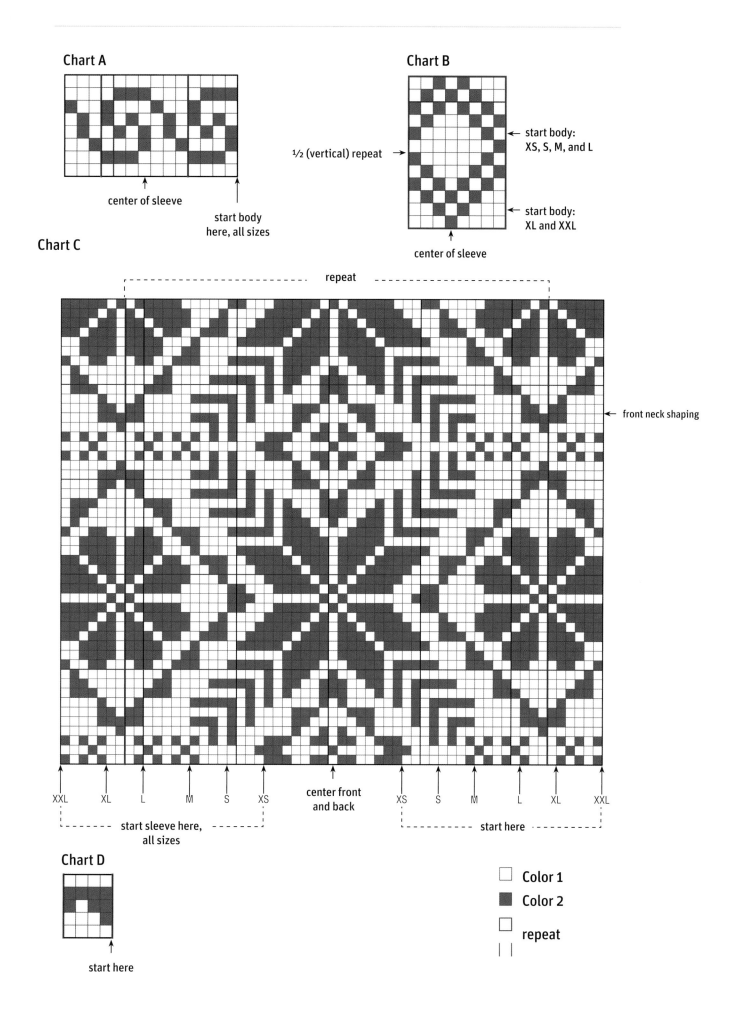

Chart A

center of sleeve

start body
here, all sizes

Chart B

½ (vertical) repeat →

← start body:
XS, S, M, and L

← start body:
XL and XXL

center of sleeve

Chart C

repeat

← front neck shaping

XXL   XL   L   M   S   XS   center front
and back   XS   S   M   L   XL   XXL

start sleeve here,
all sizes

start here

Chart D

start here

☐ Color 1
■ Color 2
☐ repeat
| |

INSTRUCTIONS

This sweater has a traditional cut with dropped shoulders and sewn-in sleeves. The body and sleeves are worked separately and in the round. When it's time for assembly, the armholes and at the center front neck shaping are cut where some extra "steek" stitches have been cast on. The sleeves are sewn in and have facings to be sewn down on the wrong side—to cover the cut edges. Finally, the neck band is knitted double to be folded in and sewn down, also covering raw, cut edges.

Pay attention to your length gauge. If yours doesn't match the recommended gauge, the length of the sweater can be adjusted by, for example, knitting or omitting a half, a whole, or more repeats of Chart B. Follow the given measurements and make adjustments as necessary.

BODY

Ribbing and Single-Color Lower Portion
With Color 1 and smaller gauge circular needle, CO 216 (232, 248, 264, 280, 296) sts. Join, being careful not to twist cast-on row. Pm for beginning of rnd. Knit 2 rnds for a slight rolled edge, then work "broken ribbing" as follows:
Rnd 1: *k2, p2, and rep from * around.
Rnd 2: Knit around.

Rep Rnds 1-2 until piece measures approx. 2½ (2½, 2½, 2¾, 2¾, 2¾) in / 6 (6, 6, 7, 7, 7) cm.

Continue in stockinette, adjusting the stitch count evenly spaced on first rnd:

XS: Inc 1 st
S: Dec 1 st
M: Dec 3 sts
L: Inc 2 sts
XL: No change
XXL: Inc 5 sts

You should now have 217 (231, 245, 266, 280, 301) sts.

Continue around in stockinette until body measures 5 (5¼, 5¾, 6, 6, 6½) in / 12.5 (13.5, 14.5, 15.5, 15.5, 16.5) cm.

Chart A (1st time)
Change to larger gauge circular needle and start pattern following Chart A. Start as shown, working rep framed in red to the last 3 sts of rnd; complete chart. The chart is worked once lengthwise. After completing Chart A, k 1 rnd with Color 1, *at the same time*, adjusting stitch count:
XS: Dec 1 st
S: Inc 1 st
M: Inc 3 sts
L: Dec 2 sts
XL: No change
XXL: Inc 3 sts

You should now have 216 (232, 248, 264, 280, 304) sts, and the body should measure approx. 6 (6½, 6¾, 7¼, 7¼, 7¾) in / 15.5 (16.5, 17.5, 18.5, 18.5, 19.5) cm.

Chart B
Work in pattern following Chart B. Begin at arrow for your size. Work complete repeats around. After working Chart B once lengthwise, rep the

entire chart another 6 times. Now the body measures approx. 17 (17¼, 17¾, 18, 19, 19½) in / 43 (44, 45, 46, 48.5, 49.5) cm. If you need to, adjust length with more or fewer whole or half chart repeats.

After completing Chart B, knit 1 rnd with Color 1, while adjusting the st count as follows:
XS: Inc 1 st
S: Dec 1 st
M: Dec 3 sts
L: Inc 2 sts
XL: No change
XXL: Dec 3 sts.

You should now have 217 (231, 245, 266, 280, 301) sts.

Chart A (2nd time)
Begin Chart A pattern again. Begin as shown, working repeat framed in red to the last 3 sts; complete chart. The chart is worked once in length. On the last rnd (the single color rnd), knit 1 rnd with Color 1, *at the same time*, adjusting stitch count:
XS: Dec 3 sts
S: Dec 1 st
M: Inc 1 st
L: no change
XL: Inc 2 sts
XXL: Inc 1 st

You should now have 214 (230, 246, 266, 282, 302) sts, and the body should measure approx. 18 (18¾, 19, 19½, 20¼, 20¾) in / 46.5 (47.5, 48.5, 49.5, 51.5, 52.5) cm.

Chart C
Knit 1 rnd with Color 1, *at the same time* placing side markers: Pm at beginning of rnd, k 107 (115, 123, 133, 141, 151), pm, knit to end of rnd.

Work in pattern following Chart C. *Begin at arrow for your size. Widthwise, work repeat (up to the left red frame), work entire rep (between red lines), first once, then start rep (in red frame) again but end at arrow for your size (= side marker). Rep from * once, for front. Knit Chart C vertically to arrow for "Front Neck Shaping."

FRONT AND BACK NECK SHAPING
Note: Please read entirely through this section (up to "Sleeves") before continuing, because several steps take place simultaneously.

Begin at "Front Neck Shaping," *at the same time* finishing Chart C.

When Chart C is complete and body measures about 25½ (26, 26½, 26¾, 27½, 28) in / 65 (66, 67, 68, 70, 71) cm, knit next rnd with Color 1: BO steek sts at center front and place the center 41 (43, 43, 45, 47) sts of back on a holder. Knit to end of rnd. Cut yarn and then begin at front neck, right side. The rest of the body is worked back and forth, each side separately.

Work in pattern following Chart D, continuing neck shaping as described below. At back, BO 1 st at neck edge on every other row a total of 2 times. Make sure pattern remains symmetrical on both sides of markers.

When Chart D is complete, the piece measures

about 26½ (26¾, 27¼, 27½, 28¼, 28¾) in / 67 (68, 69, 70, 72, 73) cm and 124 (136, 152, 168, 184, 200) sts rem, with 31 (34 38, 42, 46, 50) sts for each shoulder. Place sts on a holder. Set body aside and knit sleeves.

Front Neck Shaping
Place the center 23 (25, 25, 27, 27, 29) sts of the front on a holder; CO 5 steek sts and work to end of rnd. Shape neckline as follows: Knit to 2 sts before steek, k2tog, work across steek, ssk, complete row = 2 sts decreased.

Work this dec rnd every rnd 6 times, and then work dec rnd every other rnd 5 times.

SLEEVES
Ribbing and Single-Color Section at Lower Edge
With smaller gauge dpn and Color 1, CO 60 (60, 64, 64, 68, 68) sts. Divide sts onto dpn and join. Knit rolled edge and ribbing as on lower edge of body.

Change to larger gauge dpn and continue in stockinette. On Rnd 1, inc 4 (6, 4, 6, 4, 6) sts evenly spaced around = 64 (66, 68, 70, 72, 74) sts. When sleeve measures 2¾ (2¾, 3¼, 3½, 3½, 3½) in / 7 (7, 8, 9, 9, 9) cm, begin shaping sleeve at underarm. Pm at beg of rnd.

Inc Rnd: M1, knit up to last st, M1, k1.

Rep the inc rnd every 1 (1, ¾, ¾, ¾, ¾) in / 2.5 (2.5, 2, 2, 2, 2) cm until sleeve is 4¼ (4¾, 5¼, 5½, 5¼, 5½) in / 11 (12, 13, 14, 13, 14) cm long.

Pattern
Note: Read the following section up to ASSEMBLY before continuing.

The sleeve is now worked in pattern (Charts A + B + A) *at the same time* as the incs at the underarm continue as est. Work the new sts into pattern as they appear. Work the inc rnd 16 (16, 18, 18, 20, 20) times = 96 (98, 104, 106, 112, 114) sts. Change to short circular needle when dpn are overcrowded.

General information for sleeve: From here on, the last st of the rnd is always knitted with Color 1 as a marker st. The center of rem sts is center of sleeve—count back from center of sleeve to the st where the charted pattern begins (see arrow marked "center of sleeve"). Pattern B is symmetrical on both sides of marker st. There should be 2 rnds with Color 1 between the different motifs.

Chart A (1ˢᵗ time): The chart is worked once in length. K 1 rnd with Color 1. The sleeve now measures approx. 5¾ (6, 6½, 7, 6 ½, 7) in / 14.5 (15.5, 16.5, 17.5, 16.5, 17.5) cm.

Chart B: Begin at row marked with arrow "begin sleeve: all sizes" and work repeat until sleeve measures 18¼ (18¾, 19, 19½, 20, 20¼) in / 46.5 (47.5, 48.5, 49.5, 50.5, 51.5) cm (or 1½ in / 3.5 cm shorter than desired total length). End with either a whole or half rep lengthwise, as neatly as possible. Continue with 1 rnd in Color 1.

Chart A (2ⁿᵈ time): Work the charted rows once in length. Cut Color 2.

Knit 1 rnd in stockinette (or more if necessary) until sleeve measures about 19¾ (20, 20½, 21, 21¼, 21¾) in / 50 (51, 52, 53, 54, 55) cm. Make the sleeve facing: Turn to WS and work back and forth in stockinette for ¾ in / 2 cm. BO loosely. Set sleeve aside and make the second one the same way.

ASSEMBLY

Neck opening: Tightly machine-stitch down center front neck, on each side of the center steek st.

Armhole: Baste (optionally with contrasting color) on both sides of the side marker, from the top down as far as width of sleeve—approx. 8 (8, 8½, 8¾, 9¼, 9½) in / 20 (20.5, 21.5, 22, 23.5, 24) cm. Tightly machine-stitch on both sides of the basting thread(s). Carefully cut open armholes between the seams.

Join shoulders with Kitchener st or, on the WS, with 3-needle BO. Attach sleeves. Lay facings over cut edges and sew down on WS.

NECK BAND

Use smaller gauge circular and Color 1. Slip held sts to needle. Beg at center back, k across back neck, pick up and k 21 sts along neck shaping up to sts from holder at front and knit them. Finally, pick up and k 21 sts on other side of neck shaping = 106 (110, 110, 114, 114, 118) sts. Work around in stockinette for 1 in / 2.5 cm; p 1 rnd for foldline and then k around for 1 in / 2.5 cm (= facing). BO loosely.

Turn neck in at foldline and sew down edge on WS. Weave in all ends neatly on WS.

HILLS AND VALLEYS SWEATER

Chart from *Norwegian Knitting Designs*: figure 50, page 49.

This fine and adaptable color pattern has found its place on a women's sweater. Your fingers will fly across the bands of pattern, and with no long floats, it's easy to get a tiptop look. The pattern also works well on other garments— socks, pullovers, and hats.

SKILL LEVEL
Experienced

SIZES
Women's XS (S, M, L, XL, XXL)

FINISHED MEASUREMENTS
Chest: 35 (37, 39¾, 41¾, 44¼, 46¼) in / 89 (94, 101, 106, 112.5, 117.5) cm
Total Length: 23¼ (23¾, 24½, 24¾, 25½, 25½) in / 59 (60, 62, 63, 65, 65) cm
Sleeve Length: 17¾ (17¾, 18¼, 18¼, 18½, 18½) in / 45 (45, 46, 46, 47, 47) cm

YARN
CYCA #2 (sport, baby) Hifa Ask (100% wool, 344 yd/315 m / 100 g)

YARN AMOUNTS
Color 1: approx. 350 (350, 350, 400, 400, 450) g
Color 2: approx. 75 (75, 75, 100, 100, 100) g
Color 3: approx. 60 (65, 65, 75, 75, 75) g

COLORS SHOWN
Gray/Blue Version
Color 1: Light Warm Gray 316106
Color 2: Dark Blue-Gray 316104
Color 3: Steel Gray 316052

Ecru/Terracotta/Cyclamen Version
Color 1: Ecru 316107
Color 2: Dark Cyclamen 316135
Color 3: Dark Terracotta 316003

SUGGESTED NEEDLE SIZES
US 1.5 / 2.5 mm: 24 and 32 in / 60 and 80 cm circulars and set of 5 dpn
US 2.5 / 3 mm: 16 in / 40 cm circulars and set of 5 dpn
US 4 / 3.5 mm: 24 and 32 in / 60 and 80 cm circulars and set of 5 dpn

GAUGE
24 sts and 32 rnds in single-color stockinette on US 2.5 / 3 mm needles = 4 x 4 in / 10 x 10 cm.
26 sts in single-color stockinette for neck band on US 1.5 / 2.5 mm needles = 4 in / 10 cm.
24 sts and 28-30 rnds in pattern on US 4 / 3.5 mm needles = 4 x 4 in / 10 x 10 cm.
23 sts in seed st on US 1.5 / 2.5 mm needles = 4 in / 10 cm.
Adjust needle size to achieve correct gauge if necessary.

NOTIONS
7 buttons. Optionally, tape to cover raw edges along steek.

BUTTONS SHOWN
Gray/Blue Version: MJØLNER ¾ in / 20 mm, K342969 from Hjelmtvedt
Ecru/Terracotta/Cyclamen Version: SYNNØVE ¾ in / 20 mm, K342919 from Hjelmtvedt

INSTRUCTIONS

Begin by knitting the lower edge of the body back and forth on a circular needle. Next, cast on steek stitches at center front. (These sts will later be cut open for the front opening.) You begin working in the round at this point.

Steek stitches are also cast on at the armhole so you can continue knitting in the round. Just as on the armholes, a steek is set up at the neck so you knit in the round until the final shoulder shaping. Each sleeve is knitted in the round up to the armhole and then worked back and forth while shaping the sleeve cap.

The sweater is cut open in the front and at armholes; the button/buttonhole bands are knitted and sewn onto the front edges. Next up is the neck band. Facings on the neck band and button bands are sewn down on wrong side. Finally, the sleeves are attached. Done!

BODY

Color 1 is the background (main) color and Colors 2 and 3 are the pattern (contrast) colors.

With smallest gauge circular and Color 1, CO 205 (217, 229, 241, 255, 267) sts. Work back and forth in seed st for 1½ in / 3.5 cm. End with a WS row.

Switch to largest gauge circular, and work next row: K1, pm. *At the same time*, inc 6 (6, 10, 10, 12, 12) sts evenly spaced across, knit up to last st, pm, k1. CO 5 sts at end of row. The 5 new sts + 1 st on each side of the seed st edge are the 7 steek sts. (Do not work steek sts in pattern and do not count them in total stitch counts. On pattern rnds, work steek sts in vertical stripes, alternating colors, the first and last sts with Color 1.) When increases are complete, total (as noted, not counting 7 steek sts) = 209 (221, 237, 249, 265, 277) sts.

Now you will work in the round in pattern on front and back, with p1 in Color 1 marking the side "seams" and separating pattern panels front and back. The color pattern will meet symmetrically at center front and at both sides. Arrows below chart show where individual sections begin and end for each size.

On next rnd, set up pattern as follows:

Right front: Start at beg of chart and k 52 (55, 59, 62, 66, 69) sts in pattern, ending at the arrow marked "end right front and back."

Side marking st, right side: Optionally, pm. P1 with Color 1.

Back: Begin back at arrow marked "start back and left front" for your size, and k 103 (109, 117, 123, 131, 137) sts in pattern. End back at arrow indicated for your size.

Side marking st, left side: Optionally, pm. P1 with Color 1.

Left front: Begin left front at arrow indicated for desired size and complete chart = 52 (55, 59, 62, 66, 69) sts.

Work steek sts in vertical stripes, starting and ending with Color 1.

When piece measures 3¼ in / 8 cm, begin shaping waist:

Dec Rnd: *Knit until 2 sts before side st, ssk, p1 (side st), k2tog; rep from * once = 4 sts dec (see page 18, "Tips for Decreasing in a Color Pattern"). **Note:** After each dec, the beg or ending st next to the side p st shifts one st right or left on the chart.

Work a dec rnd every 1 (1, 1¼, 1¼, 1¼, 1¼) in / 2.5 (2.5, 3, 3, 3, 3) cm, 5 times. Each front now has 47 (50, 54, 57, 61, 64) sts and the back has 93 (99, 107, 113, 121, 127) sts + 2 side sts = 189 (201, 217, 229, 245, 257) sts total. (Remember not to count steek sts.)

After completing dec rnds, knit around for 1½ (1½, 1½, 1¾, 1¾, 1¾) in / 4 (4, 4, 4.5, 4.5, 4.5) cm. Then begin increasing.

Inc Rnd: *K up to side st, M1, p1 (side st), M1; rep from * once = 4 inc sts. Work the new sts into pattern as they appear. **Note:** With each inc, the beg or ending st next to the side p st shifts one st right or left on the chart.

Work the inc rnd every 1¼ in / 3 cm, 5 times. Each front now has 52 (55, 59, 62, 66, 69) sts and the back has 103 (109, 117, 123, 131, 137) sts + 2 side sts = 209 (221, 237, 249, 265, 277) sts total.

Continue in pattern until body measures 15½ (15½, 16⅛, 16⅛, 16½, 16½) in / 39 (39, 41, 41, 42, 42) cm. On the next rnd, bind off for armholes as follows: *Knit until 3 (3, 5, 5, 6, 7) sts before side st, BO 7 (7, 11, 11, 13, 15) sts; rep from * once

more and then knit to end of rnd = 49 (52, 54, 57, 60, 62) sts on each half front and 97 (103, 107, 113, 119, 123) sts on back.

ARMHOLES

Knit 1 rnd and CO 5 steek sts between the front and back of each armhole. Set up and work steek as at center front; do not include steek sts in your stitch count.

Dec Rnd: *Knit in pattern until 2 sts before steek, ssk, work steek sts, k2tog; work from * once more (on opposite side) = 4 dec sts. (See page 18, "Tips for Decreasing in a Color Pattern.")

Work dec rnd *every* rnd 4 (4, 4, 5, 4, 5) times. Then work dec rnd *every other* rnd 4 (5, 5, 5, 5, 5) times.

The sts are now divided as: back = 81 (85, 89, 93, 101, 103) sts; each front = 41 (43, 45, 47, 51, 52) sts.

Continue until armhole depth is 4¾ (5⅛, 5⅛, 5½, 6, 6) in / 12 (13, 13, 14, 15, 15) cm, or 2¾ in / 7 cm less than finished length.

NECK SHAPING

BO center front steek sts and place 8 (9, 9, 10, 11, 12) sts on each side of steek on a holder. Knit 1 rnd and, at end of this rnd, CO 5 new steek sts. Neckline will be decreased at each side of the steek.

Dec Rnd: *K2tog, knit until 2 sts before steek at center front, ssk. (See page 18, "Tips for Decreasing in a Color Pattern.")

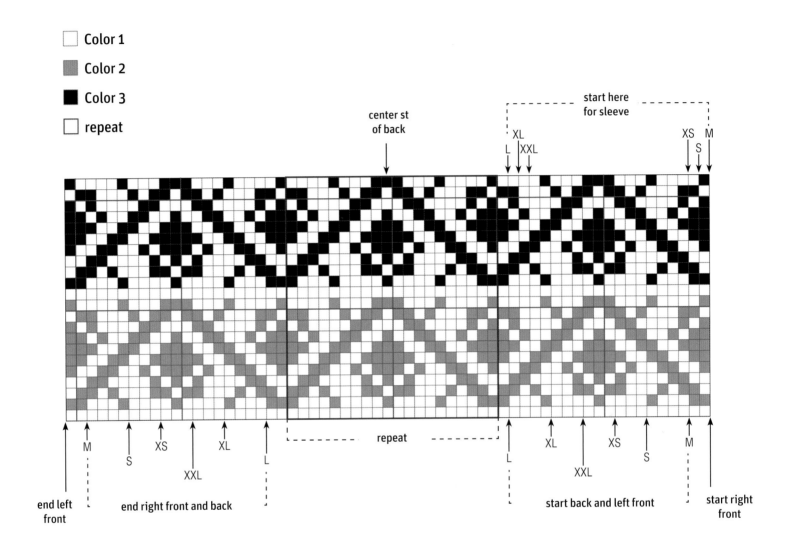

Color 1

Color 2

Color 3

repeat

center st of back

start here for sleeve

XL

L XXL

XS M

S

repeat

M

S

XS

XXL

XL

L

end left front

end right front and back

L

XL

XXL

XS

S

M

start back and left front

start right front

Work dec rnd *every* rnd a total of 7 times. Work dec rnd *every other* rnd 4 (4, 4, 4, 5, 5) times.

Each front now has 22 (23, 25, 26, 28, 28) sts while the back still has 81 (85, 89, 93, 101, 103) sts.

Continue in pattern until armhole depth is 7½ (7½, 8, 8¼, 8¾, 8¾) in / 19 (19, 20, 21, 22, 22) cm.

On the last rnd, BO steek sts at center front and at armholes. Place center 33 (35, 35, 37, 41, 43) sts of back on a holder.

SHOULDERS
Now work back and forth (k on RS and p on WS) to shape shoulders. Continue pattern as far as is reasonable. That is, if a band of pattern is just completed, it's not reasonable to start a new band if only a couple of rnds rem to be knitted. In that case, continue without pattern in Color 1.

Right Front Shoulder
Begin on RS at center front. Work 1 row. At beg of next row and every second following row, BO: 5,6,5 (5,6,6; 6,6,6; 6,7,6; 7,7,7; 7,7,7) sts. On the next (RS) row, BO rem 6 (6, 7, 7, 7, 7) sts. Cut yarn.

Left Front Shoulder
Begin on WS at center front. Work 1 row. At beginning of next (WS) row and every second following row, BO: 5,6,5 (5,6,6; 6,6,6; 6,7,6; 7,7,7; 7,7,7) sts. On the next (WS) row, BO rem 6 (6, 7, 7, 7, 7) sts. Cut yarn.

Right Back Shoulder
Begin on WS at back of neck. Shape shoulder as for left front shoulder, but, *at the same time*, after the 1st row, BO 1 st at each neck edge on every other row 2 times.

Left Back Shoulder
Begin on RS at back of neck. Shape shoulder as for right front shoulder, but, *at the same time*, after the 2nd row, BO 1 st at neck edge on every other row 2 times.

Set body aside while you knit the sleeves.

SLEEVES
Note: Inc rnds start near the end of the color pattern. Be sure to read section on increasing before starting color pattern.

With US 1.5 / 2.5 mm dpn and Color 1, CO 49 (51, 53, 55, 57, 59) sts.

Join and work around in seed st (see page 23, "Tips for a Firmer Seed Stitch") for 1½ in / 3.5 cm. Change to dpn US 4 / 3.5 mm. K 1 rnd, increasing 8 sts evenly spaced around = 57 (59, 61, 63, 65, 67) sts. The last st of the rnd will be the center of the underarm. P this st in Color 1 as a marker in all rnds.

Work in pattern following chart. The arrows above chart show where to start for desired size. Make sure pattern is centered on sleeve (see arrow on chart). Work charted pattern once in length. Cut Colors 2 and 3.

Change to US 2.5 / 3 mm dpn and continue in single-color stockinette with Color 1.

At the same time, when sleeve measures 2½ in / 6 cm, begin shaping sleeve at underarm.

Inc Rnd: *M1, knit in pattern up to last (marker) st, M1, k1.*

Work inc rnd every 1½ (1½, 1¼, 1¼, 1, 1) in / 3.5 (3.5, 3, 3, 2.5, 2.5) cm until you have 11 (12, 13, 14, 15, 15) inc rnds = 79 (83, 87, 91, 95, 97) sts. Change to a short circular needle (US 2.5 / 3 mm) when sts get overcrowded on dpn.

Continue until sleeve measures 17¾ (17¾, 18¼, 18¼, 18½, 18½) in / 45 (45, 46, 46, 47, 47) cm or desired length. On next rnd, BO 7 (7, 11, 11, 13, 15) sts for armhole, centered on sleeve as follows: BO the first 3 (3, 5, 5, 6, 7) sts, knit until 4 (4, 6, 6, 7, 8) sts rem in rnd, BO rem sts = 72 (76, 76, 80, 82, 82) sts rem.

The sleeve cap is now worked back and forth *at the same time* as it is shaped with decs:

BO 2 sts at beg of the next 4 rows = 64 (68, 68, 72, 74, 74) sts rem.

BO 1 st at each side of sleeve cap on every other row 15 (17, 15, 16, 17, 18) times = 34 (34, 38, 40, 40, 38) sts rem.

BO 1 st on each side of sleeve cap on every row 4 (4, 6, 5, 5, 4) times = 26 (26, 26, 30, 30, 30) sts rem.

BO 2 sts at beg of the next 6 (6, 6, 8, 8, 8) rows = 14 sts rem.

On next row, BO rem 14 sts. Cut yarn.

Make the second sleeve the same way.

ASSEMBLY
With small stitches, machine-stitch on each side of the center steek st: center front, front neck, and each armhole. Cut open each steek between the seams. Join shoulders on WS by sewing or 3-needle bind off.

BUTTON/BUTTONHOLE BANDS
With RS facing you, smallest gauge needles and Color 1, pick up and k sts along each front edge, in the space between the steek and body sts. The bands are worked back and forth in seed st and the 1st row is on the WS. The row vs. stitch gauge is different: pick up and knit about 23 sts for every vertical 4 in / 10 cm on front—this corresponds roughly to picking up 7 sts every 10 rows. (If you're uncertain, try this out on 4 in / 10 cm of the lower edge of the right front. There should be no puckering.) The stitch count should be a multiple of (2)+1. On the right front, start at bottom of the seed st edge, and, on left front, begin at the neck. The choice of which will have buttons and which will have buttonholes is up to you!

Button Band Without Buttonholes:
Work a total of 10 rows in seed st. BO in seed st.

Button Band With Buttonholes:

Rows 1-4: Work back and forth in seed st.

Row 5 (WS): Continue in seed st and, *at the same time*, make 7 buttonholes. The buttonholes are made by binding off 2-3 sts (depending on size of buttons). The first and last buttonholes are worked 3 sts in from the edge and the rest spaced evenly in between. You can place pins on the right front edge of the body as guides.

Row 6 (RS): Work in seed st and CO 2-3 sts (same number as were bound off) over each gap in previous row.

Continue in seed st until you've worked a total of 10 rows. BO in pattern.

NECK BAND

The neck band is worked back and forth in stockinette and has a contrast-color facing that peeks nicely over the top edge. Move held sts to smallest gauge circular needle. With RS facing you and Color 1, beg at center of right button band, pick up and k 4 sts, k sts along front neck edge; pick up and knit 31 (31, 31, 31, 33, 33) sts on right side of neck edge; knit back neck sts; pick up and knit 31 (31, 31, 31, 33, 33) sts on left side of neck edge; pick up and knit sts on left front neck edge and, finally, pick up and knit 4 sts to center of left button band = 119 (123, 123, 127, 137, 141) sts.

Row 1 (WS): Purl and, *at the same time*, dec 3 (3, 3, 3, 9, 9) sts evenly spaced across = 116 (120, 120, 124, 128, 132) sts. Work another 6 rows; the last row is on WS. Cut Color 1 with a tail of approx. 4 in / 10 cm.

Join Color 2—or Color 3, if you prefer—and knit a facing: k 2 rows (one on WS to create a foldline), then work 7 rows in stockinette. BO loosely.

Turn neck band at foldline and sew down somewhat loosely on WS. Seam the short ends with mattress st.

FINISHING

Sew in sleeves. Match center of each sleeve cap to shoulder seam, and be sure that center sts of underarms and side "seams" match. Sew down cut edges to WS. If you like, sew on tape to cover raw edges.

Sew on buttons and, if necessary, reinforce buttonholes.

Weave in all ends neatly on WS.

ROSE CARDIGAN

Chart from *Norwegian Knitting Designs*: figure 11, page 18 and figure 27, page 32.

A stocking and a mitten—both from Selbu—were the basis of the pattern for
this lovely sweater. The rounded eight-petaled roses fit together beautifully—
yet another example of how you can combine several patterns to create
something completely new, but still recognizably traditional. The cut
of this pretty and feminine cardigan seems created to go with a skirt,
either A-line or loose and flowy.

SKILL LEVEL
Experienced

SIZES
Women's XS (S, M, L, XL, XXL)

FINISHED MEASUREMENTS
Chest: 35 (36, 39¾, 41¾, 44¼, 46) in / 89 (94, 101, 106, 112.5, 117.5) cm
Length: 20½ (21, 21¾, 22, 22½, 22) in / 52 (53, 55, 56, 57, 56) cm
Sleeve Length: to underarm, 17¾ (17¾, 18¼, 18¼, 18½, 18½) in / 45 (45, 46, 46, 47, 47) cm

YARN
CYCA #2 (sport, baby) Hifa Ask 100% wool yarn (315 m / 100 g)

YARN AMOUNTS
Color 1: approx. 250 (300, 300, 300, 350, 350) g
Color 2: approx. 200 (200, 200, 200, 250, 250) g

COLORS SHOWN
Old Rose and Brown Version
Color 1: Old Rose Heather 346574
Color 2: Dark Brown Heather 316103

Light Gray/Dark Blue-Gray Version
Color 1: Light Gray Heather 316054
Color 2: Dark Blue-Gray 316104

White/Dark Gray-Blue Version
Color 1: Unbleached White 316057
Color 2: Dark Gray-Blue Heather 316104

SUGGESTED NEEDLE SIZES
US 2.5 / 3 mm: 24 in / 60 cm circular and 5 dpn
US 4 / 3.5 mm: 16, 24, and 32 in / 40, 60, and 80 cm circulars and 5 dpn

GAUGE
24 sts and 28 rnds in pattern on US 4 / 3.5 mm needles = 4 x 4 in / 10 x 10 cm.
Adjust needle size to obtain correct gauge if necessary.

NOTIONS
7 buttons

BUTTONS SHOWN
Old Rose and Brown Version: URNES 20 mm, K342984 from Hjelmvedt
Light Gray and Dark Gray-Blue Version: SNORRE 20 mm, K342970 from Hjelmvedt.
White and Dark Gray-Blue Version: SNORRE 20 mm, K342970 from Hjelmvedt.

INSTRUCTIONS

Work the ribbed lower edge first, back and forth on a circular needle. After that, you'll cast on steek sts at the front, which will later be cut apart. From that point on, everything is worked in the round. The body and the sleeves are worked separately up to the underarm; then all parts are placed on the same circular needle and continued up into a yoke with decreases on both sleeves and shoulders, in a smooth approximation of set-in sleeves. The shoulders are sloped and sewn or bound off together and the sleeve tops are sewn in. Next, the jacket front is cut open, button bands are knitted and sewn onto the cut edges. Finally, you'll tackle the neck band and sew in facings for the button/buttonhole bands to cover the cut edges. Done!

BODY

With smaller gauge circular needle and Color 1, CO 200 (212, 224, 236, 248, 260) sts. Work k2, p2 ribbing back and forth with the first and last sts as edge sts:

Row 1 (WS): Slip 1 p-wise with yarn in front, work k2, p2 ribbing until 3 sts rem, end with p3.

Row 2 (RS): Slip 1 k-wise with yarn in back, work k2, p2, ribbing until 3 sts rem, end with k3.

Rep Rows 1 and 2. When ribbing is ¾ in / 2 cm long, make a buttonhole on the knit side right edge: Slip 1 k-wise with yarn in back, k2, p2, BO the next 3 sts, continue ribbing as est to end of row. On next row (WS), CO 3 sts over the bound

off sts. Continue with ribbing until work measures 3½ in / 9 cm. End with a WS row.

Work the first 11 sts in the ribbed edge. Place these 11 sts and the 11 sts on the opposite end on a piece of scrap yarn or other holder. (These form the bases of the button/buttonhole bands.)

Change to larger gauge circular. K 1 row, and inc 11 (11, 15, 15, 19, 19) sts evenly spaced = 189 (201, 217, 229, 245, 257) sts. CO 5 sts at the end of the rnd for a steek (cutting stitches). Do *not* work these in pattern, and do not include them in your st count. Optionally, pm on both sides of these sts. Work the steek in 1-st vertical stripes with a Color 1 st at each end.

Next, you will join and start charted pattern on both sides of front and back with a single p st at each side as a "side seam" marker. The pattern will be symmetrical on both sides of the front steek and both sides of the purl "side seam" marker. Arrows under the chart at right show where each part starts and ends in every size. Set up pattern on next rnd as follows:

Right front: Start pattern at point indicated for chosen size, and work 47 (50, 54, 57, 61, 64) sts. Stop at arrow marked "end here, right front and back."

Side "seam" marker (right side): Purl 1 st in Color 1.

Back: Start at arrow marked "start here, back and left front," k 93 (99, 107, 113, 121, 127) sts, and stop at arrow marked "end here, right front and back."

Side "seam" marker (left side): Purl 1 st in Color 1.

Left front: Start at arrow marked "Start here, back and left front" and knit through the chart = 47 (50, 54, 57, 61, 64) sts.

Continue in the round in pattern until work measures 4¾ in / 12 cm. Now begin a gradual inc at the sides moving toward the armhole, as follows:

Inc Rnd: *Work pattern up to the p marking st, M1, p1 (side marker), M1,* repeat from * once = 4 inc sts. Work new sts into pattern as you go. Remember, starting/ending position in the chart will shift right or left as you inc.

Rep the inc rnd every 1½ in / 3.5 cm until there are 5 inc rnds = 209 (221, 237, 249, 265, 277) sts total. Now, continue in pattern until body measures 12 (12½, 13, 13, 13, 13½)in / 31 (32, 33, 33, 33, 34) cm. On last rnd, BO for armholes: *Work up to 3 (3, 5, 5, 6, 7) sts before the side marker st, BO 7 (7, 11, 11, 13, 15) sts, rep from * once; finish the rnd = 49 (52, 54, 57, 60, 62) sts on each front and 97 (103, 107, 113, 119, 123) sts on back.

Set body aside and knit sleeves.

SLEEVES

With smaller gauge dpn and Color 1, CO 48 (52, 52, 56, 56, 60) sts. Work k2, p2 ribbing for 2½ in

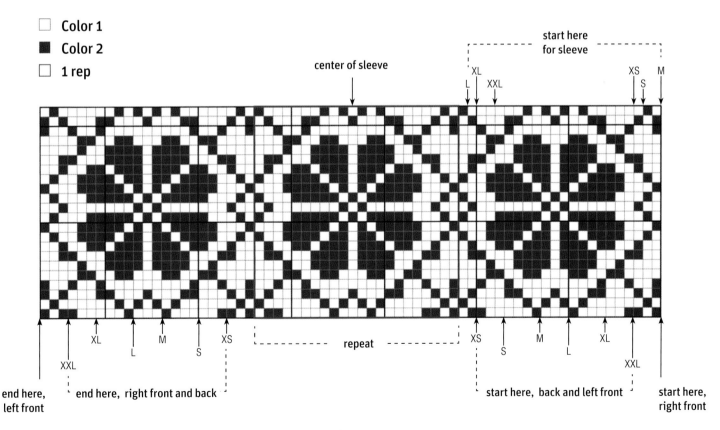

/ 6 cm. Change to larger gauge dpn. K 1 rnd, and inc 14 (12, 16, 14, 16, 16) sts, evenly spaced = 62 (64, 70, 70, 72, 76) sts. From now on, always p the last st in Color 1 (the underarm "seam" marker).

Before continuing, you should decide how long a sleeve you want and on which row of the chart to start. This is because the pattern on the sleeve has to end in exactly the same row as the pattern on the body. To figure out which row of the chart to start on, you can use the following example:

A. Say the body measures 13 in / 33 cm to the underarm, and the ribbed edge is 3½ in / 9 cm. 13 minus 3½ = 9½ in (or 33 minus 9 = 24 cm).

B. And perhaps you want a sleeve that measures 18 in / 46 cm. The ribbed cuff is 2½ in / 6 cm. 18 minus 2½ = 15½ in (or 46 minus 6 = 40 cm).

C. Therefore, the difference between the color-patterned portion of the sleeves and the body is 15½ minus 9½ in = 6 in (or 40 minus 24 = 16 cm).

D. Lay the body on a flat surface, measure from the armhole to the highest full vertical rep, and then down 6 in / 16 cm. That row is the row in the chart where you should start the pattern on the sleeve.

Where the pattern starts is actually a little chancy: It depends both on your vertical knitting tension and your desired sleeve length. Sometimes the pattern will look better if it's started either a couple of rows before or after the row you calculated, so you can start on a whole or a half vertical

repeat. This can be adjusted on a case-by-case basis by, for example, shortening or lengthening the ribbing on the sleeve, or working a few single color (Color 1) rnds before starting the pattern.

Arrows above chart show where to start for each size. Be sure pattern is centered (see arrow marked "center of sleeve") and remember to always purl last st of rnd.

When sleeve measures 4 (4, 4¾, 3½, 3½, 2¾) in / 10 (10, 12, 9, 9, 7) cm, beg inc at underarm on both sides of the marking p st:

Inc Rnd: M1, work in pattern up to last st, M1, p1 (seam marker). Work new sts into the color pattern as they appear.

Rep this inc rnd every 1½ (1½, 1¼, 1¼, 1¼, 1¼) in / 3.5 (3.5, 3, 3, 3, 3) cm until you have worked 10 (10, 11, 12, 12, 13) inc rnds = 82 (84, 90, 94, 96, 102) sts. Shift to a short circular needle when sts become crowded. Continue in pattern until sleeve measures 17¾ (17¾, 18¼, 18¼, 18½, 18½) in / 45 (45, 46, 46, 47, 47) cm (or desired length to underarm). End pattern as on body: On last rnd, BO the first 3 (3, 5, 5, 6, 7) sts and the last 4 (4, 6, 6, 7, 8) sts of the rnd = 7 (7, 11, 11, 13, 15) sts bound off in total, and 75 (77, 79, 83, 83, 87) sts rem. Set sleeve aside and make another one just like it.

JOINING THE SLEEVES AND THE BODY
Place sleeve sts on same circular as body sts, one sleeve above each underarm BO on the body, bind offs matching = 345 (361, 373, 393, 405, 421) sts. Beg of rnd is center of steek sts in front.

Knit around, continuing pattern as before: Work 1 rnd with M1 st at every join point of the sleeves and body (marking sts) = 349 (365, 377, 397, 409, 425) sts. P these marking sts through the back of the st in Color 1. You will dec at this joining point, first on both sides of it, then only on the sleeve side. **Note:** You will also BO for neckline eventually, and this takes place *at the same time* as the other decs. Please read ahead up to "Assembly" before you continue.

Dec Rnd: *Knit in pattern up to 2 sts before the marking st, ssk, p1 through back of st, k2tog, rep from * 3 more times = 8 sts dec.

Work dec rnd *every* rnd 4 (4, 4, 5, 4, 5) times. Then work dec rnd *every other* rnd 4 (5, 5, 5, 5, 5) times = 81 (85, 89, 93, 101, 103) sts for back; 41 (43, 45, 47, 51, 52) sts for each half front; 59 (59, 61, 63, 65, 67) sts for each sleeve.

Now you will dec *only* on the sleeves. Remember, neckline decs will be worked after each sleeve dec. (See next paragraph.)

Dec Rnd: *Knit to the marking st, k it; k2tog, knit to 2 sts before the next marking st, ssk. Repeat from * once, and then work the rest of the rnd = 4 sts dec, 2 on each sleeve.

Work this dec rnd *every 3ʳᵈ* rnd 4 (4, 4, 4, 4, 3) times. Then work this dec rnd *every other* rnd 3 (3, 4, 3, 5, 6) times. Then work the dec rnd *every* rnd 9 (9, 9, 10, 9, 10) times.

At the same time that sleeve decs continue, when armhole measures 5 (5, 5½, 6, 6¼, 6¼) in / 13

(13, 14, 15, 16, 16) cm, BO starts on the front neckline. BO steek sts. Place the 7 (8, 8, 9, 10, 11) sts on each side of steek on a holder. From here on, knit back and forth (or use an alternative technique, see instructions below). Marking sts are knitted (through the back loop) on the WS, and decs on sleeve cap are purled, but otherwise the same as on the RS. The outermost st at edge of neckline is worked as an edge st and is knitted on all rows; at the ends of rows, it is knitted with both colors to "lock" the yarn at the edge.

BO for neck opening at beg of *every other* rnd 3, 2, 2, 1, 1, 1 sts.

When all sleeve decs are complete, 27 (27, 27, 29, 29, 29) sts rem on each sleeve cap and armhole measures approx. 5½ (5¾, 6, 6, 6¼, 6½) in / 14 (14.5, 15.5, 15.5, 16, 16.5) cm. On next rnd, BO sleeve sts (saving, however, the marking sts) and fronts and back are knitted separately back and forth. Marking sts act as edge sts from here on: they're counted in st totals for front and back, and worked with both colors as for edge sts on neckline.

Methods to Avoid Purling Color Patterns
Here are two alternatives if you want to avoid purling color patterns. Take care that the dominant color remains so!

Method 1: Work the "wrong side" from the right side, but in the other direction. Do this: With RS still facing you, k mirror-image to your usual knitting: put the left needle into the first st through the back loop, slip it. Now, think about how you usually knit: If you knit two-handed, switch the colors, holding the dominant color in your right rather than your left hand. If you pick both colors from your *left* index or middle finger, move both strands to your *right* index or middle finger, holding the dominant color closer to the work—that is, closer to your second joint—and picking the non-dominant color from above it. If you always hold both colors in your right hand, continue to do so, but remember to take the dominant color from *underneath* the non-dominant color. This method takes a little practice, but many find they can work just as speedily as they do in the usual direction. **Remember:** Work left to right. Put the needle through the back loop of each st. Be careful to maintain the same color dominance.

Method 2: Continue to knit in the round: When the steek has been BO, and the sts on both sides of it are on a stitch holder, CO 5 new steek sts at the front of the neckline and continue to work in the round. Dec for the front of the neckline on both sides of the new steek. Sew and cut open the new steek as you would for the front edges. **Note:** With this method, a double neck band works best, because it can be folded inward and hemmed down to cover the cut edges.

FRONTS

From this point, the two front shoulders are worked separately. They're worked the same, but mirror-image.

Continue with decs for the front neckline. When neckline decs are complete, there will be 25 (26, 28, 29, 32, 32) sts on each shoulder part, including the edge stitch toward the armhole, which

was the "marking st" earlier. Work in pattern until armhole measures 7½ (7½, 8, 8¼, 8¾, 8¾) in / 19 (19, 20, 21, 22, 22) cm.

Shoulder bind-off: The shoulders fit best if they are a little sloped. Accomplish this by binding off in stages. BO on the side toward the armhole—which means the right shoulder will be BO on the WS, and the left shoulder on the RS. BO at the beg of every other row 4 times: 6, 6, 6, 7 (6,7,6,7; 7,7,7,7; 7,7,7,8; 8,8,8,8; 8,8,8,8) sts.

THE BACK

Work in pattern until armhole measures 7½ (7½, 8, 8¼, 8¾, 8¾) in / 19 (19, 20, 21, 22, 22) cm. Place the center 33 (33, 33, 35, 37, 39) sts on a holder. From here, work each shoulder separately, and BO shoulders as on the front.

ASSEMBLY

Sew the shoulders together. Sew in the sleeve caps and stitch the underarm seams.

Machine stitch tightly down the front on both sides of the center steek st. Cut between the two seams.

BUTTON BANDS

Button Band Without Buttonholes

Transfer sts from holder onto a needle of the size used for the ribbing. These instructions are written as if this button band will be on the left; if you want it on the right, then Row 1 will be a WS row (i.e., knits and purls, etc., must be reversed).

Row 1 (RS): K2, p2 twice, end with k3.

Row 2 (WS): Slip 1 p-wise with yarn in front (wyf), p2 (k2, p2) twice, CO four sts (for a facing to cover the cut steek edges).

Row 3 (RS): P4 (for facing), (k2, p2) twice, end with k3.

Row 4 (WS): Sl 1 p-wise wyf; p2, (p2, k2) twice, k4.

Rep Rows 3 and 4 until the button band, lightly stretched (it should have ended up approx. 1 in / 2-3 cm shorter) reaches the neckline of the body. BO the 4 facing sts and place the remaining 11 sts on a holder. Figure and mark the position of 6 buttons—the 7th button will be halfway up the neck band.

Button Band With Buttonholes
Transfer sts from holder onto smaller gauge needle. These instructions are written as if this button band will be on the right; if you want it on the left, then Row 1 will be an RS row (i.e., knits and purls, etc., must be reversed).

Row 1 (WS): (P2, k2) twice, end with p3.

Row 2 (RS): Slip 1 k-wise wyb, k2, (p2, k2) twice, CO 4 sts for facing.

Row 3 (WS): K4, (p2, k2) twice, end with p3.

Row 4 (RS): Slip 1 k-wise, wyb, k2 (p2, k2) twice, p4.

Rep Rows 3 and 4 as on the first button band, but make buttonholes (as on the ribbed bottom edge) that correspond with the button marks on the first button band. When the buttonhole band is as long as the matching button band, BO the 4 sts of the facing and place the remaining 11 sts on a holder.

Sew both button bands in place in the space between steek sts and front edge of pattern. Wait to sew down facing until neck band is complete.

NECK BAND
With Color 1 and smaller gauge, short circular, start at right buttonhole band. Transfer 11 sts from holders onto needle and pick up and knit sts along neck edge for a total of 120 (120, 124, 124, 128, 132) sts. (The number must be a multiple of 4.)

Work k2, p2 ribbing. After 1 cm, make top buttonhole, in line with other buttonholes. Work ribbing until neck band measures 1¼ in / 3 cm. BO in ribbing.

FINISHING
Fasten facings over cut edges and sew them down on the WS. Weave in and trim all ends on WS. Sew on the buttons.

STORSKARVEN SWEATER—
THE BIG RASCAL

Charts from *Norwegian Knitting Designs*, figure 19, page 26; figure 59, page 53;
and figure 63, page 56.

The mountain peak at the juncture point of Selbu, Stjørdal, and Meråker in Trøndelag is called Storskarven in Norwegian, which means "The Big Rascal." The patterns on this jacket are bands of zigzag, small Selbu roses, stars, and crosses from the pattern on a Selbu stocking. Imagine yourself under a starry sky, nearing the peak and that the cross is the meeting point of the three places. With a bit of imagination, you can see that the zigzags are the mountains that you can see all around from the top of The Big Rascal—Storskarven.

SKILL LEVEL
Experienced

SIZES
Men's S (M, M/L, L, XL, XXL)

FINISHED MEASUREMENTS
Chest: 38¼ (40¼, 42½, 44¾, 47¼, 49¼) in / 97 (102, 108.5, 113.5, 120, 125) cm
Full Length: 27½ (28, 28¼, 28¼, 28¾, 29) in / 70 (71, 72, 72, 73, 74) cm
Sleeve Length: 21¼ (21¼, 21¾, 21¾, 21¾, 22) in / 54 (54, 55, 55, 55, 56) cm

YARN
CYCA #2 (sport, baby) Hifa Ask 100% wool yarn (344 yd/315 m / 100 g)

YARN AMOUNTS AND COLORS SHOWN
Color 1: Gray Heather 316055, approx. 300 (400, 400, 450, 450, 500) g
Color 2: Lilac Brown 316099, approx 200 (200, 200, 200, 250, 250) g
Color 3: Light Farmer Blue 316037, approx. 75 (75, 75, 75, 100, 100) g

SUGGESTED NEEDLE SIZES
US 2.5 / 3 mm: 24 and 32 in / 60 and 80 cm circular and set of 5 dpn
US 4 / 3.5 mm: 16, 24, and 32 in / 40, 60, and 80 cm circular and set of 5 dpn

GAUGE
24 sts in pattern on larger gauge needles = 4 in / 10 cm.
Adjust needle size to obtain correct gauge if necessary.

NOTIONS
9 buttons

BUTTONS SHOWN
JOTUN 22 mm, K362909 from Hjelmvedt

Hand stitch the button/buttonhole bands down along the front edges, in the space between the front and the steek, not including the facings (which are to be tacked down when the neck band is completed).

NECK BAND

Using smaller gauge circular and Color 1, start at right button band. Place sts from holder onto needle and pick up and knit sts along neck edges and left buttonhole band, until you have a total of 116 (120, 120, 124, 128, 128) sts (a multiple of 4). Work p2, k2 ribbing as before. After ½ in / 1 cm, make a buttonhole, in line with the buttonholes in the buttonhole band.

Single neck band: Work in ribbing until neck band measures 1¼ in / 3 cm. BO in ribbing.

Double neck band: Work in ribbing until neck band measures 6 cm, placing a second buttonhole to match the one on the outside. BO in ribbing. Hem the bound-off edge of the neck band on the inside (over the cut edges) and sew the inner and outer buttonholes together carefully.

FINISHING

Sew in sleeves. Lay facings over cut edges and sew them to WS. Weave in all ends. Sew buttons on where marked and, optionally, reinforce buttonholes. Done!

A MOST ELEGANT SWEATER

Chart from *Norwegian Knitting Designs*, figure 19, page 26.

This smart pattern is too marvelous to be tucked away in a book.
It has to be brought out and used again and again. In *Norwegian Knitting Designs*, we see it used as an area pattern on a beautiful knee-high sock. Here we've used it for a striking women's jacket, but it would be magnificent on a man's pullover as well. The pattern was slightly altered to make it more symmetrical.

SKILL LEVEL
Experienced

SIZES
Women's XS (S, M, L, XL, XXL)

FINISHED MEASUREMENTS
Chest: 35 (37, 39¾, 41¾, 44¼, 46¼) in / 89 (94, 101, 106, 112.5, 117.5) cm
Full Length: 22¾ (22¾, 24, 24½, 25¼, 25) in / 58 (58, 61, 62, 64, 64) cm
Sleeve Length: 18¼ (18¼, 18¼, 18½, 18½, 18½) in / 46 (46, 46, 47, 47 47) cm

YARN
CYCA #2 (sport, baby) Hifa Ask 100% wool yarn (344 yd/315 m / 100 g)

YARN AMOUNTS
Color 1: approx. 250 (250, 300, 300, 300, 350) g
Color 2: approx. 250 (250, 300, 300, 350, 350) g
Color 3: approx. 50 (50, 50, 100, 100, 100) g
Color 4: approx. 25 g (all sizes)

COLORS SHOWN
Blue Version
Color 1: Dark Air Force Blue 316136
Color 2: Light Turquoise Green 316127
Color 3: Terracotta 316096
Color 4: Pale Rose 316108

Brown Version
Color 1: Semi-bleached White 316047
Color 2: Brown Heather 316102
Color 3: Burgundy 316143
Color 4: Pale Rose 316103

SUGGESTED NEEDLE SIZES
US 2.5 / 3 mm: 24 in / 60 cm circular and set of 5 dpn
US 4 / 3.5 mm: 16, 24, and 32 in / 40, 60, and 80 cm circulars and set of 5 dpn
US B-1 and C-2 / 2.5 and 3 mm: crochet hooks

GAUGE
24 sts and 32 rnds in plain stockinette on smaller gauge needles = 4 x 4 in / 10 x 10 cm
24 sts and 28 rnds in pattern on larger gauge needles = 4 x 4 in / 10 x 10 cm
Adjust needle size to obtain correct gauge if necessary.

NOTIONS
9 buttons; sharp mid-sized tapestry needle for optional embroidery

BUTTONS SHOWN
Blue Version: NUMEDAL ¾ in / 18 mm, K312983 from Hjelmvedt
Brown Version: VIKING ¾ in / 18 mm, K312982 from Hjelmvedt

Chart A Cuff

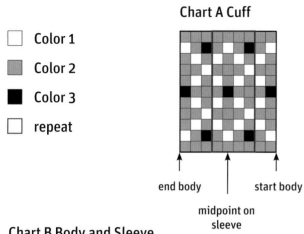

- Color 1
- Color 2
- Color 3
- repeat

end body

midpoint on sleeve

start body

Chart B Body and Sleeve

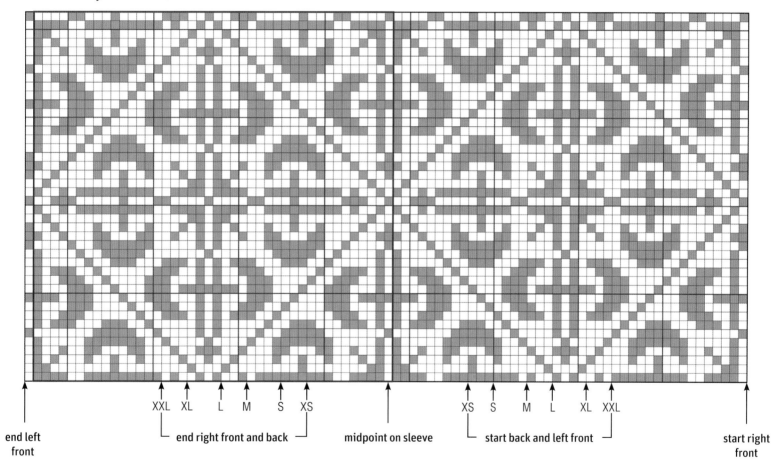

XXL XL L M S XS

XS S M L XL XXL

end left front

end right front and back

midpoint on sleeve

start back and left front

start right front

INSTRUCTIONS

The main pattern on this sweater has large motifs. It looks nice that way! It's also easier to knit if the patterns on the sleeves and body match up nicely when the three parts are worked together on the yoke; so we have deliberately calculated a body length that is one half repeat shorter than the sleeves. If your vertical tension matches ours, a half repeat is 3 in / 7.5 cm. We recommend working the sleeves first.

The sleeves and body are worked separately up to the underarm. The parts are then transferred to the same circular needle and continued in the round with decreases on both yoke and sleeve caps. The tops of the sleeve caps are sewn into the armholes. The sweater is cut open in front, and the neck band and the button bands are doubles—knitted to start, with the last bit crocheted.

SLEEVES

With smaller gauge dpn and Color 3, CO 52 (52, 56, 56, 60, 60) sts. Join, being careful not to twist cast-on row. Work around in stockinette for 1½ in / 4 cm (hem). Purl 1 rnd (turning edge). From this point all measurements are from this edge.

Change to larger gauge dpn and begin pattern on Chart A. Count back from middle of rnd on sleeve to find starting point for desired size on chart. Join Colors 1 and 2, and work chart once vertically. Cut Color 3.

With Color 1, k 1 rnd and inc 4 (6, 4, 6, 4, 6) sts evenly spaced around = 56 (58, 60, 62, 64, 66) sts. The last st of the rnd marks the underarm

"seam," and is worked as a p st in every rnd. Start color pattern on Chart B, counting from center st of sleeve to find where to start Chart B in desired size. The pattern should meet symmetrically at the p st underarm marker.

When sleeve measures 2½ in / 6 cm, begin inc on both sides of underarm "seam" marking st:

Inc Rnd: M1, work rnd in pattern up to marking st, M1, p1. Work new sts into pattern as they are added.

Rep this inc rnd every 1¼ (1¼, 1, 1, 1, ¾) in / 3 (3, 2.5, 2.5, 2.5, 2) cm until there are 13 (13, 15, 16, 16, 18) inc rnds = 82 (84, 90, 94, 96, 102) sts. Switch over to a short circular needle when sts become crowded on dpn. Continue until sleeve measures 18¼ (18¼, 18¼, 18½, 18½, 18½) in / 46 (46, 46, 47, 47, 47) cm, or desired length. On last rnd, BO the 7 (7, 11, 11, 13, 15) sts centered on the underarm marking st: BO the first 3 (3, 5, 5, 6, 7) sts and the last 4 (4, 6, 6, 7, 8) sts = 75 (77, 79, 83, 83, 87) sts rem. Set the sleeve aside and knit another one just like it.

BODY

With smaller gauge circular and Color 3, CO 211 (223, 239, 251, 267, 279) sts.

Facing: The first row is p, on the WS. Work back and forth in stockinette for 1½ in / 4 cm. End with a p row on the WS.

Fold line: Work 1 p row on RS. From this point, all measurements are taken from this fold line. At end of row, CO 3 new sts. These 3 new sts along with the 2 outer edge sts are a steek. The 5 steek sts are not worked in the color pattern and are not counted in st counts. Optionally, pm on both sides of the steek. It's a good idea to work the steek in 1-st vertical stripes on the rnds with more than 1 color.

The body now has 209 (221, 237, 249, 265, 277) sts. Change to larger gauge circular and start color pattern on Chart A. Start right front at Chart A's first st, rep area within red frame, and end where indicated. Work Chart A once vertically. Cut Color 3.

Work 1 rnd stockinette with Color 1 and proceed to Chart B. Starting on this rnd and continuing to armhole, you will p 1 st with Color 1 on each side as side "seam" markers.

On next rnd, set up color pattern following Chart B. The pattern should meet symmetrically at front and at each side seam marker. Arrows on chart show where each part begins and ends within color pattern for desired size:

Right front: Start at right lower corner of Chart B and work 52 (55, 59, 62, 66, 69) sts in pattern, ending at arrow marked "end back and right front."

Side "seam" marker, right side: P1 with Color 1. Optionally, pm here.

Back: Start at arrow marked "start back and left front here" for desired size and knit 103 (109, 117, 123, 131, 137) sts in pattern, ending at arrow marked "end back and right front here."

Side "seam" marker, left side: P1 with Color 1. Optionally, pm here.

Left front: Start at arrow marked "start back and left front" for desired size and work in pattern to end of Chart B = 52 (55, 59, 62, 66, 69) sts for left front, and (with marking p sts) = 209 (221, 237, 243, 265, 277) sts total.

Continue in pattern until work measures 3 (3, 3, 3, 3½, 3½) in / 8 (8, 8, 8, 9, 9) cm from folding edge. Begin shaping waist. If you prefer an unshaped sweater, skip the next 3 paragraphs.

Shaping Waist
Dec Rnd: *Work to 2 sts before the side marker st, ssk, p1 (marker st), k2tog, rep from * once = 4 sts decreased. Rep dec rnd about every 1 (1, 1¼, 1¼, 1¼, 1¼) in / 2.5 (2.5, 3, 3, 3, 3) cm until there are 5 dec rnds = 189 (201, 217, 229, 245, 257) sts.

Continue in pattern for 4 cm.

Inc Rnd: *Work up to side seam marker, M1, p1 (marker st), M1, repeat from * once = 4 inc sts. Rep inc rnd about every 1¼ in/3 cm until there are 5 inc rnds = 209 (221, 237, 249, 265, 277) sts again.

Continue until work measures about 15¼ (15¼, 15¼, 15½, 15½, 15½) in / 38.5 (38.5, 38.5, 39.5, 39.5, 39.5) cm. End pattern so it matches last rnd on sleeves—that is, you are at the same place in the pattern—either in lower or upper part of Chart B, which looks right but is turned sideways (see photos). At the same time, on last rnd, BO for armhole: *Work to 3 (3, 5, 5, 6, 7) sts before side seam marker, BO 7 (7, 11, 11, 13, 15) sts, rep from

115

* once, and finish rnd = 49 (52, 54, 57, 60, 62) sts for each front part, and 97 (103, 107, 113, 119, 123) sts for back.

KNITTING SLEEVES AND BODY TOGETHER

Transfer sleeves to same circular as body, one sleeve to a side above BO areas on body = 345 (361, 373, 393, 405, 421) sts. The beg of rnd is now in center of steek, in front.

Working in the round, continue as before with Chart B on each part, BUT work 1 rnd and CO (marking st) at each joint of the parts = 349 (365, 377, 397, 409, 425) sts. Work the marking sts as twisted p sts (through the back of the st) with Color 1. There will be decs at the joints: first on both sides of each, then only on the sleeve side. Be aware that neckline BOs will occur later at the same as the other decs. Please read the whole section up to "Assembly" before continuing to knit.

Dec Rnd: *Work in pattern to 2 sts before the side marking st. Ssk, p1 through the back loop, k2tog. Work from * a total of 4 times, then finish the rnd = 8 sts dec.

Rep this dec rnd *every* rnd until there are 4 (4, 4, 5, 4, 5) dec rnds. Then work dec rnd *every other* rnd 4 (5, 5, 5, 5, 5) times = 81 (85, 89, 93, 101, 103) sts for back; 41 (43, 45, 47, 51, 52) sts for each front; 59 (59, 61, 63, 65, 67) sts for each sleeve; plus the four marker sts.

Continue dec, but *only* on the sleeve caps. Remember there will be a BO for neck opening, to be worked part way through this.

Dec Rnd: *Work up to and including the marking st, k2tog, work to the last 2 sts before the next marking st, ssk, repeat from * once, finish the rnd = 4 sts dec (2 sts on each sleeve).

Rep this dec rnd *every 3rd* rnd until there are 4 (4, 4, 4, 4, 3) dec rnds. Then rep this dec rnd *every other* rnd 3 (3, 4, 3, 5, 6) times. Then rep this dec rnd *every* rnd 9 (9, 9, 10, 9, 10) times.

At the same time as decs continue on sleeves, when armhole measures 5¼ (5¼, 5½, 6, 6¼, 6¼) in / 13 (13, 14, 15, 16, 16) cm, BO for neck-line on both front sections. BO steek sts. Place 7 (8, 8, 9, 10, 11) sts on each side of steek sts on a holder. From this point, work in stockinette back and forth (or use an alternative method described below). When working back and forth, marking sts are k1 into back loop on WS; WS sleeve decs are worked just as on RS, but purled. Outer sts at neckline are edge sts and are knitted on all rows, and at the end of each row, edge sts are worked with both colors to "lock" the strands at the edges. BO for neckline at beg of every other row: 3, 2, 2, 1, 1, 1 sts.

When all sleeve decs are complete, 27 (27, 27, 29, 29, 29) sts rem on each sleeve and the armhole measures approx. 5½ (5¾, 6, 6, 6¼, 6½) in / 14 (14.5, 15.5, 15.5, 16, 16.5) cm. Next row: BO sleeve cap—all but marking sts. Now the parts are worked to completion separately, and back and forth, still in pattern. Marking sts now act as edge sts, and are worked as described above for neck-line edge sts.

Methods to Avoid Purling Color Patterns

Here are two methods if you would rather not work a color pattern from the WS. Take care that your dominant color stays dominant.

Method 1: Work the "wrong side" from the right side, but in the opposite direction. Do this: With RS still facing you, knit mirror-image to your usual knitting: put the left needle into the st on the right needle, *through the back loop*. Now, think about how you usually knit: If you knit two-handed, switch the colors, holding the dominant color in your right rather than your left hand. If you pick both colors from your left index or middle finger, move both strands to your *right* index or middle finger, holding the dominant color closer to the work—that is, closer to your second joint—and picking the non-dominant color from above it. If you always hold both colors in your right hand, continue to do so, but remember to take the dominant color from *underneath* the non-dominant color. This method takes a little practice, but many find they can work just as quickly as they can in the other direction. Maybe even faster. **Remember:** Work *left to right*. Put the needle through the *back loop* of each st. Be *careful* to maintain the same color dominance.

Method 2: When the steek sts are bound off and the sts on both sides are on a holder, CO 5 new steek sts at the neck, and continue to work in the round. Dec for the neckline at both sides of the new steek. Later, machine stitch and cut the steek open as at the center front. If you use this method, it's best to make a double neck band in order to cover the cut edges.

FRONTS

The front portions are now worked separately. They are worked the same way but mirror-image.

Continue decs for neckline. When neckline decs are done, 25 (26, 28, 29, 32, 32) sts rem on each front section. Continue until the armhole measures 7½ (7½, 8, 8¼, 8½, 8½) in / 19 (19, 20, 21, 22, 22) cm.

Shoulder shaping: The shoulders will fit best if they have a bit of a slope. This is accomplished by binding off shoulder sts by degrees. BO on the side toward sleeve—i.e., on right front, BO on WS, and on left front, BO on RS. BO at beg of every other row: 6,6,6,7 (6,7,6,7; 7,7,7,7; 7,7,7,8; 8,8,8,8; 8,8,8,8) sts. Be careful to include both strands when you BO.

BACK

Work in pattern until armhole measures 7½ (7½, 8, 8¼, 8½, 8½) in / 19 (19, 20, 21, 22, 22) cm. Place the center 33 (33, 33, 35, 37, 39) sts on a holder. BO shoulder as you did on front.

ASSEMBLY

Sew shoulders together. Sew sleeve caps into armholes and sew tog BO sts at underarms. Machine stitch with small sts down front on both sides of center steek st. Cut between seams. Hem facings at cuff and lower edge of body to the inside.

EDGES

The neck band and button bands will be both knitted and crocheted. First a narrow double edge is knitted; the neck edge is folded to the inside and sewn down. The button bands are next, knitted and folded over and sewn down over the steeks. The rest of the edging is crocheted, first with a single crochet, but then with a row of crab st in a contrasting color. Crab sts are single crochet sts worked backwards—that is, from left to right. They make a firm and fine edge, almost like a little string of beads.

Neck Band, Knitted Section

Use smaller gauge circular and Color 3. With RS facing, start at neck edge of right front. Transfer sts from holder to needle. Start by CO 1 st (edge st), then knit sts from holder; pick up and k 1 st in every st and 3 st per 4 rnds/rows along right side of neckline; k sts from back of neck; pick up and k along left side of neckline the same way as for right side; k the last sts from the holder and end by CO 1 st (edge st) = 115–120 (115–120, 115–120, 120–125, 120–125, 125–130) sts. Knit 1 row back (on RS), which makes a little ridge in a contrast color. Cut yarn and join Color 2. Work 3 rows stockinette, back and forth. (*Knit* the edge st on both WS and RS.) On next row (WS), k entire row (fold line). Work 4 more rows in stockinette. BO. Feel free to use one of the other colors to bind off (Color 3 was used in both versions shown). Fold over at purl row and sew edge down on the inside.

Right Button Band, Knitted Section

With smaller gauge circular and Color 3, start by CO 1 st (edge st) on the right needle. With RS facing, start at purl fold line and pick up and k sts between front edge and steek, up to and including the ridge in contrast color at edge of neckline. The last st is *knit* into the ridge—not the furthermost out. (You're just trying to create a "corner" in the contrast color.) Where there is a double layer, pick up sts through both layers. If you have trouble picking up sts there with the knitting needle, try using a crochet hook as a helper. Pick up about 12 sts per 2 in / 5 cm. Work 1 row k back (another ridge in contrast color). Cut yarn.

Join Color 2. K 1 row, but don't turn yet. Pick up and k 3 sts in the last bit (for a fold line) on neck band, and at end of row, CO 1 st (edge st). Work 2 rows stockinette back and forth (always k the edge st, both sides). Next row (WS), k to end (fold line, becomes a p row on RS). Work 4 rows in stockinette, and BO. If you used a contrasting color for the BO on the neck band, do the same here. Fold edging over steek and hem it on the inside.

Left Button Band, Knitted Section

With smaller gauge circular and Color 3, on the RS, start at the contrasting color ridge of neck band (not the outermost sts) and pick up sts inside steek and down front to the p row at the very bottom. Where there is a double layer at the hem, pick up sts through both layers. Use a crochet hook if you find it hard to pick up there with a knitting needle. Pick up about 12 sts per 2 in / 5 cm. CO an extra st at the end as an edge st. P 1 row back (a contrasting color ridge). Cut yarn.

Join Color 2. First, CO 1 st on right needle (edge stitch). Beg at outer hem edge (the p rnd) of the neck band, pick up 3 sts along the neckline (up to the ridge in the contrast color), k to end of row. Work 2 rows stockinette, back and forth (always knitting the edge st). Next row (WS), k, for a p fold-over row on the RS. Work 4 rows in stockinette. BO, and if you used a different color to BO the neck band, do the same here. Fold band at p row and sew it down on the inside.

Buttonholes

Measure and mark where buttonholes should be (on right front). With a pin or other removable marker, mark the lowest buttonhole in the 5th st from the lower edge and the top one in the 3rd st from the top. Divide the other seven evenly between these. The marks correspond to the middle of each buttonhole.

All Front Bands, Crocheted Section

The rest of the edge is crocheted. Use crochet hook US C-2 / 3 mm and Color 2. Beg on RS, at bottom of right front edge. Read this whole section before you start.

Row 1: Sc in purl fold line along front and neck edges, in the outermost loop of the fold line, and work 1 st in each st when working straight, and 3 sts in every st at corners (the neck band). *At the same time*, make buttonholes on right front edge, at marks: *Crochet up to 1 st before your mark, do 3 chain sts, skip 3 p sts on the edge (the mark should fall in the center of these 3 sts), rep from * until all buttonholes are made.

Row 2 (WS): Crochet 1 chain st (= first sc); sc around edge. At buttonholes, crochet 3 sc into chain st loop. At corners, crochet 2 sc into corner st. Turn.

Row 3 (RS): Sc around edge. At corners, crochet 2 sc into corner st. Cut Color 2.

Crab Stitch

Finish the edges with a row of crab st (reverse sc) around the entire sweater edge, including the cuffs of the sleeves:

Change to crochet hook US B-1 / 2.5 mm and Color 4. Beg at the left button band and work crab st along the lower edge of the body, picking up the outmost loop of the purl hemline. When you've gone completely around, cut yarn. Don't forget to crab st the lower edge of the sleeves as well!

MORE DECORATIONS?

It's fun to decorate knitted clothes with various sequins, buttons, crocheted edges, embroidery, and whatnot. Tiny details can make a huge difference. Use your imagination and give it a try. In decorating both of these designs, we used the same yarn as for the rest of the sweater, but that doesn't have to be the case. On the blue/green turquoise, see the small flowers in Color 4. Sewn in Lazy Daisy stitch, the flower petals flare out from a single st in the middle. There's a flower on each cuff, and one at the back of the neck. The flower below the neckline also has little specks surrounding the flower, these also done with Lazy Daisy (Color 3). On the sleeves of the light brown and white version, there's a single row of embroidered chain sts (Color 1), making a transition between the cuff and the larger motifs. What other embellishments could you add?

FINISHING

Weave in all loose ends. Sew buttons on between knitted and crocheted parts of edging, carefully placed across from buttonholes.

HALLINGDAL STAR SWEATER

Chart from *Norwegian Knitting Designs*, figure 61, page 55.

Here is a side-buttoned garter-stitch jacket for the littlest kids, with a Hallingdal Star in mosaic knitting on the front. The inspiration for the star is an eight-petaled rose from Hallingdal. For the pattern to be clearly visible, it's best to use highly contrasting colors.

SKILL LEVEL
Experienced

SIZES
0 (3, 6, 12 months, 2, 3 years)

FINISHED MEASUREMENTS
Chest: 17¼ (19¼, 21, 22¾, 24½, 26½) in / 44 (49, 53.5, 58, 62.5, 67.5) cm
Length: approx. 8½ (9½, 10¼, 11½12½, 14) in / 21.5 (24, 26, 29, 31.5, 35.5) cm
Sleeve Length: 5½ (6, 6¼, 7, 8, 9) in / 14 (15, 16, 18, 20, 23) cm

YARN
CYCA #1 (sock, baby, fingering) Hifa Hjerte Kamgarn superwash (328 yd/300 m / 100 g)

YARN NEEDED
Color 1: approx. 50 (65, 75, 90, 105, 125) g
Color 2: approx. 50 (65, 75, 90, 105, 125) g

COLORS SHOWN
Rose/Brown Version:
Color 1: Brownish Old Rose 62956 and
Color 2: Semi-bleached White 62960
Gray Version:
Color 1: Dark Gray 62965 and
Color 2: Semi-bleached White 62960
Blue Version:
Color 1: Farmer Blue 62934 and
Color 2: Semi-bleached White 62960
Old Rose Version:
Color 1: Old Rose 62967; and
Color 2: Semi-bleached White 62960

SUGGESTED NEEDLE SIZES
US 1.5 or 2.5 / 2.5 or 3 mm: circular; optionally, 5 dpn in the same size, if you wish to work sleeves in the round

GAUGE
26 sts and approx. 50-52 rows in garter st = 4 x 4 in / 10 x 10 cm.
Adjust needle size to obtain correct gauge if necessary.

NOTIONS
6 (6-7, 7, 7-8, 8, 8-9) buttons

BUTTONS SHOWN
Blue, Old Rose, and Rose/Brown Versions: ROSENDAL 11 mm, K292968 from Hjelmvedt. The other versions used "recycled" buttons.

SPECIAL TECHNIQUES
Mosaic knitting: A knitting technique using 2 colors, but knitting with only one color at a time, taking turns between 2 rows/rnds of each color. The pattern is achieved by slipping some sts from the preceding row while carrying the active color as a float on the WS. Mosaic knitting can be worked in either stockinette or, as here, garter stitch. There should be a strong contrast between the two colors. Mosaic knitting is decorative and much simpler than it looks, once you get the hang of it. It has a tendency to pull up a little width-wise—the trick is to keep the active yarn rather loose when slipping sts.

Charts: The charts are read from the bottom up and from right to left on the RS and left to right on the WS. Pay attention to the row numbers on both sides of the chart: Each charted row corresponds to *two rows/rnds* of knitting—both the RS and the WS rows.

Color changes in garter stitch: When changing colors at the end of a pair of rows, always take the new color from behind the one just used.

Joining a new strand: Garter st looks best if, when a new strand is joined (or one switches to a new ball), this happens on the RS—avoiding the turn at the outside edges, because the garter st structure makes it a little difficult to fasten ends nicely at the edges.

Raglan increases: On this jacket, the raglan incs are worked with a yarnover on the RS, which will be twisted as a p st on the WS.

CHART, 0–9 MONTHS

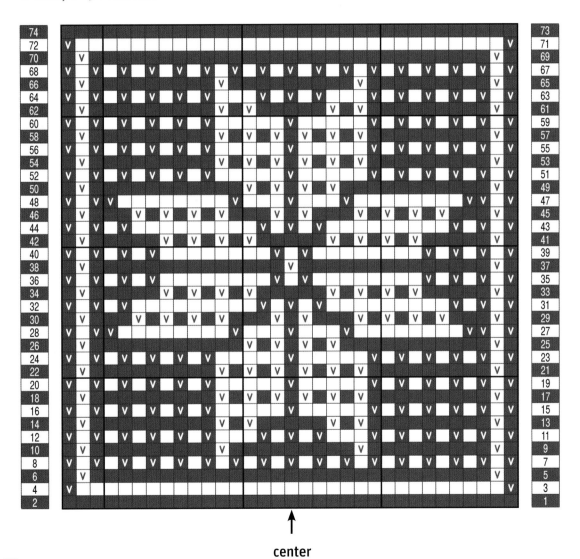

center
front

Color 1: k on RS, k on WS

Color 2: k on RS, k on WS

V Color 1: slip p-wise wyb on RS, slip p-wise wyf on WS

V Color 2: slip p-wise wyb on RS, slip p-wise wyf on WS

Background color in the row numbers on right and left indicate color actually knitted in that pair of rows. One row in the Chart indicates 2 rows of work—that is, both RS and WS. The WS row on your needles duplicates the colors on the RS row.

CHART, 12 MONTHS TO 3 YEARS.

■ Color 1: k on RS, k on WS

☐ Color 2: k on RS, k on WS

V Color 1: slip p-wise wyb on RS, slip p-wise wyf on WS

V Color 2: slip p-wise wyb on RS, slip p-wise wyf on WS

Background color in the row numbers on right and left indicate color actually used in that pair of rows.

One row in the chart indicates 2 rows of work—that is, both RS and WS. The WS row on your needles duplicates the colors on the RS row.

**center
front**

INSTRUCTIONS

The sweater is worked from the neck down and back and forth and is worked in garter st—knitted on both sides, except for the star motif on the front, which is knitted in mosaic knitting garter stitch. When the raglan increases are complete, the sleeve sts are put on holders and the body is knitted to completion. The sleeves are worked last, and then the underarms are sewn together.

YOKE

With Color 1, cast on 73 (77, 81, 85, 89, 93) sts. Work 3 rows garter st. The first row is the WS = 2 garter ridges on RS.

Next row (RS): Join Color 2 and make a buttonhole: k 4 sts, k2tog, yarn over, k2. Make another buttonhole every 20 rows (10 ridges). K to end of row.

Next row (WS): K to end of needle. Now there are 2 ridges in Color 1 and 1 ridge in Color 2. From here on, change color every second row, always starting a new color on the RS.

Next row (RS): Start raglan incs. K 4, yarn over, k 9 (left sleeve); yo, k 3, yo, k 19 (21, 23, 25, 27, 29) sts (back); yo, k 3, yo, k 9 (right sleeve); yo, k 3, yo, k 19 (21, 23, 25, 27, 29) sts (front); yo, k4 = 8 sts inc.

Next row (WS): K back and k all yarnovers through back loop.

Next row (RS): K 4, yo, k 11 (left sleeve); yo, k 3, yo, k21 (23, 25, 27, 29, 31) sts (back of sweater); yo, k 3, yo, k 11 (right sleeve); yo, k 3, yo, k 21 (23, 25, 27, 29, 31) sts (front); yo, k 4 = 8 sts inc. Next row, knit back, and knit all yarnovers through back loop.

Continue with raglan incs on RS until there are 6 (6, 8, 8, 10, 10) inc rows. There are now 9 (9, 11, 11, 13, 13) ridges and 4 (4, 5, 5, 6, 6) stripes with Color 2. There are 31 (33, 39, 41, 47, 49) sts on each front and back and 121 (125, 145, 149, 169, 173) sts total on the needle.

STAR PATTERN

Continue raglan incs, *at the same time* working color pattern on front, following chart for desired size. Center pattern at center front (arrow on chart). **Note:** In the smallest size (0 months), the first row of the chart can only be started when the total number of sts for front has reached 33 (the number of sts on chart). This should not cause a problem, though, as the first row of the chart is a solid color.

Keep working in pattern on front and continue raglan incs as est, until there are 16 (18, 20, 22, 24, 26) inc rows = 201 (221, 241, 261, 281, 301) sts.

SPLIT WORK INTO SLEEVES AND BODY

Continue in garter st and mosaic on the front, and split work into body and sleeves: K4, place the next 41 (45, 49 53, 57, 61) sts (left sleeve) on a holder; k 57 (63, 69, 75, 81, 87) sts, place the next 41 (45, 49, 53, 57, 61) sts (right sleeve) on a holder; k the last 58 (64, 70, 76, 82, 88) sts, and leave 119 (131, 143, 155, 167, 179) sts for body.

BODY

Continue in garter st and pattern as before. Don't forget to work a buttonhole every 20 rows. When charted pattern is complete, continue in ridges/stripes until work from the armhole measures 5 (5¾, 6¼, 7, 7½, 9) in / 12.5 (14.5, 15.5, 17.5, 19.5, 22.5) cm, and end with a ridge in Color 2. Now k 2 ridges with Color 1. BO.

SLEEVES

Transfer one set of sleeve sts from holder to circular or dpns = 41 (45, 49 53, 57, 61) sts. K garter st stripes back and forth. After 12 rows (6 ridges), dec 1 st each side (RS, 1 st in from the edge) and after that every 10 rows (5 ridges), until you have worked 6 (6, 6, 7, 8, 9) dec rows = 29 (33, 37, 39, 41, 43) sts rem. When sleeve measures 4¾ (5, 5½, 6¼, 6¾, 8) in / 12 (13, 14, 16, 17, 20) cm, or is ¾ (¾, 1, 1, 1¼, 1¼) in / 2 (2, 2.5, 2.5, 3, 3) cm shorter than desired full length, work rem sts in garter st in Color 1. BO all sts when sleeve measures 5½ (6, 6¼, 7, 8, 9) in / 14 (15, 16, 18, 20, 23) cm. Knit another sleeve just like this one.

ASSEMBLY

Sew sleeves together with mattress stitch. Weave in all ends. Sew on buttons.

WAVES ON WAVES SWEATER

Diagram from *Norwegian Knitting Designs*, figure 11, page 18.

A little band of pattern from a Selbu mitten is used here as an area pattern on a
child's sweater in sizes from six months all the way to 10 years old.
It would be pretty in many different color combinations, and it will be extra
beloved if the child gets to pick out the colors themselves.

SKILL LEVEL
Experienced

SIZES
6-9 months (12-18 months, 2, 4, 6, 8, 10 years)

FINISHED MEASUREMENTS
Chest: 21 (23, 24, 26½, 27½, 29½, 32) in / 53 (58.5, 61, 67, 69.5, 75, 81) cm
Full Length: 11 (13½, 15, 16½, 18, 19¾, 21½) in / 28 (34, 38, 42, 46, 50, 54.5) cm
Sleeve Length: 6¾, 8¼, 10, 11, 12¼, 13½, 14½) in / 17 (21, 25, 28, 31, 34, 37) cm

YARN
Color 1 (main color): CYCA #2 (sport, baby) Hifa Vilje Lamb's wool (410 yd / 375 m / 100 g)
Colors 2 and 3 (contrast colors): CYCA #2 (sport, baby) Sølje Pelsullgarn (383 yd/350 m / 100 g)

YARN AMOUNTS
Color 1: Vilje—approx. 100 (150, 150, 150, 200, 250, 250) g
Color 2: Sølje—approx. 50 (50, 50, 50, 50, 100, 100) g
Color 3: Sølje—approx. 50 (50, 50, 50, 50, 100, 100) g

COLORS SHOWN
Color 1: Vilje—Natural White 57400
Color 2: Sølje—Red 642132
Color 3: Sølje—Light Brown 642102

SUGGESTED NEEDLE SIZES
US 1.5 / 2.5 mm: 24 and, optionally, 32 in / 60 and, optionally, 80 cm circulars and set of 5 dpn
US 2.5 or 4 / 3 or 3.5 mm: 16, 24, and, optionally, 32 in / 40, 60, and, optionally, 80 cm circulars and set of 5 dpn

GAUGE
25 sts and 32 rnds in stockinette and pattern on larger gauge needles = 4 x 4 in / 10 x 10 cm.
25 sts in seed st on smaller gauge needles = 4 in / 10 cm.
Adjust needle sizes to obtain correct gauge if necessary.

NOTIONS
5 (6, 6, 7, 7, 8, 8) buttons
Optional: tape to cover cut steek edge

BUTTONS SHOWN
ROSENDAL 15 mm, K312968 from Hjelmvedt

INSTRUCTIONS

The body ribbing is worked first, back and forth. A steek is set up in front, to be cut open later, and from there on, the sweater is worked in the round. The body and the sleeves are worked separately up to the armholes, the parts are transferred to a single circular needle, and work continues with raglan decreases on the yoke. The front is cut open, and button bands are knitted onto the front edge. Finally, the neck band: the cut edges are folded to the inside and can be hidden with a knitted facing or textile tape, or simply hemmed down on the wrong side.

BODY

With smaller gauge circular and Color 1, CO 123

(137, 143, 157, 163, 177, 191) sts. Work seed st back and forth (see page 23, "Seed Stitch") until work measures 1 (1, 1¼, 1¼, 1½, 1½, 1½) in / 2.5 (2.5, 3, 3, 3.5, 3.5, 4) cm. Finish with 1 row on WS.

Change to larger gauge circular and work next row: k 1, pm, k to end of row and inc 6 (6, 7, 7, 8, 8, 8) sts evenly spaced, pm before the last st, k 1, CO 3 sts at the end of the row. The 3 new sts + 1 st from each side of seed st edge become a 5-st steek, which is not included in color pattern or st counts. In rnds with color pattern, work steek with 1-st vertical stripes, starting and ending with Color 1. There are now 127 (141, 148, 162, 169, 183, 197) sts, not counting steek. Now, pm on each side "seam": Allow 32 (35, 37, 41, 42, 46, 49) sts for each front and 63 (71, 74, 80, 85, 91, 99) sts for the back.

Start color pattern, knitting in the round and following chart. Continue in pattern until work measures approx. 6¾ (8¼, 9½, 10¾, 11¾, 13, 14¼) in / 17 (21, 24, 27, 30, 33, 36) cm. On last rnd, BO for armhole: K to 4 (3, 4, 4, 4, 5, 4) sts before side marker, BO 7 (7, 7, 7, 9, 9, 9) sts; k to 3 (4, 3, 3, 5, 4, 5) sts before the next side marker, BO 7 (7, 7, 7, 9, 9, 9) sts; and finish the rnd. Each front now has 28 (32, 33, 37, 38, 41, 45) sts and back has 57 (63, 68, 74, 75, 83, 89) sts. Set body aside and make sleeves.

SLEEVES
With smaller gauge dpn and Color 1, CO 37 (37, 39, 41, 41, 43, 45) sts. Join to work in the round, being careful not to twist cast-on row. Work around in seed st until work measures 1 (1, 1¼, 1¼, 1½, 1½, 1½) in / 2.5 (2.5, 3, 3, 3.5, 3.5, 4) cm. Change

to larger gauge dpn. Work a rnd in stockinette and inc 3 (5, 5, 5, 7, 7, 7) sts, evenly spaced = 40 (42, 44, 46, 48, 50, 52) sts. Work 0 (0, 3, 3, 3, 3, 3) rnds stockinette before starting color pattern.

The last st of rnd is centered at underarm and is knitted with Color 1 in all rnds (marking st). The marking st is not worked in pattern, but is included in st count. The midpoint of sts in rnd is center of sleeve. Count out from center point of sleeve to find starting point on chart. Work pattern following chart. After 6 rnds of pattern (top of first wave), inc on both sides of underarm "seam":

Inc Rnd: M1, work in pattern to the marking st, M1, k 1. The new sts are worked into pattern as they appear.

Rep this inc rnd every 1 (1, 1, 1, ¾, ¾, ¾) in / 2.5 (2.5, 2.5, 2.5, 2, 2, 2) cm until there are 5 (6, 8, 9,11, 13, 14) inc rnds = 50 (54, 60, 64, 70, 76, 80) sts. Continue in pattern until sleeve measures 6¾ (8¼, 9¾, 11, 12¼, 13½, 14½) in / 17 (21, 25, 28, 31, 34, 37) cm. End pattern in same rnd as final rnd of body, and in that rnd, BO 7 (7, 7, 7, 9, 9, 9) sts at the underarm: BO the first 3 (3, 3, 3, 4, 4, 4) sts and the last 4 (4, 4, 4, 5, 5, 5) sts = 43 (47, 53, 57, 61, 67, 71) sts. Set sleeve aside and make another just like it.

YOKE
Transfer all parts to one larger gauge circular needle in this order: right front, right sleeve, back, left sleeve, left front = 199 (221, 240, 262, 273, 299, 321) sts. Pm at each juncture of parts (raglan dec marker). The pattern continues from

where you stopped, but knit the last 2 sts before and the first 2 sts after the raglan marker in Color 1. Work 1 (3, 2, 3, 2, 1, 1) rnds. Continue pattern and beg raglan decs.

Dec Rnd: *Work in pattern up to 2 sts before the raglan marker. With Color 1, k2tog, ssk. Rep from * 4 times = 8 sts dec.

Then work 1 rnd with no decs, knitting the 2 sts before and after markers in Color 1.

Repeat dec rnd *every other* rnd until there are 11 (13, 15, 17, 18, 20, 22) dec rnds. End with a rnd without decs = 111 (117, 120, 126, 129, 139, 145) sts rem, as follows: 17 (19, 18, 20, 20, 21, 23) sts for each half front; 35 (37, 38, 40, 39, 43, 45) sts for back; 21 (21, 23, 23, 25, 27, 27) sts for each sleeve.

NECKLINE

Now there are 5 more raglan dec rnds. Try to ensure the color pattern will not be chopped off in the middle of a vertical repeat at the end. If it looks as if it will, end the color pattern a little early and work the last few rnds in only Color 1. The last bit is worked back and forth, and the neck opening is bound off.

BO steek. Place 4 (5, 5, 6, 6, 7, 7) sts from each side of the steek on a holder. Cut yarn and start afresh from right side of neckline. Work back and forth and continue to BO for neckline at beg of each row: 2,2,1,1,1 (2,2,1,1,1; 2,2,1,1,1; 3,2,1,1,1; 3,2,1,1,1; 3,2,1,1,1; 3,3,2,1,1) sts, *at the same time* continuing raglan decs *every other* row (RS). Finish neck BOs. You should have 16 (18, 20, 22,

23, 25, 27) raglan dec rnds/rows total (count on the back of the sweater). Take out raglan markers on last row. Either leave sts on circular or transfer them to a holder.

ASSEMBLY

Machine stitch a tight seam on both sides of the center steek st. Cut between the seams.

BUTTON BANDS

With right side toward you, smaller gauge needle, and Color 1, pick up and k sts along the front edge, in the space between the body and the steek. On right front, start at bottom at seed-st edge; on left, start at neckline.

Assuming your knitting gauge is constant, pick up about 25 sts per 4 in / 10 cm in length, or about 3 sts every 4 rows. For safety's sake, measure your gauge on the seed st lower edge. The final st count on the button bands should be a multiple of (2)+1. Work the band back and forth in seed st, starting on the WS. Traditionally, girls' and women's sweaters have the buttonholes on the right side, and boys' and men's on the left; but in the end, it's up to you.

Button Band Without Buttonholes
Work 8 (10, 10, 10, 12, 12, 12) rows seed st. Next row: BO in seed st.

Button Band With Buttonholes
Work 3 (4, 4, 4, 5, 5, 5) rows in seed st. Next row: Continue in seed st while making 5 (6, 6, 7, 7, 8, 8) buttonholes. Make the buttonhole by BO 2 sts (or adjust for button size). The bottom buttonhole is placed ½ in / 1 cm from lower edge and the

top buttonhole is in the vertical center of the neck band (to be worked later). The remainder should be spaced evenly between them.

Next row: Work across in seed st; CO 2 sts above the BO sts.

Continue in seed st until there are 8 (10, 10, 10, 12, 12, 12) rows. BO in seed st.

NECK BAND
The neck band is worked back and forth in seed st and Color 1. Transfer sts from holder to smaller gauge circular. With RS facing you, and Color 1, start at top of right button band. Pick up 4-5 (5, 5, 5, 5, 6, 6) sts from each button band, pick up about 1 st per bound off st along the neckline, and knit sts from the holder. Work a row in seed st and, *at the same time*, adjust stitch count (not including button bands) to 79 (83, 87, 93, 99, 103, 107) sts. Work seed st back and forth for 3 (4, 4, 4, 5, 5, 5) rows. Form top buttonhole in next 2 rows, in line with other buttonholes. Continue in seed st until there are 8 (10, 10, 10, 12, 12, 12) rows. BO in seed st.

FINISHING
Weave in all ends. Sew underarm BOs together. Sew on buttons.

The cut steek edges are turned to the inside. They can either be sewn down overhand on the WS, or covered with tape or a knitted facing, as you wish. If you use cotton tape, it's wise to preshrink it, either by steaming or laundering it.

If you choose to knit a facing to hide the raw steek edge, do this: With the larger gauge needle you used for the body, and Color 1, pick up and knit into the loops on back of first row of button band. Pick up 1 st per st in button band along steek. Work 4 rows stockinette, BO loosely, and sew facing to WS of the sweater.

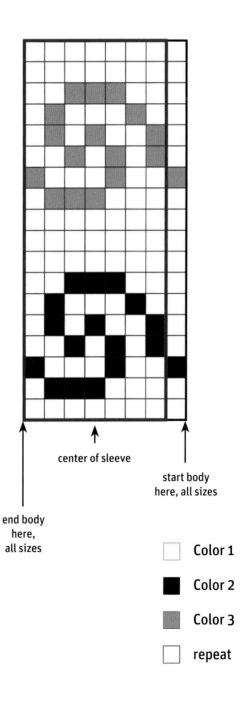

center of sleeve

start body here, all sizes

end body here, all sizes

☐ Color 1

■ Color 2

▨ Color 3

☐ repeat

CIRCLE OF DANCERS DRESS

Chart from *Norwegian Knitting Designs*, figure 31, page 36.

The circle dancers and the stars were originally on a hat in *Norwegian Knitting Designs*. The pattern lit up my imagination and inspired both the Summer Solstice Pullover (p. 143) and this little dress. A super dress to grow into, it has generous width at the bottom, and it will surely be good to spin around in. Most of us who wore dresses and skirts as children remember the wonderful feeling of spinning around and around, our skirts lifting and twirling out—and spinning and spinning some more, until we were completely dizzy and giddy. It was so much fun!

SKILL LEVEL
Experienced

SIZES
1 (2, 4, 6) years

FINISHED MEASUREMENTS
Chest: 22¾ (24, 25¼, 26½) in / 57.5 (61, 64, 67) cm
Full Length: measured at center front, 16 (18, 21, 23) in / 40 (46, 53, 58) cm
Short Sleeve Length: at underarm, 1 (1, 1¼, 1) in / 2.5 (2.5, 3, 3) cm
Long Sleeve Length: at underarm, 8¼ (9¾, 11, 12¼) in / 21 (25, 28, 31) cm

YARN
CYCA #2 (sport, baby) Hifa Vilje Lamb's wool (410 yd/375 m / 100 g); and/or CYCA #2 (sport, baby) Hifa Sølje Pelsullgarn (383 yd/350 m / 100 g)

YARN AMOUNTS
Color 1: about 150 (150, 200, 250) g for short-sleeved version; about 150 (200, 250, 300) g for long-sleeved version
Color 2: about 50 g (all sizes)
Color 3: about 50 g (all sizes)

COLORS SHOWN
White/Blue/Black Version
Color 1: Vilje, Natural White 57400
Color 2: Vilje, Light Air Force Blue 57411
Color 3: Sølje, Black 642109 or Vilje, Black 57414

Blue/Rose/White Version
Color 1: Vilje, Light Air Force Blue 57411
Color 2: Sølje, Dusty Rose, 642137
Color 3: Vilje, Natural White 57400

SUGGESTED NEEDLE SIZES
US 1.5 / 2.5 mm: 16 and 24 in / 40 and 60 cm circulars and set of 5 dpn
US 2.5 / 3 mm: 16, 24, and 32 in / 40, 60, and 80 cm circulars and set of 5 dpn
Optionally, if you knit more tightly in colorwork, **US 6 / 4 mm:** 16, 24, and 32 in / 40, 60, and 80 cm circulars

GAUGE
25 sts and 32 rnds in stockinette on US 2.5 / 3 mm needles = 4 x 4 in / 10 x 10 cm
25 sts and approx. 30 rnds in color pattern on US 2.5 / 3 mm needles = 4 x 4 in / 10 x 10 cm
Adjust needle size to obtain correct gauge if necessary. (If US 2.5 / 3 mm needles are too small, give US 6 / 4 mm needles a try.)

INSTRUCTIONS

The dress is worked in the round and from the top down. Start with the neck band, continue onto the yoke, set sleeve sts to wait, finish up the bodice and the skirt, and then knit the sleeves, either long or short.

NECK BAND

With Color 2 and smallest gauge needles, CO 90 (96, 102, 108) sts. Join to work in the round, being careful not to twist cast-on row. Pm at beg of rnd, which will be middle of back. Work k1, p1 ribbing for ¾ (1, 1, 1⅛) in / 2 (2.5, 2.5, 3) cm. Change to medium-gauge circular (or largest circular, if it gave you the correct color pattern gauge) and work a single rnd stockinette.

PATTERN ON THE YOKE

Beg to k color pattern following chart at right. Be careful to follow chart for desired size. The pattern repeats 15 (16, 17, 18) times around. If you want to alternate between dancing men and women, be aware that in Sizes 1 and 4 years, perfect alternation isn't possible because of the odd number of repeats. Inc at the points shown in the chart. Pay attention to the symbols on the charts: "x" is a color, "+" is an inc. Be aware that the chart calls for 3 colors in some rnds; drawing the third color up through the circular knitting helps avoid tangles. Hold the third color as a dominant color in this case. Change to a longer circular if sts become crowded. Complete the chart = 210 (224, 238, 252) sts.

If you needed the largest suggested size to work the color pattern to the right gauge, switch to the medium-gauge (US 2.5 / 3 mm) needles to continue. Work in stockinette in Color 1, and k 1 rnd. On the next rnd, inc 8 (8, 12, 12) sts as follows:

Size 1 yr: K 18, M1, (k 25, M1) 7 times, k 17 = 218 sts.

Size 2 yr: K 14, M1, (k 28, M1) 7 times, k 14 = 232 sts.

Size 4 yr: K 9, M1, (k 20, M1) 11 times, k 9 = 250 sts.

Size 6 yr: K 11, M1, (k21, M1) 11 times, k 10 = 264 sts.

K 0 (2, 2, 4) more rnds. The yoke, including neck band, should come out to approx. 5¾ (6⅛, 6¾, 7) in / 14.5 (15.5, 17, 18) cm, measured at center front.

DIVIDE WORK INTO SLEEVES AND BODY

On next rnd, divide sts into sleeves and body/skirt sections. Work 33 (34, 37, 38) sts, place the next 44 (48, 52, 56) sts on scrap yarn (right sleeve); CO 4 sts, pm (right side and start of new rnd); CO 3 (4, 3, 4) sts, k 65 (68, 73, 76) sts (front); place the next 44 (48, 52, 56) sts on scrap yarn (left sleeve); CO 7 (8, 7, 8) sts (underarm), and k to new marker, removing marker at center back as you pass.

SKIRT

There are now 144 (152, 160, 168) sts on the needle. Work in stockinette for 1¼ (1¼, 1½, 1½) in / 3 (3, 3.5, 3.5) cm.

1 year, dancing woman

1 year, dancing man

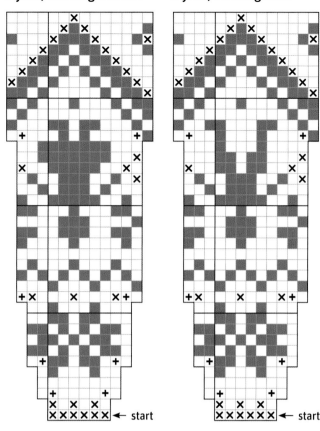

← start

← start

2–6 years, dancing woman

2–6 years, dancing man

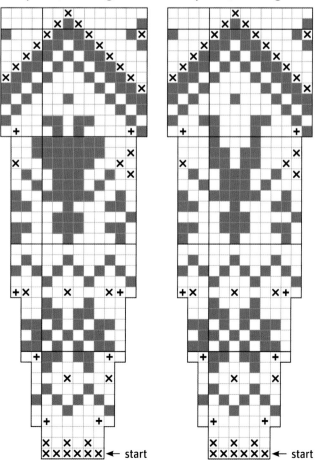

← start

← start

	Color 1
X	Color 2
■	Color 3
+	Inc 1 st

Border

← start

On next rnd, divide sts into 8 sections: pm after every 18th (19th, 20th, 21st) st. You now have 8 markers per rnd. It's a good idea to have the marker for beg of rnd in a different color. Then, inc:

Inc Rnd: *K1, M1L, k until 1 st rem before next marker, M1R, k1, rep from * 8 times = 16 sts inc.

Rep this inc rnd approx. every 1¼ (1¼, 1½, 1½) in / 3 (3, 3.5, 3.5) cm until there are 8 (9, 9, 10) inc rnds = 272 (296, 304, 328) sts. Change to a longer circular when stitches become crowded.

K around until skirt measures approx. 9¼ (11, 13½, 15) in / 23.5 (28, 34, 38) cm (or until whole dress, measured at center front, is ¾ in / 2 cm shorter than desired length).

PATTERNED BORDER

Change back to largest gauge circular, if needed to work color pattern to gauge. Work pattern following "Border" chart. Cut Color 1 and Color 3.

HEM EDGE AND FACING

Switch back to US 2.5 / 3 mm circular, if you used largest gauge for the color-pattern border. Continue with Color 2 and p 1 rnd (fold line for hem).

Knit 1 in / 2.5 cm stockinette, or as much as necessary to cover WS of border pattern when hem is folded in on fold line. BO all sts loosely.

SLEEVES

Transfer held sts for one sleeve to dpn of same size used for plain stockinette on the skirt.

With Color 1, beg in the middle of the sts CO at the underarm of the body, and pick up 1 st in each of 4 CO sts there; k the 44 (48, 52, 56) sleeve sts; and pick up the last 3 (4, 3 4) sts at the underarm. Pm here for beg of rnd = 51 (56, 59, 64) sts. K 1 rnd and adjust the st count to an even number: Inc 1 (0, 1, 0) st = 52 (56, 60, 64) sts.

SHORT SLEEVES

Switch to smallest gauge dpn and work k1, p1 ribbing for ¾ (¾, 1, 1) in / 2 (2, 2.5, 2.5) cm. Change to Color 2. Turn to WS and BO with k sts on WS.

LONG SLEEVES

Work around in stockinette until sleeve measures 1¼ (1¼, 1, 1¼) in / 3 (3, 2.5, 3) cm. Then start decreasing:

Dec Rnd: K 1, k2tog, k to 3 sts before marker, ssk, k1 = 2 sts decreased.

Repeat this dec rnd about every ¾ (1, 1, 1) in / 2 (2.5, 2.5, 2.5) cm, until you've worked 6 (6, 8, 8) dec rnds = 40 (44, 44, 48) sts rem.

Work until sleeve measures 6¼ (8, 8¾, 9¾) in / 16 (20, 22.5, 25) cm, or until sleeve is roughly 2 (2, 2¼, 2½) in / 5 (5, 5.5, 6) cm shorter than desired length. Switch to largest gauge needle, if needed to work color pattern to gauge. Join Colors 2 and 3 and work pattern from "Border" chart.

Next rnd: Dec 4 (6, 4, 6) sts evenly spaced around = 36 (38, 40, 42) sts rem.

Continue with Color 2 and switch to smallest gauge dpn. Work k1, p1 ribbing for 1¼ (1¼, 1½, 1½) in / 3 (3, 3.5, 4) cm in Color 2. BO in ribbing.

FINISHING
Fold over hem at bottom and sew it down some-what loosely to WS. Weave in all loose ends.

SUMMER SOLSTICE PULLOVER

Chart from *Norwegian Knitting Designs*, figure 31, p. 36.

You will recognize the circle dancers and the stars from the "Circle of
Dancers Dress" on p. 135. Here the dancers have found their way onto a
child's pullover. Flowers bloom in the background, and the dancers
also have small flowers in their hands. They're surely going to make
beautiful flower crowns for the Summer Solstice.

SKILL LEVEL
Experienced

SIZES
1 (2, 4, 6) years

FINISHED MEASUREMENTS
Chest: 21¾ (24, 25½, 27¼) in / 58.5 (61, 65, 69) cm
Full Length: 12¾ (14½, 16, 17¾) in / 32.5 (37, 41, 45) cm
Sleeve Length: 8¼ (9¾, 11, 12¼) in / 21 (25, 28, 31) cm

YARN
CYCA #2 (sport, baby) Hifa Vilje lamb's wool (100% wool yarn, 410 yd/375 m / 100 g) and/or CYCA #2 (sport, baby) Hifa Sølje pelsull yarn (100% wool yarn, 383 yd/350 m / 100 g)

YARN AMOUNTS
Color 1: 100 (100, 150, 200) g
Color 2: 25 (25, 50, 50) g
Color 3: 25 (25, 50, 50) g

COLORS SHOWN
Light Gray/Blue/Red Version
Color 1: Vilje, Light Gray Heather 57413
Color 2: Vilje, Light Air Force Blue 57411
Color 3: Vilje, Red-Orange 57405

Light Gray/Blue/Turquoise Version (photo, p. 141)
Color 1: Vilje, Light Gray Heather 57413
Color 2: Vilje, Light Air Force Blue, 57411
Color 3: Sølje, Blue Turquoise 642129

SUGGESTED NEEDLE SIZES
US 1.5 / 2.5 mm: 16 and 24 in / 40 and 60 cm circulars and set of 5 dpn
US 2.5 / 3 mm: 16, 24, and 32 in / 40, 60, and 80 cm circulars and set of 5 dpn
Optionally, US 4 / 3.5 mm (if you knit more tightly in color pattern): 16, 24, and 32 in / 40, 60, and 80 cm circulars and set of 5 dpn

GAUGE
25 sts and approx. 32 rnds stockinette on US 2.5 / 3 mm needles = 4 x 4 in / 10 x 10 cm
25 sts and approx. 30 rnds in color pattern on US 4 / 3.5 mm needles = 4 x 4 in / 10 x 10 cm
Adjust needle size to obtain correct gauge if necessary.

INSTRUCTIONS

This pullover is worked in the round and from the top down. Start with the neck band, continue onto the yoke, set sleeve sts to wait, finish up the body and finally knit the sleeves.

NECK BAND
With Color 2 and short, smaller gauge circular needle, CO 90 (96, 102, 108) sts. Join to work in the round, being careful not to twist cast-on row. Pm at beg of rnd, which will be center of back. Work k 1, p 1 ribbing for ¾ (1, 1, 1¼) in / 2 (2.5, 2.5, 3) cm. Switch to larger gauge circular (the one you need to knit to gauge in colorwork), and k 1 rnd.

PATTERN ON THE YOKE
Start color pattern on yoke using chart for desired size. The pattern repeats 15 (16, 17, 18) times per rnd. If you want the dancing men and women to alternate, be aware that for Sizes 1 and 4 years, perfect alternation is impossible because of the odd number of repeats. Pay attention to the symbols on the chart: "x" is a color, "+" is an inc. Be aware that the chart calls for 3 colors in some rnds; drawing the third color up through the circular knitting helps avoid tangles. Hold the 3rd color as a dominant color.

Inc as shown on chart and switch to a longer needle if the sts become overcrowded. Finish the chart(s) = 210 (224, 238, 252) sts.

Switch back to medium-gauge needle, if you found you knit more tightly in colorwork. Continue in stockinette with Color 1 and k 1 rnd.

In the next rnd, you will inc 8 (8, 12, 12) sts thus:
Size 1: k 18, M1, (k 25, M1) 7 times, k 17 = 218 sts.
Size 2: k 14, M1, (k 28, M1) 7 times, k 14 = 232 sts.
Size 4: k 9, M1, (k 20, M1) 11 times, k 9 = 250 sts.
Size 6: k 11, M1, (k 21, M1) 11 times, k 10 = 264 sts.

K 0 (2, 2, 4) more rnds.

DIVIDE WORK INTO SLEEVES AND BODY
On next rnd, divide work into sleeves and body. K 33 (34, 37, 38) sts, place the next 44 (48, 52, 56) sts onto scrap yarn (right sleeve); CO 4 (4, 4, 5) sts, pm here (right side "seam" and new beg of rnd); CO 4 (4, 4, 5) sts, k 65 (68, 73, 76) sts (front); and place next 44 (48, 52, 56) sts onto scrap yarn (left sleeve), CO 8 (8, 8, 10) sts at underarm, k in stockinette to new beg of rnd, and discard marker at center back.

BODY
There are 146 (152, 162, 172) sts on needle for body. K onward around in stockinette until body from underarm measures 6 (7½, 8¾, 9½) in / 15 (19, 22, 24) cm, or until about 2 (2, 2¼, 2½) in / 5 (5, 5.5, 6) cm less than desired length.

On last rnd, dec 2 (0, 2, 0) sts evenly spaced = 144 (152, 160, 172) sts.

PATTERNED BORDER
Switch to a heavier gauge needle if you need to, to maintain gauge while knitting colorwork. Work pattern using "Border" chart. On last rnd, dec 6 (8, 8, 10) sts evenly spaced = 138 (144, 152, 162) sts. Cut Colors 1 and 3.

RIBBING

Continue with Color 2, and switch to smallest gauge circular. Work k1, p1 ribbing for 1¼ (1¼, 1½, 1½) in / 3 (3, 3.5, 4) cm. BO in ribbing.

SLEEVES

Transfer sts for one sleeve from scrap yarn to dpn of same gauge as for body.

With Color 1, beg in the middle of CO sts for underarm on body, and pick up and k 1 st in each of the first 4 (4, 4, 5) sts there; k the 44 (48, 52, 56) sleeve sts, and pick up and k 1 st in each of the last 4 (4, 4, 5) underarm CO sts. Pm here for beg of rnd = 52 (56, 60, 66) sts.

K around in stockinette until sleeve measures ¾ (1, 1, ¾) in / 2 (2.5, 2.5, 2) cm. Then beg dec:

Dec Rnd: K1, k2tog, k to 3 sts before marker, ssk, k1 = 2 sts decreased.

Rep dec rnd about every ¾-1 (1-1¼, 1, 1) in / 2-2.5 (2.5-3, 2.5, 2.5) cm, until 6 (6, 8, 9) dec rnds have been worked = 40 (44, 44, 48) sts rem.

Work until sleeve measures 6¼ (8, 9, 9¾) in / 16 (20, 22.5, 25) cm, or until sleeve is 2 (2, 2¼, 2½) / 5 (5, 5.5, 6) cm shorter than desired length.

BORDER PATTERN

Switch back to largest gauge dpn, if needed to work color pattern to gauge. K border pattern from "Border" chart (7 rnds). On next rnd, dec 4 (6, 4, 6) sts evenly spaced = 36 (38, 40, 42) sts rem.

RIBBING

Continue with Color 2, and switch to smallest gauge dpn. Work k1, p1 ribbing for 1¼ (1¼, 1½, 1½) in / 3 (3, 3.5, 4) cm. BO in ribbing.

FINISHING

Weave in all loose ends. Done!

1 year, dancing woman

1 year, dancing man

2–6 years, dancing woman

2–6 years, dancing man

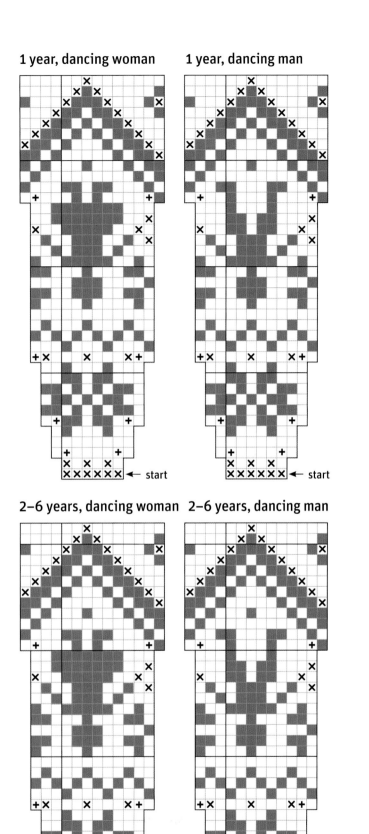

← start
← start
← start
← start

	Color 1
☒	Color 2
■	Color 3
✚	Inc 1 st

Border

← start

CLOVER MEADOW CHILDREN'S SWEATER

Chart from *Norwegian Knitting Designs*, figure 56, page 52.

The Nordenfjeldske (Northern Mountains) clover border is super chic and can be used for lots of things. Here, it has found its way onto a children's sweater. Two color combinations are presented here, but this pattern would also look great in countless other combinations. Choose from among your own favorite colors and knit your own little clover meadow.

SKILL LEVEL
Experienced

SIZES
2 (4, 6, 8, 10) years

FINISHED MEASUREMENTS
Chest: 24¾ (26¾, 28¾, 30¾, 32¾) in / 63 (68, 73, 78, 83) cm
Full Length: 14½ (16, 17¾, 19¼, 21) in / 37 (41, 45, 49, 53) cm
Sleeve Length: 9¾ (11, 12¼, 13½, 14½) in / 25 (28, 31, 34, 37) cm

YARN
CYCA #2 (sport, baby) Hifa Ask 100% wool yarn (344 yd/315 m / 100 g)

YARN AMOUNTS
Color 1: 150 (150, 200, 200, 200–225) g
Color 2: 100 (100, 100, 150, 150) g
Color 3: approx. 50 (100, 100, 100, 100) g

COLORS SHOWN
Pale Rose Version
Color 1: Pale Rose 316108
Color 2: Light Blue-Gray 316050
Color 3: Dark Blue-Gray 316104

Light Blue-Gray and Brown Version
Color 1: Light Blue-Gray 316050
Color 2: Chocolate Brown 316115
Color 3: Dark Brown Heather 316103

SUGGESTED NEEDLE SIZES
US 2.5 / 3 mm: 24 in / 60 cm circular and set of 5 dpn
US 4 / 3.5 mm: 24 and 32 in / 60 and 80 cm circulars and set of 5 dpn

GAUGE
24 sts and 30 rnds in pattern on larger gauge needles = 4 x 4 in / 10 x 10 cm
Adjust needle size to obtain correct gauge if necessary.

NOTIONS
7 (7, 7, 8, 8) buttons; optionally, tape to cover cut edges

BUTTONS SHOWN
Pale Rose Version: MØRE 15 mm K292913 from Hjelmvedt
Light Blue-Gray and Brown Version: STJERNE 20 mm K342958 from Hjelmvedt

INSTRUCTIONS

After the ribbing is worked back and forth, the sweater is knitted in the round with a steek in front, to be cut open later. The body and sleeves are knitted separately up to the armholes. The parts are collected onto a single circular, and the shoulders are finished with raglan decreases on the yoke. The steek is cut open and button bands are knitted along the front edges. The neck band is worked last. The cut steek edges are turned in and can be hidden with a knitted facing or fabric tape, or simply hemmed down on the inside.

BODY

With the smaller gauge circular and Color 2, CO 136 (148, 156, 168, 180) sts. Work ribbing back and forth:

Row 1 (WS): K1 (edge st), work p 2, k 2 ribbing until the last 3 sts, p 2, k1 (edge st).
Row 2 (RS): K1 (edge st), work k 2, p 2 ribbing until the last 3 sts, k 2, k1 (edge st).
Rep these two rows until ribbing measures 1¼ (1¼, 1½, 1¾, 1¾) in / 3.5 (3.5, 4, 4.5, 4.5) cm.

Switch to larger gauge circular needle (60 cm). K 1 rnd and inc 10 (10, 14, 14, 14) sts evenly spaced = 146 (158, 170, 182, 194) sts.

Work to end of rnd and CO 5 new sts between end and beg of rnd. The 5 new sts, combined with the 2 outer edge sts in the ribbing, will be a steek, to be cut apart for the front opening = 7 steek sts. Do *not* work steek sts in pattern and do not include them in st count. Pm on each side of steek. You may find it helpful to k steek sts in vertical stripes

when working colorwork rnds—Color 1 on 1st, 3rd, 5th, and 7th st across.

Join Color 1 (and later Color 3) and work color pattern following chart. There are 12 (13, 14, 15, 16) widthwise repeats per rnd. Pm on each side with 36 (39, 42, 45, 48) sts for each front and 72 (78, 84, 90, 96) sts for the back.

Work in pattern until body measures approx. 9½ (10½, 11¾, 13, 14¼) in / 24 (27, 30, 33, 36) cm. On last rnd, BO for armhole: K to 4 (4, 4, 5, 5) sts before first side marker, BO 8 (8, 8, 10, 10) sts, knit to 4 (4, 4, 5, 5) sts before the next side marker, BO 8 (8, 8, 10, 10) sts, finish rnd = 32 (35, 38, 40, 43) sts for each half front, and 64 (70, 76, 80, 86) sts for back. Set body aside and knit sleeves.

SLEEVES

With smaller gauge dpn, and Color 2, CO 40 (40, 44, 44, 48) sts. Join to work in the round, being careful not to twist cast-on row. Work around in k2, p2 ribbing for 1½ (1½, 1¾, 2, 2) in / 4 (4, 4.5, 5, 5) cm. Switch to larger dpn, k 1 rnd stockinette, and inc 6 (8, 6, 10, 8) sts evenly spaced = 46 (48, 50, 54, 56) sts.

Next rnd: Join Color 1 and k to last st, p 1. From now on, p last st of rnd with Color 1 in all rnds. This is the underarm "seam," and is not knitted in pattern, but is included in st counts; incs will occur here.

Next rnd: Beg pattern, following chart. Check arrows under chart to see where to start for desired size, but repeat pattern through whole rnd. After 6 rnds, inc on both sides of the p st:

Inc Rnd: M1, knit in pattern to the last st (the p st), M1, p1. New sts are worked into pattern as they appear.

Work this inc rnd every 1 (1, 1, 1¼, 1¼) in / 2.5 (2.5, 2.5, 3, 3) cm, until there are 7 (8, 9, 9, 10) inc rnds = 60 (64, 68, 72, 76) sts.

Then continue working around until sleeve measures just under 9¾ (11, 12¼, 13½, 14½) in / 25 (28, 31, 34, 37) cm; end on same row of pattern as for body. On last rnd, BO 8 (8, 8, 10, 10) sts at underarm—the first 4 (4, 4, 5, 5) sts and the last 4 (4, 4, 5, 5) sts, including the p st = 52 (56, 60, 62, 66) sts. Set sleeve aside and knit another just like it.

YOKE

Knit the body and the sleeves onto the same (larger gauge) circular. Beg at right front, continuing color pattern, and CO 1 st at each juncture of body and sleeves; these new sts will be twisted p sts with Color 1 in all rnds and will be called "the purl st(s)" = 236 (256, 276, 288, 308) sts (including the 4 p sts). K 2 (1, 2, 3, 2) more rnds in pattern.

RAGLAN DECREASES

Dec Rnd: *K pattern as est to 2 sts before the p st. Ssk, twisted p1, k2tog and repeat from * for the remainder of the rnd (4 times total) = 8 sts decreased.

Work dec rnd *every other* rnd 17 (19, 20, 21, 23) times total. Change to a shorter circular needle, as fewer sts pull at the rnd.

Now work dec rnd *every* rnd 3 times = 20 (22, 23, 24, 26) total rnds with raglan decs. Your stitch count on the needle after finishing the decs is 76 (80, 92, 96, 100) sts: 12 (13, 15, 16, 17) sts for each front; 24 (26, 30, 32, 34) sts for back; and 12 (12, 14, 14, 14) sts for each sleeve. BO 5 center steek sts.

NECK BAND

With smaller gauge needle and Color 2, work k2 p2 ribbing back and forth.

Row 1 (WS): K1 (edge st), *k2, p2, rep from * to the last 3 sts, k2, k1(edge st).

Row 2 (RS): K1 (edge st), *p2, k2, rep from * to the last 3 sts, p2, k1 (edge st).

Rep these 2 rows until neck band measures about 1 (1, 1, 1¼, 1¼) in / 2.5 (2.5, 2.5, 3, 3) cm. BO in ribbing. Take care to ensure BO is comfortably loose.

ASSEMBLY

Closely machine stitch on each side of center st of steek and cut carefully between seams.

BUTTON BANDS

With RS facing, use smaller gauge dpn and Color 2 to pick up sts along front end in the space between steek and body sts. On right front, start at ribbing at bottom, and for left front, start at edge of neck band. Pick up 3 sts for every 4 rnds along front edge, and 2 sts for every 3 rows along ribbed bands. The st count should be a multiple of 4. Work back and forth and start on WS.

Row 1 (WS): k 1 (edge st), *p 2, k 2, rep from * to the last 3 sts, p 2, k 1 (edge st).
Row 2 (RS): k 1 (edge st), *k 2, p 2, rep from * to the last 3 sts, k 2, k 1 (edge st).

Traditionally, girls' and women's sweaters have the buttonholes on the right side, and boys' and men's on the left; but in the end, it's up to you.

Button Band Without Buttonholes
Work 9 (9, 9, 9, 11) rows of ribbing. BO in ribbing.

Button Band With Buttonholes
Work 4 (4, 4, 4, 5) rows of ribbing. On next row, continue ribbing but start 7 (7, 7, 8, 8) buttonholes by BO 2 sts. Place the top buttonhole midway up the neck band, and the lowest, about ½ in / 1.5 cm from the bottom edge; space the rest evenly between them.

On next row, CO 2 sts over the BO sts. Continue ribbing for 3 (3, 3, 3, 4) more rows. BO in ribbing.

FINISHING
Weave in all ends. Sew BO sts at underarm.

The steek edges are turned to the inside of the front edges. They can either be sewn down (over-cast st) on the WS, or covered with a decorative tape or a knitted facing, as you wish. If you use cotton tape, it's wise to preshrink it beforehand, either by steaming or laundering it.

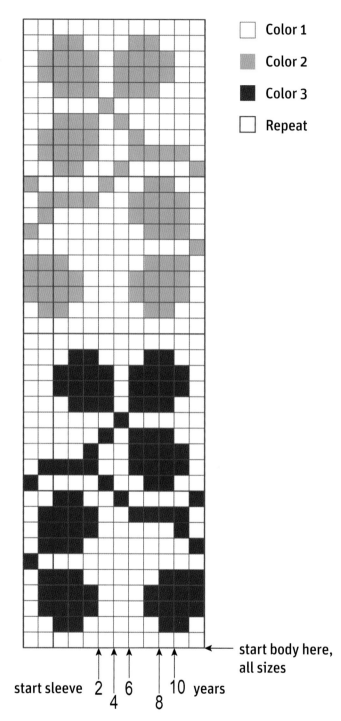

☐ Color 1
▨ Color 2
■ Color 3
☐ Repeat

start body here, all sizes
start sleeve 2 6 10 years
4 8

153

If you choose to knit a facing to hide the steek edges: With smaller gauge needle and preferred color, pick up sts on WS from sts of first row of ribbed button bands. Pick up 1 st for each st in button band, but only between neck band and ribbing. Work 4 rows in stockinette and BO loosely. Whipstitch facing to the inside.

If you made a double neck band, fold it in toward WS and sew it down neatly.

Sew on buttons and, if needed, reinforce buttonholes.

CHILDREN'S SELBU ROSE SWEATER AND HAT

Chart from *Norwegian Knitting Designs*, figure 3, page 12 and figure 51, page 49.

Isn't this perfect? This Selbu rose set with a sweater and matching hat suits a two-year-old as well as a 10-year-old. Flip the colors, or choose other colors, and express your own creativity. The band of eight-petaled roses is repeated in the hat, but the hat has "lice" instead of cross-hatches on the body,

SWEATER

SKILL LEVEL
Experienced

SIZES
2 (4, 6, 8, 10) years

FINISHED MEASUREMENTS
Chest: 24¾ (27, 29, 30¾, 33) in / 63.5 (68.5, 73.5, 78.5, 83.5) cm
Full Length: 14½ (16, 17¾, 19¼, 21) in / 36.5 (41, 45, 49, 53.5) cm
Sleeve Length: 9¾ (11, 12¼, 13½ 14½) in / 25 (28, 31, 34, 37) cm

YARN
CYCA #2 (sport, baby) Hifa Ask 100% wool yarn (344 yd/315 m / 100 g)

YARN AMOUNTS
Color 1: 100 (150,150, 200, 200) g
Color 2: 150 (150, 150, 200, 200) g
(Yarn amounts for hat are listed separately below.)

COLORS SHOWN
Turquoise/White Version
Color 1: Light Green-Turquoise Heather 346584
Color 2: Natural White 316057

Corn Yellow/White Version
Color 1: Corn Yellow Heather 346502
Color 2: Semi-bleached White 316047

SUGGESTED NEEDLE SIZES
US 2.5 / 3 mm: 24 in / 60 cm circular and set of 5 dpn
US 4 / 3.5 mm: 16, 24, and 32 in / 40, 60, and 80 cm circulars and set of 5 dpn

GAUGE
24 sts and 30 rnds in pattern on larger gauge needles = 4 x 4 in / 10 x 10 cm.
Adjust needle size to obtain correct gauge if necessary.

NOTIONS
7 (7, 7, 8, 8) buttons; optionally, tape to face steek edges

BUTTONS SHOWN
Turquoise/White Version: VIKING 18 mm, K312982 from Hjelmvedt
Corn Yellow/White Version: MØRE light 15 mm, K292913 from Hjelmvedt

HAT

SKILL LEVEL
Experienced

SIZES AND MEASUREMENTS
2–4 (6–8, 10) years. The hat has a circumference of roughly 17¼ (18, 20½) in / 44 (46, 52) cm and a height of 8 (8½, 9) in / 20.5 (21.5, 22.5) cm, measured flat.

YARN
CYCA #2 (sport, baby) Hifa Ask 100% wool yarn (344 yd/315 m / 100 g)

YARN AMOUNTS
Color 1: 25 (25, 30) g
Color 2: 30 (35, 40) g, of which 10 g are for an optional pompom

158

COLORS SHOWN
Colors are listed under "Sweater," above.

SUGGESTED NEEDLE SIZES
For Sizes 2–4 years and 10 years, **US 2.5 / 3 mm:**
16 in / 40 cm circular and set of 5 dpn
For Size 6–8 years, **US 4 / 3.5 mm:** 16 in / 40 cm
circular and set of 5 dpn

GAUGE
Note: The different sizes are achieved with different numbers of sts, but also through different gauges and needle sizes.
25 (24, 25) sts in pattern on US 2.5 / 3 mm (US 4 / 3.5 mm, US 2.5 / 3 mm) needles = 4 in / 10 cm. Adjust needle size to obtain correct gauge if necessary.

INSTRUCTIONS, SWEATER

The sweater body is first, starting with the ribbing, worked back and forth on a circular needle. Next, a steek is cast on at center front, where you will later cut the front opening. From this point, knitting is in the round. The body and the sleeves are worked separately to the armholes. The parts are assembled on a circular needle and worked around with raglan decreases on the yoke. The sweater is cut open and button bands knitted along the front edges. Finally, you knit a neck band or a collar. The steek is folded to the inside and can be hidden with either a knitted facing or a fabric tape or it can be hemmed to the inside.

BODY
With smaller gauge circular and Color 1, CO 139 (149, 159, 169, 181) sts.

Work ribbing back and forth:
Row 1 (WS): k1, (p1, k1) rep to end of row.
Row 2 (RS): k1, (k1, p1) rep to end of row.

Rep these 2 rows until ribbing measures 1¼ (1¼, 1½, 1¾, 1¾) in / 3.5 (3.5, 4, 4.5, 4.5) cm.

Switch to larger gauge circular, and k 1 rnd while you inc 8 (10, 12, 14, 14) sts evenly spaced around = 147 (159, 171, 183, 195) sts.

Continue around, and at end of row, CO 5 new sts at center front. These 5 new sts and the 2 edge sts of the ribbing form a 7-st steek, which will later be cut apart. Do *not* work steek sts in the color pattern, and do not include them in st counts. Pm on each side of steek. It's helpful to knit it with 1-st vertical stripes in rnds where you're knitting with 2 colors.

Join Color 2 and work 1 rnd stockinette (in Color 2). Pm at each side of work: k 36 (39, 42, 45, 48) sts (right front), pm; k 73 (79, 85, 91, 97) sts (back), pm; k 36 (39, 42, 45, 48) sts (left front).

Beg pattern following Chart A, and work in pattern until piece measures about 9¾ (11, 12¼, 13½, 14½) in / 25 (28, 31, 34, 37) cm. End with a full vertical rep. On last rnd, BO for armholes: Work to 3 (3, 3, 4, 4) sts before first side marker, BO 7 (7, 7, 9, 9) sts, work to 4 (4, 4, 5, 5) sts before next side marker, BO 7 (7, 7, 9, 9) sts, work to end of rnd = 33 (36, 39, 41, 44) sts for each half front, and 65 (71, 77, 81, 87) sts for back.

Set body aside and knit sleeves.

SLEEVES
With smaller gauge dpn and Color 1, cast on 40 (42, 44, 48, 48) sts. Join, being careful not to twist cast-on row. Work around in k1, p1 ribbing for 1¼ (1¼, 1½, 1¾, 1¾) in / 3.5 (3.5, 4, 4.5, 4.5) cm. Change to larger gauge dpn. Work 1 rnd stockinette, inc 6 (6, 6, 6, 8) sts evenly spaced = 46 (48, 50, 54, 56) sts.

Next rnd: Join Color 2 and work stockinette until the last st. P1. From this point, always p last st of rnd in Color 2; this is underarm "seam" st, and is not knitted in pattern, but (unlike steek sts) is included in st count.

Beg working Chart A. The square marked with X on chart is the midpoint of sleeve, widthwise. Count backwards from that st on sleeve to find starting point on chart for desired size.

After 6 rnds, inc at the underarm "seam" on both sides of the p st:

Inc Rnd: M1, work in pattern up to the last st (p st), M1, p1. New sts are worked in pattern as they are added.

Rep this inc rnd every 1 (1, 1, 1¼, 1¼) in / 2.5 (2.5, 2.5, 3, 3) cm, until 7 (8, 9, 9, 10) inc rnds have been worked = 60 (64, 68, 72, 76) sts. Work in pattern until sleeve is as long as body. Finish with a complete vertical rep. On final rnd, BO 7 (7, 7, 9, 9) sts at underarm (BO the first 3 (3, 3, 4, 4) sts and last 4 (4, 4, 5, 5) sts) = 53 (57, 61, 63, 67) sts. The sleeve now measures about 9¾ (11, 12¼, 13½, 14½) in / 25 (28, 31, 34, 37) cm. Set sleeve aside and make another just like it.

YOKE

Raglan decs are going to be knitted *at the same time* as color pattern. It's important for the pattern to be positioned perfectly. Because several things have to be done at the same time, but are spelled out one after the other, please read through the next three sections before you continue. The next section gives an overview of how to place the pattern bands and their positioning on the various parts of the sweater. When you've read this, go on to the section "Knit sleeves and body together," to proceed.

COLOR PATTERN ON YOKE

Chart A (Size 2 years not included here)
Work Chart A for 0 (1, 1, 1, 2) vertical repeats.

Chart B (All Sizes)
To have the pattern meet symmetrically:
Right front: Start at first st on chart.
Both sleeves: The box marked x on the chart is the midpoint of sleeve. Count out from that st on sleeve to find starting point on chart for desired size.
Back: The box marked o on the chart is the midpoint of back. Count out from that midpoint on your knitting to find starting point on chart.
Left front: Will be worked mirror-image to the right front.

Chart B is worked once lengthwise.

Chart C (All Sizes)
Make sure cross-hatches here line up with cross-hatches farther down, under the Selbu Rose pattern. Work this chart until all raglan decs are completed (also indicated with an arrow on chart).

KNIT SLEEVES AND BODY TOGETHER

The body and sleeves are now knitted onto the same circular. With larger gauge needle, beginning at right front, knit pattern as described in last section and CO one new st at each joining point between sleeves and body; these new sts are worked as twisted p in all rnds and are referred to from now on as "the purl stitch(es)" = 241 (265, 281, 293, 313) sts in rnd (including these 4 new sts). K 0 (0, 1, 1, 0) more rnd in pattern.

RAGLAN DECREASES

Dec Rnd: *Work est pattern up to 2 sts before p st, ssk, twisted p1, k2tog, rep from * 3 more times = 8 sts decreased. Work dec rnd *every other* rnd 17 (19, 20, 22, 26) times. Then rep dec rnd *every* rnd 3 (3, 3, 2, 0) times.

Switch to a shorter circular needle whenever there are fewer sts and your work is starting to stretch. After raglan decs are complete, 81 (85, 97, 101, 105) sts rem: 13 (14, 16, 17, 18) sts for each front; 25 (27, 31, 33, 35) sts for back; and 13 (13, 15, 15, 15) sts for each sleeve. BO steek sts, and either leave the rem sts on needle, or transfer them to scrap yarn.

CUT FRONT OPEN

Machine stitch 2 tight seams down front on each side of center steek st. Carefully cut between seams.

BUTTON BANDS

With RS facing, smaller gauge needles, and Color 1, pick up an *odd number* of sts along front edges, in the transition between steek and body sts. On right front, start at bottom on ribbed edging. On left front, start at neck. Pick up approx. 3 sts per 4 rnds along front edge—that is, skip every 4th rnd—and approx. 2 sts every 3 rnds along edge of ribbing. You will be working back and forth, and the first row is on the WS.

Row 1 (WS): k1 (edge st), p1 (k1, p1) until the last st, k1 (edge st).
Row 2 (RS): k1 (edge st), k1 (p1, k1) until the last st, k1 (edge st).

Now, follow the directions for button bands, one with and one without buttonholes. Traditionally, girls' and women's sweaters have the buttonholes on the right side, and boys' and men's on the left; but in the end, it's up to you.

Button Band Without Buttonholes
Work 9 (9, 9, 9, 11) rows k1, p1 ribbing. BO in ribbing.

Button Band With Buttonholes
Work 4 (4, 4, 4, 5) rows k1, p1 ribbing.

Next row: Continue in ribbing and make 7 (7, 7, 8, 8) buttonholes. Place top buttonhole 3 sts down from top edge, and bottom buttonhole 4 sts up from lower edge; space the rest evenly between these two. BO 2 sts to make a buttonhole.

Next row: Continuing in ribbing, CO 2 sts over BOs in the previous row.

Continue in ribbing for 3 (3, 3, 3, 4) more rows. BO in ribbing.

NECK BAND

With RS facing, smaller gauge needle, and Color 1, beg at top in middle of short side of right button band. Pick up and k 4 (4, 4, 4, 5) sts from button band, k across waiting 81 (85, 97, 101, 105) neckline sts, and pick up and k 4 (4, 4, 4, 5) sts from middle of left button band = 89 (93, 105, 109, 115) sts.

Single neck band: Work k1, p1 ribbing back and forth (as described for the body) for 1 (1, 1, 1, 1¼,

1¼) in / 2.5 (2.5, 2.5, 3, 3) cm.

Double neck band: Work k1, p1 ribbing back and forth for approx. 2 (2, 2, 2½, 2½) in / 5 (5, 5, 6, 6) cm.

BO all sts in ribbing. Make sure to BO loosely.

COLLAR

Optional; see corn yellow version. With WS facing, smaller gauge needle, and Color 1, beg at top in middle of short side of left button band. Pick up and k 4 (4, 4, 4, 5) sts from button band, k across waiting 81 (85, 97, 101, 105) neckline sts, and pick up and k 4 (4, 4, 4, 5) sts up to middle of right button band = 89 (93, 105, 109, 115) sts.

Work k1, p1 ribbing back and forth for approx. ¾ (¾, 1, 1, 1) in / 2 (2, 2.5, 2.5, 2.5) cm. Switch to larger gauge needle and continue in ribbing until collar measures 2½ (2½, 2¾, 3¼) in / 6 (6.5, 7, 7.5, 8) cm. BO loosely. Cut yarn.

FINISHING

Weave in loose ends. Sew underarm seams.

Fold steek edges to the inside. They can be sewn down with whipstitch on the WS or covered with decorative tape or a knit facing, if you wish. If you use a cotton tape, it's wise to pre-shrink it, either by washing or steaming it.

If you choose to knit a facing, this is one way: With smaller gauge needle and desired color, pick up and knit sts from back of first row of button bands. Pick up 1 st for every st in button band, but only between neck band and ribbing at bottom edge. Work 4 rows stockinette. BO rather loosely, then hem facing nicely on the WS, covering raw edges of steek.

If you've made a double neck band, turn it inside and sew it down neatly.

Sew on buttons and reinforce buttonholes if necessary.

INSTRUCTIONS, HAT

Use US 1.5 / 2.5 mm needles for sizes 2-4 and 10 years. Use US 2.5 / 3 mm for size 6-8. See information on p. 158.

Note: The different sizes are achieved with different numbers of sts, but also through different gauges/needle sizes.

With smaller (medium, smaller) gauge needles and Color 2, CO 98 (98, 114) sts. Join, being careful not to twist cast-on row. Pm at beg of rnd, if you wish. Make sure CO sts are nice and loose.

Work k1, p1 ribbing around; continue in ribbing until piece measures 1¼ (1½, 1½) in / 3 (3.5, 4) cm.

Switch to medium (larger, medium) gauge needles. Knit 1 rnd and inc 14 sts: K 0 (0, 2), *k 7 (7, 8), M1. Rep from * to end of rnd = 112 (112, 128) sts.

Join Color 1 and start following Chart D. There are 7 (7, 8) widthwise repeats per rnd. After complet-

CHARTS FOR SWEATER

Chart A

X

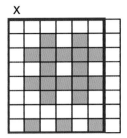

■ Color 1
□ Color 2
□ Repeat

Chart B

O   X

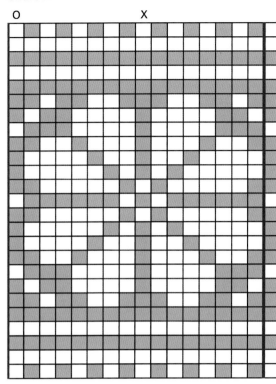

Chart C

last rnd

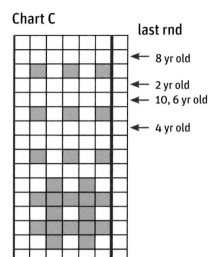

← 8 yr old
← 2 yr old
← 10, 6 yr old
← 4 yr old

CHARTS FOR HATS

Chart D

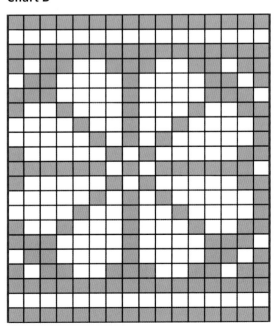

Chart E

4
3
2
1

SYMBOLS

■ Color 1
□ Color 2
□ Repeat

ing Chart D, continue to Chart E. On first rnd of Chart E, adjust st count to a multiple of 16: Dec 2 (dec 2, inc 2) sts evenly spaced around = 110 (110, 130) sts. Rep Chart E until work measures 6 (6¼, 6¾) in / 15 (16, 17) cm. If you want a shorter or longer hat, adjust length here, before beg decs. End on Row 2 or Row 4 of Chart E.

DECREASING CROWN

Continue in pattern and dec as described below. On Rnds 1–15, dec *every other* rnd, then end with Rnd 16 as a final dec rnd.

There are 11 (11, 13) decs per dec rnd. Switch to dpn as sts become strained on circular.

Rnd 1 (dec rnd): *K8, k2tog, rep from * around = 99 (99, 117) sts rem.
Rnds 2, 4, 6, 8, 10, 12, 14: Work in pattern.
Rnd 3 (dec rnd): *K7, k2tog, rep from * around = 88 (88, 104) sts.

Rnd 5 (dec rnd): *K6, k2tog, rep from * around = 77 (77, 91) sts.
Rnd 7 (dec rnd): *K5, k2tog, rep from * around = 66 (66, 78) sts.
Rnd 9 (dec rnd): *K4, k2tog, rep from * around = 55 (55, 65) sts.
Rnd 11 (dec rnd): *K3, k2tog, rep from * around = 44 (44, 52) sts.
Rnd 13 (dec rnd): *K2, k2tog, rep from * around = 33 (33, 39) sts.
Rnd 15 (dec rnd): *K1, k2tog, rep from * around = 22 (22, 26) sts.
Rnd 16 (dec rnd): *K2tog, rep from * around = 11 (11, 13) sts remain.

Cut yarn. With a blunt tapestry needle, pull end through rem sts, and pull together firmly.

FINISHING

Weave in loose ends. If you wish, make a pompom with Color 2 and fasten it on top of hat.

NOSTALGIA SWEATER

Charts from *Norwegian Knitting Designs*, figure 55, page 51.

This children's sweater is knitted in cozy lamb's wool and has a sweet, old-timey feel. It's perfect for every kid. The small pattern band is elegant in its simplicity, and can be used on many other projects: How about a hat, a pair of half-mitts, a muffler, or a neck warmer? Or how about using the band of pattern as an all-over pattern on a sweater for yourself?

SKILL LEVEL
Experienced

SIZES
2 (4, 6, 8, 10, 12) years

FINISHED MEASUREMENTS
Chest: 24½ (25½, 29½, 30, 32, 34¼) in / 62.5 (65, 70.5, 76, 81.5, 87) cm
Full Length: 15¼ (16¾, 18¼, 20, 21¼, 22) in / 38.5 (42.5, 46.5, 50.5, 54, 56) cm
Sleeve Length: 9¾ (11, 12¼, 13½, 14½, 15¾) in / 25 (28, 31, 34, 37, 40) cm

YARN
CYCA #2 (sport, baby) Hifa Sol lamb's wool yarn (317 yd/290 m / 100 g)

YARN AMOUNTS
Color 1: 150 (150, 200, 200–225, 250, 250–275) g
Color 2: 50 (100, 100, 100, 100, 100) g
Color 3: 50 (50, 50, 100, 100, 100) g

COLORS SHOWN
Pale Blue-Gray and Orange Version
Color 1: Pale Blue-Gray 58409
Color 2: Red-Orange 58405
Color 3: Pale Yellow 58401

Beige and Blue Version
Color 1: Beige 58402
Color 2: Light Air Force Blue 58411
Color 3: Natural White 58400

Note: With this version, there's relatively little contrast between the beige background color on the body and sleeves and the unbleached white lice pattern. This was a deliberate choice, creating a soft, delicate impression.

SUGGESTED NEEDLE SIZES
US 2.5 / 3 mm: 24 and 32 in / 60 and 80 cm circulars and set of 5 dpn
US 4 / 3.5 mm: 16, 24, and 32 in / 40, 60, and 80 cm circulars and set of 5 dpn
Optionally, if you knit more tightly in colorwork, **US 6 / 4 mm:** 16, 24, and 32 in / 40, 60, and 80 cm circulars

GAUGE
22 sts in pattern on larger gauge needles = 4 in / 10 cm
Adjust needle size to obtain correct gauge if necessary.

NOTIONS
6 (6, 7, 7, 8, 8) buttons

BUTTONS SHOWN
Pale Blue-Gray and Orange Version: GJENDE 18 mm, K332910, from Hjelmtvedt
Beige and Blue Version: VIKING 18 mm, K312982 from Hjelmtvedt

Color 1

Color 2

Color 3

Repeat

Chart A

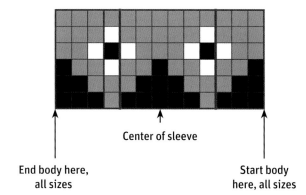

Center of sleeve

End body here,
all sizes

Start body
here, all sizes

Chart C

End here,
all sizes

Start here,
all sizes

Chart B

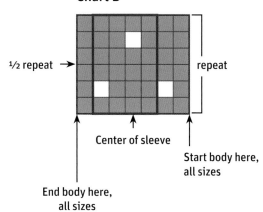

½ repeat

repeat

Center of sleeve

Start body here,
all sizes

End body here,
all sizes

Chart D

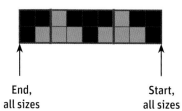

End,
all sizes

Start,
all sizes

INSTRUCTIONS

The sweater is worked in the round from the bottom up. It has lengthwise button bands and a circular yoke. The body and sleeves are knitted separately to the underarm. The parts are then assembled on one circular. Except on the two smallest sizes, the yoke starts with raglan decreases before the colorwork. When the color pattern is completed, a section is worked in one-color stockinette with gradual decreases. The yoke ends with a little band of pattern and the stitches are put on hold until it's time to work the neck band. Button bands are knitted and sewn along the front edges, which have been cut open by that point. Finally, the neck band is knitted and facings for the button bands are sewn on the inside.

BODY

With smallest circular and Color 2, CO 147 (153, 165, 177, 189, 201) sts. Join, being careful not to twist cast-on row. The ribbing will be worked back and forth. The first and last sts are edge sts.

Row 1 (WS): Slip 1 p-wise wyf (edge st), (p1, k1) until 2 sts rem, end with p2.
Row 2 (RS): Slip 1 k-wise wyb (edge st), work k1, p1 ribbing until 2 sts rem, k2.

Rep Rows 1 and 2. When ribbing is ¾ in / 1.5 cm long, make a buttonhole on whichever side you prefer, on RS: BO 2 sts, 3 sts in from edge. Next row: CO 2 sts over BO sts. Continue ribbing until piece measures 1¼ (1¼, 1½, 1½, 1¾, 1¾) in / 3 (3, 3.5, 3.5, 4, 4) cm. End with Row 1 (WS).

Work first 7 sts of ribbing. Place these sts and 7 outer sts at other end of row onto a st holder; these will be the bases of the button bands. There are now 133 (139, 151, 163, 175, 187) sts rem. Switch to medium-gauge circular needle (or largest gauge, if needed to work color pattern to gauge). Work the rest of row, and CO 5 sts at end of row. These are steek sts; do *not* work in pattern, and do *not* include in st counts. Pm if you like on both sides of these sts. You may want to knit steek sts in single st vertical stripes (main color/pattern color) on rnds with more than one color in use.

Work in pattern following Chart A. Start at arrow, rep area in red frame, and end where indicated. The pattern is worked once vertically.

Note: For size 2 years *only*, on last rnd of color pattern, dec 2 sts at the beg and the end of the round: k1, k2tog, k until 3 sts rem, k2tog, k1 = 131 sts rem.

Proceed to Chart B and knit "lice." Start rnd at arrow, rep area in red frame, and end rnd where indicated. Continue until work measures 9½ (10½, 11¾, 13, 14, 14½) in / 24 (27, 30, 33, 35.5, 36.5) cm. End with a whole or a half vertical rep (shown on Chart B) and on last rnd, BO for armholes: k 28 (31, 34, 36, 39, 42) sts (right front); BO 7 (7, 7, 9, 9, 9) sts; k 61 (63, 69, 73, 79, 85) sts (back); BO 7 (7, 7, 9, 9, 9) sts, k to end of rnd. Set body aside and make sleeves.

SLEEVES

With smallest gauge dpn and Color 2, CO 36 (38,

40, 40, 42, 44) sts. Work k1, p1 ribbing around until piece measures 1¼ (1¼, 1½, 1½, 1¾, 1¾) in / 3 (3, 3.5, 3.5, 4, 4) cm. Switch to medium or larger gauge dpn, whichever is needed to work color pattern to gauge, and k 1 rnd in stockinette. Work color pattern following Chart A. The last st of rnd is center of underarm, and is purled (with Color 1 when possible) in every rnd, as underarm "seam" marker st. The center of rnd is center st of sleeve: Count back from middle on sleeve to find starting point for chart. The pattern should meet symmetrically at "seam" marker st. Work Chart A once vertically, then proceed to Chart B. Here also, count back from center st on sleeve to find starting point for pattern on chart for desired size. *At the same time*, when piece measures 2 (2, 2, 2¼, 2¼, 2¼) in / 5 (5, 5, 6, 6, 6) cm, beg to inc at underarm on both sides of marker st:

Inc Rnd: M1, knit up to marker, M1, p1 (2 sts inc). The new sts are knitted in pattern, wherever they appear.

Rep this inc rnd every 1 (1, 1, 1, 1, 1¼) in / 2.5 (2.5, 2.5, 2.5, 2.5, 3) cm until you have worked 7 (8, 9, 10, 10, 10) inc rnds = 50 (54, 58, 60, 62, 64) sts. Switch to a circular when dpn become overcrowded.

When incs are complete, k until sleeve measures 9¾ (11, 12¼, 13½, 14½, 15¾) in / 25 (28, 31, 34, 37, 40) cm. End with a half or a whole vertical rep, and, on same rnd, BO 7 (7, 7, 9, 9, 9) sts centered at underarm: BO 3 (3, 3, 4, 4, 4); k until there are 4 (4, 4, 5, 5, 5) sts rem in rnd; BO rem sts in rnd = 43 (47, 51, 51, 53, 55) sts rem. Set sleeve aside and knit another just like it.

YOKE

Place all parts on same circular (either medium or large gauge, whichever is needed to work color pattern to gauge) in this order: right front, right sleeve (the sleeves are identical), back, left sleeve, left front = 203 (219, 239, 247, 263, 279) sts.

Size 2 years: Skip to section "*Continue here, all sizes.*"

Sizes 4 and 6 years: The pattern continues as before from where it ended on each piece individually. Work 3 rnds. Move on to section "*Continue here, all sizes.*"

Sizes 8 to 12 years: Pm in each space between parts. The pattern continues as before from where it ended on each piece individually. Work - (-, -, 2, 2, 3) rnds.

Now work a few rnds with raglan decs, *at the same time* as lice pattern continues, but work the last st before, and the first st after, markers with Color 1:

Dec Rnd: *Work in pattern up to 2 sts before marker; with Color 1, ssk, k2tog. Rep from * 3 more times = 8 sts dec.

Rep dec rnd *every other* rnd until there are - (-, -, 2, 2, 3) dec rnds.

Continue here, all sizes
There are now 203 (219, 239, 231, 247, 255) sts rem in the rnd. The last rnd should be a one-color rnd, following 1 rnd with lice. Work 1 rnd with Color 1 and dec 22 (26, 22, 2, 6, 2) sts evenly spaced around = 181 (193, 217, 229, 241, 253) sts.

Remove raglan markers, if there are any (Sizes 2, 4, 6 years have none).

Start color pattern on Chart C. Beg at arrow, rep area within red frame, and end rnd where indicated (at arrow). When Chart C is complete once through vertically, work stockinette in Color 1. Work first rnd in stockinette and adjust st number by dec 1 = 180 (192, 216, 228, 240, 252) sts.

There's a choice of ways to dec in single-colored portion above pattern band:

On the pale blue-gray version, a more discreet decrease was used, where the decrease sts lean toward a central st.

On the beige version, the decrease is a little more marked. The decs are a type called "centered k3tog," which can look like they twine up over each other, almost like a little mini-cable.

Choose your preferred method of decrease.

Dec Rnd (Light Blue-Gray Version)
On next rnd, dec 24 sts: *K5 (5, 6, 7, 7, 8) sts, ssk, k1, k2tog, k 5 (6, 7, 7, 8, 8) sts. Rep from * to end of rnd.

Dec Rnd (Beige Version)
On next rnd, dec 24 sts: *k 6 (6, 7, 8, 8, 9) sts, k3tog (centered dec), k 6 (7, 8, 8, 9, 9). Rep from * to end of rnd.

Work your chosen dec rnd every 3 rnds. Each time, there will 1 st fewer before the first dec, 2 sts fewer between decs, and 1 st fewer after last dec in rnd. Positioning decs accurately will line them up with one another with either method. Continue until 4 (4, 5, 5, 6, 6) dec rnds have been worked = 84 (96, 96, 108, 96, 108) sts rem. Check that your decs are centered above decs from previous rnds.

Work Chart D. Inc 1 in 1st line/rnd of pattern to make pattern meet symmetrically in front = 85 (97, 97, 109, 97, 109) sts. Complete Chart D (2 rnds). K 1 rnd stockinette with Color 2 and, *at the same time*, dec 4 (14, 10, 18, 4, 14) sts = 81 (83, 87, 91, 93, 95) sts rem. BO steek sts. Put rem sts aside until it's time to work neck band—either leave them on needle, pushed aside, or transfer them to holder or strand of scrap yarn.

ASSEMBLY
Machine stitch a tight seam down center front on each side of center st of steek. Cut between seams.

BUTTON BANDS
First, work the button band on the side that will have buttons. Traditionally, girls' and women's sweaters have the buttons on the left side, and boys' and men's on the right; but in the end, it's up to you. Set sts from holder at top of waist ribbing over on smaller gauge dpn. CO 4 sts for a facing (you will knit this along with the button band), and start knitting from the side against sweater front; whether this is on RS or WS will depend on which side you choose for the buttons. Work button band in k1, p1 ribbing, as for lower edge, and the 4-st facing in reverse stockinette—p on RS, k on WS. Knit button band until, when slightly stretched, it reaches neckline. BO the 4 sts of facing and put rem 7 sts on a holder.

Sew button band firmly onto front edge, in the transition between steek and sweater front and by edge of button band itself, leaving facing loose to WS of sweater front. Place markers evenly spaced for buttons—remember, the top button will be in the middle of the neck band, which will be knitted last.

The other button band—with buttonholes—is knitted like the first, but with buttonholes matching the markers for buttons. Make buttonholes as for the one you already made in the waist ribbing. Sew buttonhole band firmly along edge of front, as for button band, leaving facing hanging loose.

NECK BAND
With Color 2, transfer sts on hold to smaller gauge circular = 95 (97, 101, 105, 107, 109) sts.

With RS facing, pick up the 7 sts from right button band onto right needle (without knitting them; this avoids joining yarn at edge of a row). Work 1 row of stockinette up to the last 7 sts (left button band), then work those in ribbing, as before. Continue in ribbing, until neck band measures about $^3/_8$ in / 1 cm. On next 2 rows, make the last buttonhole, carefully lined up above the others. Work in ribbing until neck band measures 1¼ in / 3 cm. BO in ribbing.

FINISHING
Lay facings over steek edges and sew them on WS. Weave in all loose ends on WS. Sew on buttons and reinforce buttonholes if necessary.

AN ELEGANT HAT

Chart from *Norwegian Knitting Designs*, figure 19, page 26.

The area pattern that you can see on a pair of fine kneehose in *Norwegian Knitting Designs* still tempts us to try new variations; I've used parts of this pattern both on the Most Elegant Sweater and on the Star Hat. This time it's modified a bit to give it more symmetry and a lovely concentric decrease at the top.

SKILL LEVEL
Experienced

SIZES
Adult S (M). Both sizes are worked following the same instructions. The two sizes are achieved by using different weights of yarn.

SMALL SIZE
Measurement: 19 in / 48.5 cm around, 9-9½ in / 23-24 cm long, laid flat.
Yarn: CYCA #2 (sport, baby) Hifa Sølje (283 yd/350 m / 100 g) or Hifa Vilje (403 yd/375 m / 100 g)
Yarn Amounts: Color 1: about 50 g; Color 2: about 25 g; Color 3: about 10 g
Needles: US 1.5 / 2.5 mm for ribbed edge and US 2.5 / 3 mm or US 4 / 3.5 mm for patterned portion
Gauge: 26 sts and 30 rnds in pattern on larger gauge needles = 4 x 4 in / 10 x 10 cm. Adjust needle size to obtain correct gauge if necessary.

MEDIUM SIZE
Measurement: 20½ in / 52.5 cm around; 9½-10 in / 24-25 cm long, laid flat.
Yarn: CYCA #2 (sport, baby) Hifa Ask 100% wool yarn (345 yd/315 m / 100 g)
Yarn Amounts: Color 1: about 50 g; Color 2: about 25 g; Color 3: about 10 g
Needles: US 1.5 / 2.5 mm for ribbed edge and US 4 / 3.5 mm for patterned portion
Gauge: 24 sts and 28 rnds in pattern on larger gauge needles = 4 x 4 in / 10 x 10 cm. Adjust needle size to obtain correct gauge if necessary.

COLORS SHOWN
White/Brown Heather Version, Hifa Ask (shown)
Color 1: Semi-bleached White 316047.
Color 2: Brown Heather 316102.
Color 3: Light Turquoise Green 346584.

INSTRUCTIONS

Color 1
Color 2
| | Repeat
K2tog
Ssk2tog
k3tog

Both sizes have the same number of sts, but are worked with different yarns and at a different gauge—this results in different sizes.

With smaller gauge needles and Color 3, CO 120 sts. Cut Color 3.

Join Color 1, and join to work in the round, being careful not to twist cast-on row. Knit first rnd, then begin k1, p1 ribbing. Continue ribbing until work measures 1¼ in / 3 cm.

Change to larger gauge needle (= size required to work color pattern to gauge). K 1 rnd while increasing 6 sts evenly spaced around = 126 sts. Join Color 2 and begin pattern following chart at right. The chart shows 1 rep, worked 3 times around and once vertically. Pm, if you like, at beg of rnd and between repeats (that is, at the 42nd and 84th st).

Dec as indicated on chart. **Note:** The decs at center of repeat start a few rnds later than the decs at edges of motif.

When you've completed decs, 12 sts remain. Cut both strands, and, with a yarn needle, pull end through remaining sts. Tighten firmly to close top.

Weave loose ends into WS.

Using Color 3, if you wish, make a pompom with a diameter of about 2 in / 5 cm, and fasten firmly to top of hat.

A DOG'S STARRY NECK WARMER

Charts are from *Norwegian Knitting Designs*, figure 17, page 24, and figure 19, page 26.

When knitting assistant Orla Dahn had knitted one of the hat and neck warmer sets for this book, she was inspired to knit neck warmers for her two greyhounds. Their neck warmers turned out so well that they also had to have a place in the book.

SKILL LEVEL
Experienced

SIZES
Sizes 1 (2, 3)

The 3 sizes have the same number of stitches; different sizes are achieved by using different needle sizes. The length of the ribbing varies among sizes and can be adjusted as you wish. **Note:** These sizes are designed for dogs with skinny necks. If your dog has a thicker neck, you can CO, for example, 28 extra sts, and knit another rep of the chart.

FINISHED MEASUREMENTS
Circumference: approx. 9½ (10½) 12 in / 24.5 (26.5, 30) cm
Length: approx. 4 (5¼, 7¼) in / 10.5 (13, 18.5) cm

YARN
CYCA #1 (sock, fingering, baby) Hifa Huldra Worsted (100% wool yarn; 465 yd/425 m / 100 g)

YARN AMOUNTS
Color 1: about 5 (7, 12) g
Colors 2 and 3: about 6 (7, 8) g each

COLORS SHOWN
The colors used on the version shown were on 200 g spools. Huldra also has a choice of colors in 100 g skeins.
Color 1: Light Gray-Blue 428102
Color 2: Light Olive 428103
Color 3: Bleached White 428027

SUGGESTED NEEDLE SIZES
Size 1: US 1.5 / 2.5 mm for both ribbing and color pattern
Size 2: US 2.5 / 3 mm for both ribbing and color pattern
Size 3: US 2.5 / 3 mm for ribbing; US 6 or 7 / 4 or 4.5 mm for color pattern

GAUGE
Size 1: 34 sts and 40 rnds in pattern with US 1.5 / 2.5 mm = 4 x 4 in / 10 x 10 cm
Size 2: 32 sts and 36 rnds in pattern with US 2.5 / 3 mm = 4 x 4 in / 10 x 10 cm
Size 3: 28 sts and 31 rnds in pattern with US 6 or 7 / 4 or 4.5 mm = 4 x 4 in / 10 x 10 cm

INSTRUCTIONS

With needles for ribbing and Color 2, CO 84 sts. CO should be fairly loose. Work around in k2, p2 ribbing. Continue in ribbing until piece measures ¾ (1, 1¾) in / 1.5 (2.5, 4.5) cm. Sizes 1 and 2 are knitted in one needle size throughout; for Size 3 only, switch to larger needles.

Now, join Colors 1 and 3 and work pattern following chart for neck warmer. The chart shows 1 rep, which is knitted 3 times around and once vertically. Pm, if you wish, at beg of rnd. When you've finished chart vertically, cut Colors 1 and 3. For Sizes 1 and 2, continue; for Size 3 only, change back to smaller gauge needles. K 1 rnd, and then work k2, p2 ribbing for ¾ (1, 1¾) in / 1.5 (2.5, 4.5) cm. BO loosely in ribbing.

Weave in loose ends on WS. It's recommended to wash the neck warmer before using it, so the stitches can settle into the knit and the yarn can fluff out a little.

STARRY HAT AND NECKWARMER

Charts are taken from *Norwegian Knitting Designs*, figure 17, page 24
and figure 19, page 26.

These patterns are examples of how one can compose something
completely new by combining parts of other patterns. In *Norwegian Knitting
Designs*, we found this star on knee socks shown on p. 25; the cross can be seen
as a detail in the pattern for knee socks shown on p. 27.

SKILL LEVEL
Experienced

SIZE
Adult

HAT
Finished measurements: 20¾ in / 52.5 cm around and approx. 9¾ in / 25 cm long (with ribbing folded double)

Yarn: CYCA #1 (fingering, sock, baby) Hifa Huldra worsted 100% wool (465 yd/425 m / 100 g)

Yarn amounts: Color 1: approx. 40 g; Color 2: approx. 30 g; Color 3: approx. 10 g

Suggested needle sizes: US 1.5 / 2.5 mm: 16 in / 40 cm circular for ribbing and single-color stockinette; US 2.5 / 3 mm for colorwork.

Gauge: 32 sts and 32 rnds in pattern with larger gauge needles = 4 x 4 in /10 x 10 cm 32 sts and 40 rnds in stockinette with smaller gauge needles = 4 x 4 in / 10 x 10 cm
Adjust needle sizes to obtain correct gauge if necessary.

NECK WARMER
Finished measurements: 21-22 in / 54-56 cm around and approx. 8¼ in / 21 cm length

Yarn: CYCA #1 (fingering, sock, baby) Hifa Huldra worsted 100 percent wool (465 yd/425 m / 100 g)

Yarn amounts: Color 1: approx. 25 g; Color 2: approx. 20 g; Color 3: approx. 25 g

Suggested needle sizes: US 1.5 / 2.5 mm: 16 in / 40 cm circular, for ribbing; US 4 / 3.5 mm: 16 in / 40 cm circular, for colorwork

Gauge: 30-31 sts and 35 rnds in pattern with larger gauge needles = 4 x 4 in / 10 x 10 cm. Adjust needle size to obtain correct gauge if necessary.

Dark Version
Color 1: Turquoise Blue 448019
Color 2: Dark Brown 448112
Color 3: Semi-bleached White 448099 (100 g skein)

Light Version
Color 1: Light Gray-Blue 428102
Color 2: Light Olive 428103
Color 3: Bleached White 428027
Note: These colors are available only in 200 g spools.

INSTRUCTIONS

HAT
With smaller gauge needles and Color 1, CO 152 sts. Join, being careful not to twist cast-on row. Work around in k2, p2 ribbing until piece measures 4 in / 10 cm. Switch to larger gauge circular and k 1 rnd, inc 16 sts evenly spaced around = 168 sts. Work pattern following chart for hat. The chart shows 1 rep, to be worked 6 times around and once vertically. Pm at beg of rnd, if you wish.

When chart is completed vertically, change back

to smaller gauge needles and work in stockinette with Color 2 until work above ribbing measures 5½-6 in / 14-15 cm. On next rnd, place 14 markers on needle, with 12 sts between markers.

Dec Rnds

Ssk, knit to marker, and rep * to * to end of rnd = 14 sts dec. Work 2 rnds. Rep * to * once more around, with 1 fewer st between decs.

Rep dec rnd *every other* rnd 9 times total = 14 sts rem. Cut yarn, leaving a tail; with tapestry needle, draw tail through rem sts and tighten firmly to close.

Finishing

Weave loose ends into WS. If you wish, make a pompom with Color 1 and fasten it securely to top of hat. The ribbing at edge of hat can be either folded in and sewn down on WS, or turned up as a brim on RS.

NECK WARMER

With smaller gauge circular and Color 2, CO 168 sts. Join, being careful not to twist cast-on row. Work around in ribbing: k2, p2 around. Work until ribbing measures 1 in / 2.5 cm in length. Switch to larger gauge needle, join Colors 1 and 3, and work pattern on chart for neck warmer. The chart shows 1 rep, to be worked 6 times around and once vertically. Pm at beg of rnd.

When chart is completed vertically, cut Colors 1 and 3 and switch back to smaller gauge needle. K 1 rnd, then work ribbing (k2, p2) for 1 in / 2.5 cm. BO loosely in ribbing.

Weave in loose ends on WS.

Knitted garments in Huldra yarn are at their absolute finest after a gentle wash or rinse. The knitting evens itself out and the yarn fluffs out and fills in the stitches.

Hat

Neck warmer

Color 1

Color 2

Color 3

STAR BAND SOCKS

Chart taken from *Norwegian Knitting Designs*, figure 59, page 53.

This handsome band of stars from Selbu goes with almost anything.
Here it's used on a pair of warm socks, but why not try it on a hat, on half-mitts,
or as the cuff for a pair of mittens?

SIZES

Women's S (M, L) / US women's 4 (7-7½, 9) shoe / European 36/37 (38/39, 40/41) shoe

YARN

CYCA #3 (DK, light worsted) Hifa Fjord sock yarn (80% wool/20% nylon; 273 yd/250 m / 100 g)

YARN AMOUNTS AND COLORS

Color 1: Natural White 03100, approx. 100 g
Color 2: Dark Gray 03130, approx. 50 g
Color 3: Black 03511, approx. 10-15 g

SUGGESTED NEEDLE SIZES

US 1.5 / 2.5 mm: 5 dpn.
US 2.5 / 3 mm: 5 dpn
US 4 / 3.5 mm: 5 dpn.

GAUGE

24 sts in pattern on US 2.5 / 3 mm needles = 4 in / 10 cm.
Adjust needle size to obtain correct gauge if necessary.

INSTRUCTIONS

THE LEG

RIBBING

With smallest gauge needles and Color 2, CO 56 sts. Join, being careful not to twist cast-on row; beg of rnd is center back. Work around in k1, p1 ribbing until ribbing measures approx. 1½ in / 3.5 cm.

PATTERN BAND

Switch to medium gauge needles and k 1 rnd. Cut Color 2 and join Color 1. K 3 rnds stockinette. Switch to largest gauge needles and work star pattern band following Chart A. The charted

pattern repeats 4 times around, and once vertically. When pattern is complete vertically, cut Color 3.

REST OF LEG

Switch back to medium gauge needles. K 2 rnds stockinette.

Next rnd: K 9, work cables on Chart B for 10 sts, k 18, work Chart B for 10 sts, k to end of rnd. Rep this rnd, but move up the chart. When only one row of chart remains, work as est but stop when 14 sts rem in rnd. *Don't cut Color 1!* You will continue from this point when heel is complete.

THE HEEL

HEEL FLAP

The heel is worked in Color 2, back and forth, on first and last 14 sts of rnd = 28 heel sts. The rem 28 sts (the instep) are put aside while the heel is knitted.

Begin on RS, on right side of heel: k 28. This is the heel flap. Work back and forth in stockinette. On every row, sl 1st st with yarn in front; last st is a k st on both RS and WS. Work back and forth until heel flap measures just under 2¼ (just under 2½, just over 2½) in / 5.5 (6, 6.5) cm. End with a WS row.

TURNING HEEL

The heel is turned with decs and short rows.
Row 1 (RS): Sl 1 (*yarn in front*), k 15, ssk, k1, turn.
Row 2 (WS): Sl 1 p-wise (*yarn in front*), p 5, p2tog, p 1, turn.
Row 3 (RS): Sl 1 (*yarn in back*), k to 1 st before the "gap" (where you turned in the preceding row), ssk2tog (1 st from each side of the "gap"), k1, turn.
Row 4 (WS): Sl 1 (*yarn in front*), p to 1 st before gap (where you turned in the last row), p2tog, p1, turn.

Rep Rows 3 and 4 until sts to each side of turn are "eaten up." End with a WS row. 16 heel sts rem. Cut Color 2.

THE FOOT

GUSSET

The heel is done. Now pick up sts along sides of heel flap and recommence working around. There are now more sts around than there were on leg portion. These extra sts will be gradually decreased, creating a gusset on each side of foot.

Beg where you left off with Color 1 before heel was worked. Pick up and k 1 st between instep (upper side of foot) and heel (to avoid a hole there), and pick up 1 st in every slipped st on sides of heel flap—it works best to pick up the inner loop of these sts and twist them into k sts. K 16 rem heel sts. Pick up 1 st in every slipped st on opposite side of heel flap, and pick up and twist 1 st between heel flap and instep of sock (again, to avoid a hole); pm here for beg of rnd.

Next rnd (instep): K 4, p1, k 18, p1, k 4 sts and knit to end of rnd.

Dec Rnd (instep): K 4, p 1, k 18, p 1, k 4, ssk, k to 2 sts rem in rnd, k2tog = 2 decs.

Rep these 2 rnds, with decs *every other* rnd, until 24 sts rem on sole of foot = 52 sts total.

REST OF FOOT

The gusset decs are complete. Work as est on instep with stockinette on sole until foot, lightly stretched, measures 7 (7½, 8¼) in / 18 (19, 20.5) cm from "point" of heel. The toe dec will measure approx. 2¼ in / 6 cm, so if length of foot needs adjustment, take that into consideration now. Cut Color 1.

Toe Decrease

Shift 1st st of rnd over to end of rnd. The new beg of rnd is after this st. Pm. Divide sts into 26 sts each for upper side and underside of foot.

Join Color 2. Work 1 rnd stockinette.

Dec Rnd: *K 1, ssk, k 20, k2tog, k 1, rep from * once = 4 sts dec around.

Next rnd: K around.

Work these 2 rnds, with decs *every other* rnd, 4 times total = 36 sts rem.

Now rep dec rnd *every* rnd until 8 sts rem. Cut yarn and, with tapestry needle, draw tail through rem sts and tighten firmly.

Weave in all ends on WS.

Chart B

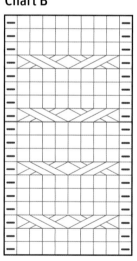

Chart A

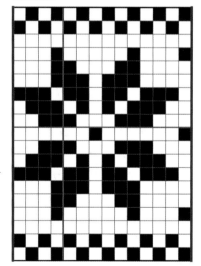

☐   knit
⊟   purl

⬚   Color 1
■   Color 3
❘ ❘   **Rep within frame**

⬚⬚   C4B
⬚⬚   C4F

GRANDMOTHER'S SOCKS

Chart from *Norwegian Knitting Designs*, figure 41, page 43.

Many a busy grandmother—and sometimes grandfather—has supplied their families with homemade socks, stockings, hose; or, depending on the age of the recipient, perhaps these objects have a name more along the lines of sockses, footies, footlets ... (As we say in Norway, beloved children have many names!) Grandma's socks have always been the very best: the ones that are hardwearing, and keep their shape. These ribbed socks with their simple, small border pattern from Selbu can certainly be said to be typical "Grandma's sockses."

SKILL LEVEL
Experienced

SIZES
Women's S (M, L) / US women's 4 (7-7½, 9) shoe / European 36/37 (38/39, 40/41) shoe

YARN
CYCA #3 (DK, light worsted) Hifa Fjord sock yarn (273 yd/250 m / 100 g)

YARN AMOUNTS AND COLORS
Color 1: Light Gray 03110, 100 g
Color 2: Dark Brown 03540, 50 g
Color 3: Natural White 03100, 20 g

SUGGESTED NEEDLE SIZES
US 1.5 / 2.5 mm: 5 dpn
US 2.5 / 3 mm: 5 dpn
If your gauge has a tendency to be tighter on color patterns than one-color stockinette, you may want to try knitting the color pattern with US 3 or 4 / 3.25 mm or 3.5 mm dpn.

GAUGE
24 sts in stockinette on US 2 or 3 / 3 mm = 4 in / 10 cm
Adjust needle size to obtain correct gauge if necessary.

INSTRUCTIONS

LEG

RIBBING
With smaller gauge needles and Color 2, CO 56 sts. Join, being careful not to twist cast-on row; beg of rnd is at center back. Work around in twisted ribbing: *p1, k1 through back loop (tbl), and rep from * around. **Note:** Rnd *begins* with a p st.

Work ribbing for 12 rnds, approx. 1¼ in / 3.5 cm. Switch to larger gauge needles and k 1 rnd in stockinette while increasing 4 sts evenly spaced around = 60 sts.

PATTERN BAND
Join Color 1. Work pattern following chart. If you work more tightly on color patterns, go up a half or whole needle size for this part. The pattern reps 5 times around. When you've completed pattern vertically, cut Colors 1 and 2.

REST OF LEG
Join Color 1. If you used heavier gauge needles for color pattern, switch back to needles recommended for stockinette. Work 2 rnds stockinette. On Rnd 2, dec 4 sts evenly spaced around = 56 sts. Now, work twisted ribbing: p1, k1 tbl. **Note:** Rnd here also *begins* with a p st. Continue in ribbing until leg measures approx. 6 in / 15 cm. On last rnd, stop when 13 sts rem. Do *not* cut yarn. You will continue in Color 1 from this point when heel is finished.

HEEL

HEEL FLAP
The heel is worked in Color 2, back and forth, on first 14 and last 13 sts of rnd = 27 sts. The remaining 29 sts (instep of sock) are put aside while heel is turned.

Begin on RS, on right side of heel: K 27 sts. Now work heel flap back and forth in stockinette; on every row, sl 1st st p-wise with yarn in front, and knit last st, both on RS and on WS. Work until heel flap measures 2¼ (2³/₈, 2½) in / 5.5 (6, 6.5) cm. End with a WS row.

TURNING HEEL
The heel is turned with a combination of decs and short rows.

Row 1 (RS): Sl 1 wyf, k 15, ssk, k1. Turn.
Row 2 (WS): Sl 1 wyf, p 6, p2tog, p1. Turn.
Row 3 (RS): Sl 1 wyb, k until 1 st before the "gap" (where you turned in the last row), ssk with 1 st from each side of the gap. K1. Turn.
Row 4 (WS): Sl 1 wyf, p until 1 st before the gap (where you turned in the last row), p2tog, p1. Turn.

Rep Rows 3 and 4 until sts to each side of turn are "eaten up." End with a p row on WS. 17 heel sts rem. Cut Color 2.

FOOT

DECREASE HEEL GUSSETS

The heel is complete. Now, pick up sts along sides and bottom of heel flap and knit around again. There are now more sts around foot than there were on leg; these extra sts will be gradually decreased on both sides, creating a triangular gusset on each side.

Beg where you dropped Color 1 before knitting heel. Pick up 1 st between instep and side of heel (to avoid a hole there), pm (side marker); pick up and k 1 st for each sl st in side of heel flap—it works best to pick up the inner loop of these sl sts and k into back loop, twisting them into k sts. K rem 17 heel sts. Pick up and k 1 st for each sl st in other side of heel flap (just as on the first side); M1 between side of heel and instep (to avoid a hole), pm (new beg of rnd and side marker).

Next rnd: Work twisted ribbing to the side marker (the first 29 sts/the instep side), k the rest of the rnd.

Dec Rnd: Work twisted ribbing to the side marker, k2tog, k until 2 sts rem in the rnd, ssk = 2 decs.

Rep these 2 rnds, working dec rnd *every other* rnd,

until there are 25 sts on the sole of the foot = 54 sts rem.

THE FOOT

The gusset dec is complete. Continue as est with twisted ribbing on instep and stockinette on sole until foot, lightly stretched, measures approx. 7 (7½, 8½) in / 18 (19, 20.5) cm. The toe dec takes approx. 2½ in / 6 cm, so if length of foot needs adjustment, take that into consideration now. Cut Color 1.

Toe Decrease

Move 1st st of rnd over to end of rnd. The new beg of rnd is now after that st. Pm here. Redistribute the sts with 27 sts each for the upper and underside of the sock. Switch to Color 2, and k 2 rnds even.

Dec Rnd: *K1, ssk, k 21, k2tog, k1. Rep from * once = 4 sts dec.
Next rnd: K around.

Work these two rnds a total of 4 times = 38 sts rem.

Then, rep the dec rnd *every* rnd 7 times = 10 sts rem.

Last rnd: *K1, k3tog, k1; rep from * once = 6 sts rem.

Cut yarn and, with tapestry needle, pull end through rem sts and tighten firmly to close.

Weave in ends on WS.

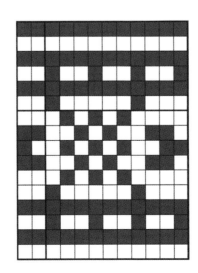

Color 2
Color 3

KONGRO SOCKS / WEAVER SOCKS

Chart from *Norwegian Knitting Designs*, figure 8, page 16.

This band of pattern, so typical of old patterns from Selbu, is an example of an endless pattern: the motifs fit together and can continue infinitely. The motif is a *kongro*, a old Norwegian word for "spider" still used in some Norwegian dialects, much as "weaver" was once used for spiders in English. The same spider motif is used in the mittens on p. 239; there, the pattern was called "Endless Roses." Take your pick of names—but together they would make a lovely, cozy gift.

SKILL LEVEL
Experienced

SIZES
Women's S (M, L) / US women's size 4 (7-7½, 9) shoe / European 36/37 (38/39, 40/41) shoe

YARN
CYCA #3 (DK, light worsted) Hifa Fjord sock yarn (273 yd/250 m / 100 g)

YARN AMOUNTS AND COLORS
Color 1: Light Gray 03110, 100 g
Color 2: Dark Gray 03130, 10-15 g
Color 3: Bleached White 03504, 10-15 g

SUGGESTED NEEDLE SIZES
US 1.5 / 2.5 mm: 5 dpn
US 2.5 / 3 mm: 5 dpn
(If you knit more tightly when working color patterns than one-color stockinette, you may want to try knitting the color pattern with US 3 or 4 / 3.25 mm or 3.5 mm dpn.)

GAUGE
24 sts in stockinette on US 2.5 / 3 mm = 4 in / 10 cm
Adjust needle size to obtain correct gauge if necessary.

INSTRUCTIONS

LEG

RIBBING
With smaller dpn and Color 1, cast on 56 sts. The beg of rnd is at center back. Work around in twisted ribbing (k1 through back loop, p1) for 12 rnds (about 1½ in / 3 cm). Switch to larger gauge needles, and k 1 rnd while increasing 4 sts evenly spaced around = 60 sts. Cut Color 1.

PATTERN BAND
Join Colors 2 and 3 and work pattern following Chart A. If you knit more tightly in colorwork, go up a needle size here. **Note:** There are 4 decs in final rnd of chart = 56 sts when color pattern is completed. Cut Colors 2 and 3.

REMAINDER OF LEG
The rest of sock is worked with Color 1. If you used even larger gauge needles on color pattern, switch back to the larger of the two needle sizes recommended. K 1 rnd.

Beg cable pattern following Chart B. (Take care that the cables don't tighten your knitting, and see page 22, "Cables," if you need more information.) The pattern reps 8 times around. Work cables until 1 rnd remains on chart. Work final rnd, but stop when 13 sts rem.

Chart A

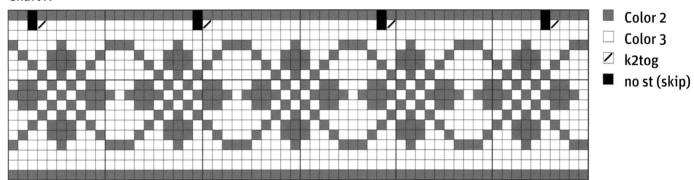

■ Color 2
□ Color 3
⊿ k2tog
■ no st (skip)

Chart B

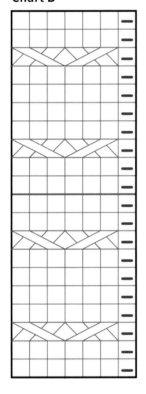

□ knit

⊟ purl

⬭ C3B

⬭ C3F

HEEL

The heel is worked back and forth on first 14 and last 13 sts of rnd = 27 heel sts. The rem 29 sts (instep of sock) are set aside while heel is turned.

Beg on RS, on right side of heel. K 27. Now work heel back and forth in stockinette. On every row, slip 1st st with yarn in front (sl 1 wyf) and k last st (on both sides). Work until heel flap measures 2¼ (2³/₈, 2½) in / 5.5 (6, 6.5) cm. End with a WS row.

TURNING HEEL

The actual heel is formed with decs and short rows.

Row 1 (RS): Sl 1 wyf, k 15, ssk, k1, turn.
Row 2 (WS): Sl 1 wyf, p 6, p2tog, p1, turn.
Row 3 (RS): Sl 1 wyb, k to 1 st before "gap" (where you turned in the last row), ssk (with 1 st from each side of gap), k1, turn.
Row 4 (WS): Sl 1 wyf, p to 1 st before gap (where you turned last time), p2tog, p1, turn.

Rep Rows 3 and 4 until sts to each side of turn are "eaten up." End with a WS row. 17 heel sts rem.

FOOT

DEC SIDE GUSSETS
The turning of heel is complete. Now pick up sts along sides of heel flap and recommence knitting around. There will be more sts around here than there were on leg; these sts will dec gradually to form a triangular gusset on each side.

Rnd 1: K the 17 heel flap sts, and pm between sts 8 and 9 (beg of rnd). Pick up and k 1 st in every sl st along side of heel flap—it works best to pick up inside loop of sl sts and k into back loop, twisting them into k sts. Pick up and k 1 st where heel flap and instep meet (to prevent a hole there), pm (side marker); k next 29 sts, continuing cable pattern (4 reps), pm (side marker); pick up and k 1 st where heel flap and instep meet, pick up and k sts along other side of heel flap (as you did on the first side) and k to end of rnd.

Next rnd: K to the side marker, continue cable pattern as est (top of foot) to next side marker, k to end of rnd.

Dec Rnd: K to 2 sts before side marker, ssk, work cable pattern as est to next side marker, k2tog, k to end of rnd = 2 sts dec.

Rep these two rnds, working decs every other rnd, until 25 sts rem on sole of foot = 54 sts around.

REST OF FOOT
The gusset decs are complete. Continue working cable pattern on instep and stockinette on sole until foot, lightly stretched, is about 7½ (8, 8½) in / 19 (20, 21.5) cm. The toe dec takes approx. 2 in / 5 cm, so if length of foot needs adjustment, take that into consideration now.

Decreasing the Toe
The sock has a decreased toe worked in the round.

K 4 rnds, without cable pattern.

Dec Rnd 1: *K4, k2tog, rep from * to end of rnd = 45 sts.
K 4 rnds.
Dec Rnd 2: *K3, k2tog, rep from * to end of rnd = 36 sts
K 3 rnds.
Dec Rnd 3: *K2, k2tog, rep from * to end of rnd = 27 sts.
K 2 rnds.
Dec Rnd 4: *K1, k2tog, rep from * to end of rnd = 18 sts.
K 1 rnd.
Dec Rnd 5: *K2tog around = 9 sts rem.

Cut yarn. With tapestry needle, draw tail through rem sts and tighten firmly to close.

Weave in any loose ends on WS.

Cable mitten with "kongro or Endless Roses" pattern. Instructions on p. 239.

HALLINGDAL STAR SLIPPER SOCKS

Chart from *Norwegian Knitting Designs*, figure 72, page 61.

Here is a mitten pattern from Hallingdal, made into slipper socks.
These are perfect as cabin slippers, guest slippers, and travel slippers. Men's
and women's sizes are knitted with the same instructions, but with
different yarn. Men's sizes are worked with a heavier sock yarn, Hifa Fjell, which
might seem a little solid, but the slippers soften when they're washed. If you
find Fjell hard to knit with, you can knit with the finer Fjord sock yarn on
heavier gauge needles and shrink or felt the slippers afterwards.

SKILL LEVEL
Experienced

SIZES
Women's sizes: S/M (L) / US women's 4 (9) shoe / European 36-38 (39-41) shoe
Men's sizes: L (XL) / US men's 9½ (12½) / European 42-43 (44-45) shoe

FINISHED MEASUREMENTS
Circumference: Women's, approx. 9½ in / 24 cm; men's, approx. 10^2/$_3$ in / 27 cm.
Length: Women's, approx. 9½-10½ in / 24.5-26.5 cm; men's, approx. 11-11½ in / 28-29.5 cm
Slippers can also be gently felted. They will shrink a little in length and width, a bit more lengthwise than widthwise.

YARN
Women's: CYCA #3 (DK, light worsted) Hifa Fjord sock yarn (80% wool/20% nylon; 273 yd/250 m / 100 g)
Men's: CYCA #4 (worsted, afghan, Aran) Hifa Fjell sock yarn (80% wool/20% nylon; 183 yd/167 m / 100 g)

YARN AMOUNTS AND COLORS SHOWN
Women's Version (3 colors)
Color 1: Medium Gray 03115, 50 g
Color 2: Natural White 03100, 30 g
Color 3: Farmer Red 03513, 30 g
Men's Version (2 colors)
Color 1: Blue-Gray 04514, 70 g
Color 2: Natural White 04100, 70 g

SUGGESTED NEEDLE SIZES
Women's Version
US 1.5 / 2.5 mm and US 2.5 / 3 mm: set of 5 dpn
Men's Version
US 2.5 / 3 mm and US 4 / 3.5 mm: set of 5 dpn
There are 2 needle gauges used for each size. They will be called "larger" and "smaller" gauge needles in the instructions.

GAUGE
Women's: 25 sts and 30 rnds in pattern on larger gauge needles = 4 x 4 in / 10 x 10 cm
Men's: 22 sts and 26 rnds in pattern on larger gauge needles = 4 x 4 in / 10 x 10 cm
Adjust needle size to obtain correct gauge if necessary.

INSTRUCTIONS

Men's and women's sizes are worked following the same instructions. If there is a difference within the directions, it will be shown like this: "K 2/2 (1/4) per rnd," that is, the two women's sizes and the two men's sizes will be separated by slashes, and the two men's sizes will be enclosed in parentheses.

There are only two colors used in the men's version. So, on the charts, read Colors 2 and 3 as a single color when working the men's version.

RIBBING
With smaller gauge needles for W (M)'s version and Color 3 (2), CO 52 sts. Join, being careful not

to twist cast-on row; beg of rnd is on left side. Work around in k1, p1 ribbing for 6 rnds.

FOOT

Switch to larger gauge needles and k 1 rnd, *at the same time* increasing 8 sts evenly spaced around = 60 sts. The rnd's first 29 sts are underside/sole, and last 31 sts are instep/top side. Join new colors and work 7 rnds of pattern following Chart A. Before knitting Rnd 8, knit first 29 sts with a piece of scrap yarn in a contrasting color—this is where the heel will be later. Walk these sts back to beg of rnd and continue in pattern following Chart A: work up to red frame at top; pay attention to arrows on right side to navigate irregularity in background net of pattern.

Women's Sizes: Skip over red-framed area and end with Chart A's last three lines of pattern.

Men's Sizes: Work entirety of Chart A.

The remainder of the slipper is worked with Color 3 (Color 2). Cut the other color(s).

Decreasing the Toe
Move last st to beg of rnd, pm. K 1 rnd.

Dec Rnd: *K1, ssk, k25, k2tog, rep from * once more = 4 sts dec.

K 1 rnd. Then rep dec rnd *every* rnd until 8 sts rem. Cut yarn and, with tapestry needle, draw tail through rem sts and tighten firmly to close.

THE HEEL

Pick up sts from above and below scrap yarn and remove it carefully. Pick up an additional st from each side. There should be 60 sts: 30 on back side and 30 on sole/underside of heel.

Join Colors 1 and 2. Beg on underside of right side: Work Chart B, *once only*, across last 30 sts. This makes the pattern the same on both sides of heel. Take care to match sts to previously worked pattern. When this half rnd is done, you are at beg of rnd.

Continue to work heel following Chart C.

Tip: There are some long floats at the sides of the decs. If you twist the strands just after the dec on the right side (ssk) and just before the dec on the left side (k2tog), you will shorten the float and the twist will be hidden by the dec in the following rnd.

Dec as shown; when chart is completed, 8 sts rem. Cut yarn, and with tapestry needle, draw tail through rem sts and tighten firmly to close.

Weave in all loose ends neatly on WS.

A

☐ Color 1

■ Color 2

▨ Color 3 (men's = Color 2)

| | Side markings

* * center of upper side

⊢ Scrap yarn for heel opening

☐ 1 repeat; length can be adjusted here

◄ Pay attention to these rows: there is an
  irregularity in the background pattern on
  sts 1 and 29 (first and last st on underside).

B

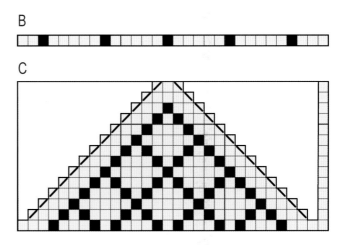

C

DANCING LADIES SOCKS

Chart from *Norwegian Knitting Designs*, figure 69, page 60.

Ladies in long lines dancing merrily! With such happy socks inside
rubber boots on a rainy day, it's easy to stay in a good mood! This pattern
can be used for a lot of other things as well. How about half-mitts? A hat?
Or a delightful children's sweater?

SKILL LEVEL
Experienced

SIZES
Women's S (M, L) / US women's 4 (7-7½, 9) shoe / European 36-37 (38-39, 40-41) shoe

YARN
CYCA #3 (DK, light worsted) Hifa Fjord sock yarn (80% wool/20% nylon; 273 yd/250 m / 100 g)

YARN AMOUNTS AND COLORS
Color 1: Light Green Turquoise 03546, 100 g
Color 2: Bleached White 03504, 20 g
Color 3: Farmer Red 03513, 10 g
Color 4: Blue-Gray 03514, 10 g

SUGGESTED NEEDLE SIZES
US 1.5 / 2.5 mm and US 2.5 / 3 mm: set of 5 dpn. If you knit more tightly when working color patterns than one-color stockinette, you may want to try going up one US size / .5 mm size to work the color pattern.

GAUGE
24 sts in stockinette on larger gauge needles = 4 in / 10 cm
Adjust needle size to obtain correct gauge if necessary.

INSTRUCTIONS

LEG

RIBBING
With smaller gauge needles and Color 1, cast on 56 sts. Join, being careful not to twist cast-on row; beg of rnd is center back of foot. Pm. K1, then work around in p2, k2 ribbing, ending with k1. Work 12 rnds of ribbing (about 1⅓ in / 3.5 cm). Switch to larger gauge needles and k 1 rnd while increasing 4 sts evenly spaced around = 60 sts. Cut Color 1.

PATTERN BAND
Join Colors 2, 3, and 4 and work pattern following chart. If you knit more tightly in colorwork, move up to a larger gauge needle—one US size / .5 mm. **Note:** You will find you are knitting the dancing women upside down. All will return to normal when the sock is completed!

When chart is complete, cut all 3 strands and join Color 1.

REMAINDER OF LEG
The rest of the sock is worked with Color 1. If you used even larger gauge needles for the color pattern, switch back to recommended large gauge needles. K 2 rnds; on 2nd rnd, dec 4 sts evenly spaced around = 56 sts.

Work ribbing as est until piece measures about 6¾ in / 17 cm. Beg *one* more rnd ribbing, but stop when 14 sts rem in rnd.

HEEL

The heel is worked back and forth on back sts, the first 14 and last 14 sts. The remaining 28 sts (instep of sock) are set aside while heel is turned.

With RS facing, beg on right side of heel. K 28 sts, and work back and forth in stockinette. On every row, slip first st with yarn in front (sl 1, wyf), and k last st on both RS and WS. Continue as est until heel flap measures 2¼ (2¹/₃, 2½) in / 5.5 (6, 6.5) cm. End with a p row.

TURNING THE HEEL

The heel is turned with a combination of decs and short rows:

Row 1 (RS): Sl 1 wyf, k 15, ssk, k1. Turn. 1 dec.
Row 2 (WS): Sl 1 wyf, p 5, p2tog, p1. Turn.
Row 3 (RS): Sl 1 with yarn back (wyb), k until 1 st before "the gap," (where you turned in the previous rnd), ssk (1 st from each side of the gap), k 1. Turn.
Row 4 (WS): Sl 1 wyf, p until 1 st before gap, p2tog (1 st from each side of gap), p1. Turn.

Rep Rows 3 and 4 until all the sts on the sides have been "eaten up" by decs. End with 1 row on WS. 16 heel sts rem.

FOOT

MAKING SIDE GUSSETS

The heel is complete. Now pick up sts along sides of heel flap and recommence working around. There are now more sts around than there were on leg; you will dec these sts gradually, forming a triangular gusset on each side.

Rnd 1: K the 16 heel sts and pm between sts 8 and 9 (beg of rnd). Pick up and k 1 st in every sl st along left side of heel flap—it works best to pick up inner loop of these sl sts and work into back loop, twisting them into k sts. Pick up and k 1 st between heel flap and instep (to prevent a hole here); pm (side marker). Work next 28 sts in ribbing: p1, then work (k2, p2) 6 times, k2, p1, pm (side marker). Pick up and k 1 st between instep and heel flap (to prevent a hole) and then pick up sts along right side of heel flap (as many and in the same way as on other side); k to end of rnd.

Next rnd: K to 2 sts before side marker, work ribbing as est to next side marker (upper), k stockinette to end of rnd.

Dec Rnd: K to 2 sts before side marker, ssk, work ribbing as est to next side marker (upper), then k2tog, k to end of rnd = 2 sts dec.

Rep these 2 rnds, working dec rnd *every other* rnd, until 22 (24, 26) sts rem on underside of foot = 50 (52, 54) sts total.

REMAINDER OF FOOT

The gusset dec is completed. Continue as est with ribbing on instep and stockinette on sole until the foot, gently stretched, measures 7½ (8, 8½) in / 19 (20, 21.5) cm. The toe dec takes approx. 2 in / 5 cm, so if length of foot needs adjustment, take that into consideration now.

Decreasing the Toe

Knit 1 rnd and dec 2 (4, 0) sts evenly spaced around = 48 (48, 54) sts.

This sock ends with a circular dec.

K 3 rnds.

Dec Rnd 1: *K 4, k2tog, rep from * to end of rnd = 40 (40, 45) sts.
K 4 rnds.

Dec Rnd 2: *K 3, k2tog, rep from * to end of rnd = 32 (32, 36) sts.
K 3 rnds.

Dec Rnd 3: *K 2, k2tog, rep from * to end of rnd = 24 (24, 27) sts.
K 2 rnds.

Dec Rnd 4: *K 1, k2tog, rep from * to end of rnd = 16 (16, 18) sts.
K 1 rnd.

Dec Rnd 5: K2tog to end of rnd = 8 (8, 9) sts rem.

Cut yarn and, with tapestry needle, draw tail through rem sts and tighten firmly to close.

Weave in all loose ends on WS.

Color 2
Color 3
Color 4

← start here

WINDOWS MITTENS

Chart from *Norwegian Knitting Designs*, figure 26, page 32, and figure 29, page 34.

Two different pairs of knee stockings in *Norwegian Knitting Designs* inspired these mittens. The cuff on the women's version is double and folds down, while the cuff on the men's version is simpler. The different sizes are achieved by changing yarn and needle gauge. For the largest men's size, we recommend Hifa Fjord sock yarn or Tinde pelsullgarn. Both make good, strong mittens.

SKILL LEVEL
Experienced

SIZES
Women's (W) and men's (M) sizes: WS (WM, WL/ MS, MM/ML)

FINISHED MEASUREMENTS
Circumference: around mitten hand above thumbhole, 8 (8½, 9, 9¾) in / 20 (21.5, 23, 25) cm
Mitten Hand Length: above the ribbing, 8 (8½, 9, 9¾) in / 20 (21.5, 22.5, 24.5) cm
Thumb Length: 2¼ (2½, 2½, 2¾) in / 6 (6.5, 6.5, 7) cm
Cuff Length, Women's: 2½ (2¾, 3, -, -) in / 6.5 (7, 7.5, -, -) cm;
Cuff Length, Men's: - (-, -, 2¾, 2¾) in / - (-, -, 7, 7) cm

YARN
Women's S, M, L and Men's S: CYCA #2 (sport, baby) Hifa Ask (100% wool; 345 yd/315 m / 100 g)
Men's M, L: CYCA #3 (DK, light worsted) Hifa Fjord sock yarn (80% wool/20% nylon; 273 yd/250 m / 100 g)
or CYCA #3 (DK, light worsted) Hifa Tinde pelsull-garn (100% wool; 284 yd/260 m / 100 g)

YARN AMOUNTS
Women's S, M, L and Men's S: Ask, 50 g each of Color 1 and Color 2
Men's M, L: Fjord or Tinde, approx. 50-55 g of Color 1 and 40 g of Color 2.

COLORS SHOWN
Women's Sea-Green Mittens
Color 1: Seagreen, Ask 316029
Color 2: Light Gray Heather, Ask 316054

Women's Blue-Gray Mittens
Color 1: Dark Blue-Gray, Ask 316104
Color 2: Light Gray Heather, Ask 316054

Men's Mittens (Ribbed Cuff)
Color 1: Light Blue-Gray, Fjord 03545
Color 2: Natural White, Fjord 03100

SUGGESTED NEEDLE SIZES
US 1.5 / 2.5 mm (US 2.5 / 3 mm; US 2.5 / 3 mm; US 3 or 4 / 3 or 3.5 mm): set of 5 dpn.
Also, set of 5 dpn one US size / .5 mm smaller, for cuff and/or ribbing.
Including smaller needles for ribbing, there will be 2 needle sizes used for each size; they will be called respectively "smaller" and "larger" gauge needles.

GAUGE
30 sts and 34 rnds (28 sts and 32 rnds, 25 sts and 26 rnds, 24 sts and 30 rnds) on larger gauge needles = 4 x 4 in / 10 x 10 cm
Adjust needle size to obtain correct gauge if necessary.

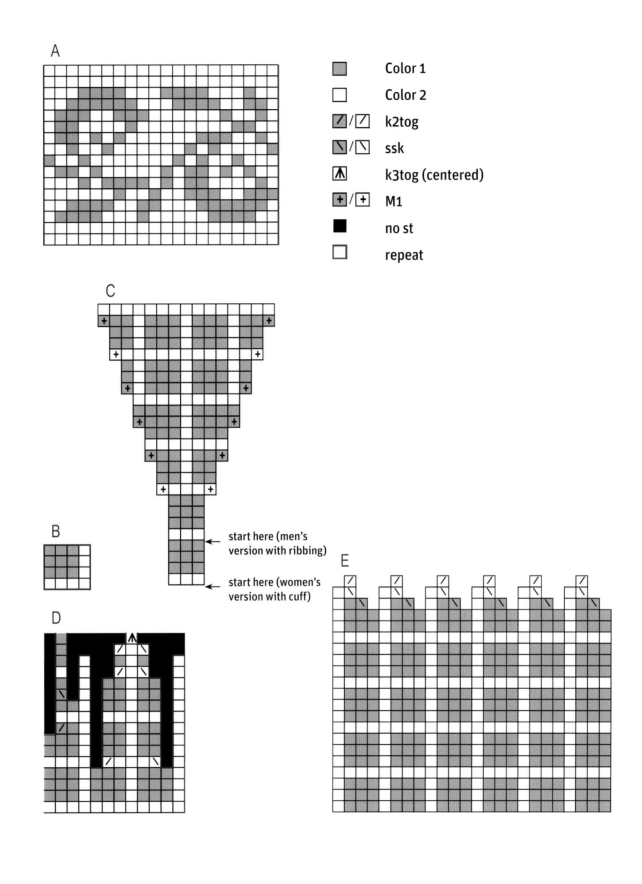

A

	Color 1
	Color 2
	k2tog
	ssk
	k3tog (centered)
	M1
	no st
	repeat

C

B

start here (men's version with ribbing)

start here (women's version with cuff)

D

E

INSTRUCTIONS

CUFF (WOMEN'S FLOWERED)

With Color 2 and smaller gauge needles, CO 60 sts. Divide sts onto 4 needles and join, being careful not to twist cast-on row. Work 3 rnds k1, p1 ribbing.

For Women's S, change to larger gauge needles now.

Join Color 1 and knit Chart A, working rep 3 times per rnd. When Chart A is complete vertically, cut Color 1 and continue with Color 2. P 1 rnd (fold line). If you used larger gauge needles for Chart A, change back to smaller gauge needles. K 2 rnds.

Next rnd: K around, while decreasing 8 sts evenly spaced = 52 sts.
Next rnd: K around.

Work k2, p2 ribbing for 1½ in / 3.5 cm. Turn work inside out, so p side faces outward.

At the very end, you will knit a short band of ribbing into the fold edge. This is described below, but first knit the rest of the mitten. Skip now to "Mitten palm and thumb gore."

RIBBED CUFF (MEN'S)

With smaller gauge needles and Color 1, CO 48 sts. Divide sts onto 4 needles and join, being careful not to twist cast-on row. Work k2, p2 ribbing until ribbing measures 2¾ in / 7 cm. K 1 rnd while increasing 4 sts evenly spaced around = 52 sts.

MITTEN PALM AND THUMB GORE

Switch to larger gauge needles and k 1 rnd and pm marker for thumb gore, thus:

Left mitten: K 21 sts, pm (beg thumb gore), k3, pm (end thumb gore), k to end of rnd.

Right mitten: K 29 sts, pm (beg thumb gore), k3, pm (end thumb gore), k to end of rnd.

Hand pattern: On men's version, be aware that Chart C (thumb gore) begins at Line 5 (see arrow). Start Chart B (area pattern) and work to first marker; then work Chart C (thumb gore) between markers. After thumb gore, continue with Chart B. Continue as est with area pattern and thumb gore (inc as indicated on chart) until thumb gore is complete. There are now 15 sts between markers.

Next rnd: K as est on Chart B to first marker; remove it. Place the 15 thumb gore sts on a piece of scrap yarn, and remove second marker. CO 11 new sts over thumbhole (casting on in colors fitting color pattern on palm), and finish rnd in pattern as est.

From here on, work around following Chart B; the pattern reps 15 times around and 7 times vertically. Once hand measures 3⅜ (3½, 3¾, 4) in / 8.5 (9, 9.5, 10) cm from thumbhole, you are ready to dec for top of mitten. The dec portion takes 4 bands of "windows" (about 1¾ (2, 2¼, 2¼, 2⅜) in / 4.5 (5, 5.5, 5.5, 6) cm). Taking this into consideration, decide now whether you need to adjust mitten length by adding or subtracting bands of windows.

DECREASING MITTEN TIP
Work following Chart D; work rep 5 times around. When Chart D has been completed vertically, 10 sts rem. Cut yarn and draw end through rem sts in Color 1. Tighten firmly to close.

THUMB
There are 24 sts on thumb. In addition to the 15 sts of thumb gore, pick up and knit 9 sts on palm side of thumbhole—that is, 2 fewer sts than you CO above thumbhole after thumb gore.

Using larger gauge needles, transfer the 15 thumb gore sts to a needle, carefully picking out the scrap yarn holding them. Pick up and k 9 sts in Color 2 above thumbhole. Divide these 24 sts onto dpn. If the corners look strained, pick up an additional st in the side corners between thumb gore and mitten palm, and then k that st together with the st next to it.

Follow Chart E, taking care that color pattern lines follow neatly onto the thumb on all sides. Dec as shown. When the chart has been completed, cut yarns and draw Color 2 through rem 6 sts. Tighten firmly to close.

RIBBED EDGE ON WOMEN'S CUFF
Turn mitten bottom up with cuff folded down, and use smaller gauge needles.

Pick up 1 st in each outer st loop in purl rnd of cuff = 60 sts. With Color 2, work 3 rnds k1, p1 ribbing. BO loosely in ribbing.

FINISHING
Weave in all loose ends on WS.

ROSE MITTENS

Chart from *Norwegian Knitting Designs*, figure 43 and figure 44, page 45 and parts of figure 68, page 59.

Three different patterns from Selbu are combined here on one mitten. Mitten knitting is a brilliant way to try out new color combinations. Just swapping colors around can give mittens a whole new expression. The various sizes are achieved by using different weights of yarn and different needle gauges.

SKILL LEVEL
Experienced

SIZES
Women's and men's sizes overlap here: WM (WL/MS, MM/ML)

FINISHED MEASUREMENTS
Circumference: around mitten hand, above thumbhole, 8½ (9, 10) in / 21.5 (23, 25.5) cm
Mitten Hand Length: above ribbing, 7¾ (8, 9) in / 19.5 (20.5, 23) cm
Thumb Length: 2½ (2¾, 3) in / 6.5 (7, 7.5) cm
Cuff Length: 2¾ (3, 3¼) in / 7 (7.5, 8) cm

YARN
Women's M: CYCA #2 (sport, baby) Hifa Ask (100% wool; 345 yd/315 m / 100 g) or Sølje Pelsullgarn (383 yd/350 m / 100 g)
Women's L and Men's S: CYCA #2 (sport, baby) Hifa Ask (100% wool; 345 yd/315 m / 100 g)
Men's M, L: CYCA #3 (DK, light worsted) Hifa Tinde pelsullgarn (100% wool, 284 yd/260 m / 100 g) or Hifa Fjord sock yarn (80% wool/20% nylon; 273 yd/250 m / 100 g)

YARN AMOUNTS
In Hifa Ask or Hifa Sølje: Color 1, approx. 40 g and Color 2, approx. 35 g.
In Hifa Fjord or Tinde: Color 1, approx. 60-70 g and Color 2, approx. 50-55 g.

COLORS SHOWN
Gray and White Version (Ask)
Color 1: Dark Gray 316051
Color 2: Natural White 316057

Red and White Version (Ask)
Color 1: Farmer Red 316013
Color 2: Natural White 316057

SUGGESTED NEEDLE SIZES
US 1.5 / 2.5 mm (US 2.5 / 3 mm, US 2.5 / 3 mm): set of 5 dpn for pattern
US 0 / 2 mm (US 1.5 / 2.5 mm, US 1.5 / 2.5 mm): set of 5 dpn for ribbing
There will be 2 needle sizes used for each mitten size: they will be called respectively "smaller" and "larger" gauge needles.

GAUGE
30 sts and 34 rnds (28 sts and 32 rnds, 25 sts and 29 rnds) on larger gauge needles = 4 x 4 in / 10 x 10 cm
Adjust needle size to obtain correct gauge if necessary.

INSTRUCTIONS

RIBBING

With smaller gauge dpn and Color 2, CO 48 sts. Divide sts evenly across 4 needles and join, being careful not to twist cast-on row. Work k3, p1 ribbing around until you've worked 8 (10, 10) rnds total. Continue in ribbing and beg stripes:

3 rnds Color 1, 2 rnds Color 2, 1 rnd Color 1, 1 rnd Color 2, 1 rnd Color 1, 1 rnd Color 2, 1 rnd Color 1, 2 rnds Color 2, 3 rnds Color 1, 2 (4, 4) rnds Color 2.

MITTEN HAND WITH THUMB GORE

Switch to larger gauge needles and continue with Color 2. Knit 1 rnd, increasing 4 sts evenly spaced around = 52 sts. K band of pattern in Chart A. There are 13 reps around, but only 1 vertically. When Chart A is completed, k 2 rnds with Color 2; on 2nd rnd, inc 4 sts evenly spaced = 56 sts.

Work Chart B for right mitten and Chart C for left mitten. On these charts, the thumb gore area is marked with a red frame: in that space, knit thumb gore (framed in red on Chart D) as you work the lower part of Chart B or C. Pm on both sides of thumb gore. As shown, incs on thumb gore are worked just after the first and before the next to last sts in the chart. When thumb gore is complete, there will be 13 sts between markers.

Next rnd: Thread these 13 sts onto a piece of scrap yarn, and CO 11 new sts over thumbhole, in colors that match charted pattern above thumb hole. Continue in pattern as est = 64 sts.

Work to end of chart, and dec as indicated. When dec is completed, cut yarn and, with tapestry needle, draw yarn through rem 8 sts. Tighten firmly to close.

THUMB

Right and left thumbs are worked the same: Transfer the 13 thumb gore sts onto a dpn and carefully pick out scrap yarn; pick up 11 sts from the top of the thumb hole and 1 st from each corner = 26 sts. Arrange sts on needles. If corners seem strained between thumb gore and palm, pick up an additional st in each corner, and then twist and k2tog with a neighboring st. Follow Chart E, Thumb.

Dec as shown on chart. Cut yarn and, with tapestry needle, draw end through rem 6 sts. Tighten firmly to close.

FINISHING

Weave in all loose ends on WS.

A. BORDER

C. LEFT MITTEN

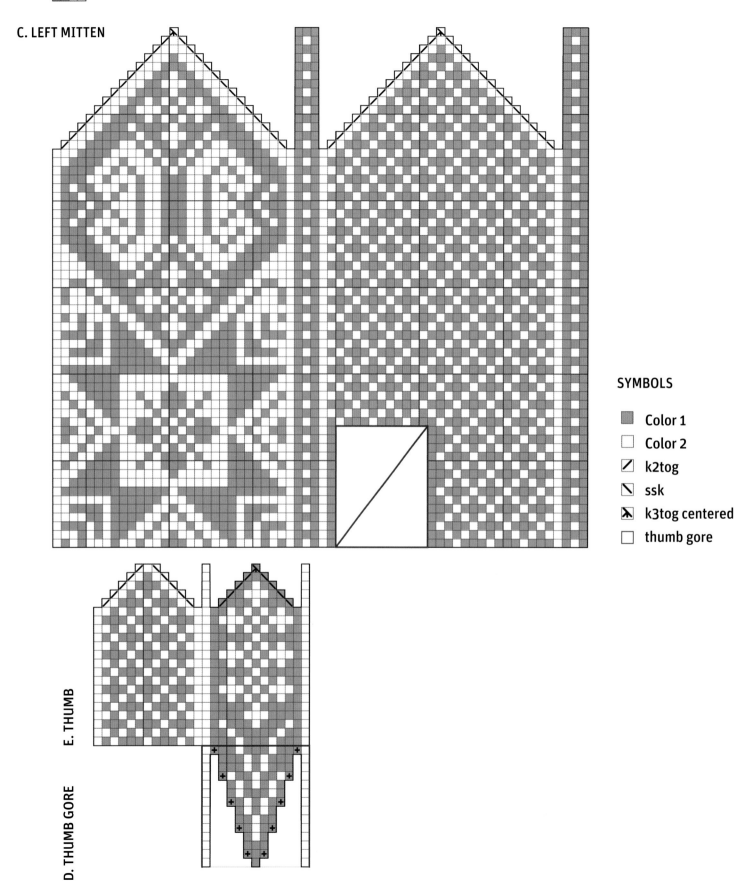

SYMBOLS

- ▨ Color 1
- ☐ Color 2
- ◩ k2tog
- ◪ ssk
- ⬟ k3tog centered
- ☐ thumb gore

E. THUMB

D. THUMB GORE

A. BORDER

B. RIGHT MITTEN

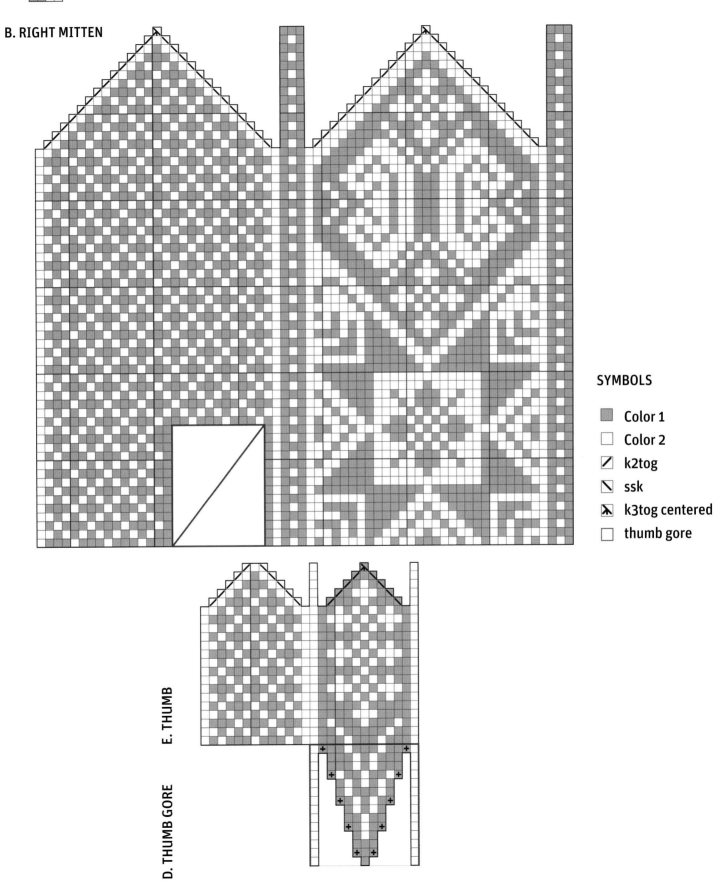

SYMBOLS

- ▨ Color 1
- ☐ Color 2
- ◪ k2tog
- ◨ ssk
- ⬩ k3tog centered
- ☐ thumb gore

E. THUMB

D. THUMB GORE

SELBU MITTENS

Chart from *Norwegian Knitting Designs*, figure 8, page 16.

These mittens are nearly identical to those shown in *Norwegian Knitting Designs*, including the "crooked path" cuff seldom seen today. Only the cuff and the length of the hand differ a bit from the original. The cuff is shortened slightly, but even so, is longer than is common today. And the hand, by contrast, is longer. The inside of the thumb, toward the palm, isn't visible in the book, so the chart for that is a free interpretation. Like the "Women on a Mitten" on p. 245, these are tight, dense mittens. Choose a thinner yarn or different needles if you find it difficult to "make the gauge," or felt them lightly when they're done.

SKILL LEVEL
Experienced

SIZES
Women's M/L

FINISHED MEASUREMENTS
Circumference: around mitten hand, above thumbhole: approx. 9 in / 23 cm
Hand Length: above cuff, approx. 7 in / 18 cm
Thumb Length: 2½ in /6.5 cm
Cuff Length: approx. 5 in / 12.5 cm

YARN
CYCA #2 (baby, sport) Hifa Ask (100% wool; 344 yd/315 m / 100 g) or Sølje Pelsullgarn (383 yd/350 m / 100 g)

YARN AMOUNTS AND COLORS SHOWN
Color 1: Hifa Ask, Natural White 316057, approx. 50-60 g.
Color 2: Hifa Ask, Moss Green 316109, approx. 35-40 g.

SUGGESTED NEEDLE SIZES
US 0 or 1 / 2 or 2.25 mm: set of 5 dpn
Note: This mitten was knitted *very* tightly. You may need to adjust needle size to obtain gauge.

GAUGE
32 sts and 36 rnds in pattern = 4 x 4 in / 10 x 10 cm.
Adjust needle size to obtain correct gauge if necessary.

INSTRUCTIONS

CUFF
With Color 1, CO 60 sts on 4 needles and join to work in the round. P 2 rnds, then knit the "crooked path" (*krokvekk*) pattern following Chart A. The 15-st chart reps 4 times around, and the 2 rnds rep vertically *at the same time* as you work width-wise stripes:

Following Chart A, work 10 rnds with Color 1; 2 rnds with Color 2; 1 rnd with Color 1; 1 rnd with Color 2; 1 rnd with Color 1; 1 rnd with Color 2; 1 rnd with Color 1; 2 rnds with Color 2; and 8 rnds with Color 1.

Work band of color pattern on Chart B. Repeat chart 5 times around and once vertically. **Note:** Even though this cuff is shorter than the original, it's still quite long; this is the traditional style. If you prefer a shorter cuff, though, work fewer single-color rnds before and after the stripes.

HAND AND THUMB GORE
Now, follow Chart C for right mitten and Chart D for left. **Note:** As you knit Rnd 1 of chart, inc 8 sts at points marked with + on chart. Also, make sure center of Chart B (marked *) lines up with center of Charts C and D (also marked *).

The thumb gore is framed in red. Pm on both sides of thumb gore sts. As chart shows, the incs for thumb gore are *after* the 2 first sts and before the last 2 sts in the red frame. When thumb gore is complete, there will be 17 sts between markers.

Next rnd: Thread a piece of scrap yarn through these 17 thumb gore sts, and CO 11 new sts over thumbhole. CO these new sts in colors that match palm pattern above thumbhole, and continue in pattern as est = 74 sts.

Continue following chart(s) and BO as shown. **Note:** The decs on back of hand start 3 rnds earlier than on palm.

When decs are completed, cut yarn; with tapestry needle, draw yarn ends through rem 8 sts. Tighten firmly to close.

THUMB
Right and left thumb are both worked the same way. Transfer the 17 thumb gore sts to a needle and carefully pick out the scrap yarn; pick up 11 sts on palm side of thumb and 1 st in each corner = 30 sts. Divide sts onto dpn. If corners seem strained between hand and thumb gore, pick up an additional st in each corner, and then twist and k2tog with a neighboring st. Work following Chart E, Thumb.

BO as indicated. Cut yarn and, with tapestry needle, draw ends through rem 4 sts. Tighten firmly to close.

FINISHING
Weave in all loose ends neatly on WS.

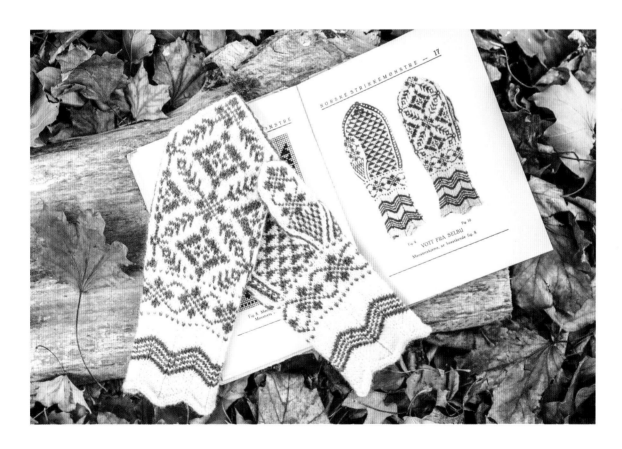

CHART, LEFT MITTEN

C. LEFT MITTEN HAND

*

SYMBOLS

- ☐ Color 1
- ⬛ Color 2
- ◪ k2tog
- ◪ ssk
- ◪ k3tog, centered
- ◉ yarn over
- ◪ k1 tbl
- ⊞ M1
- ☐ thumb gore

E. THUMB

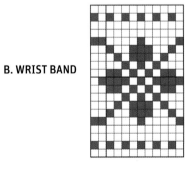

B. WRIST BAND

*

A. "CROOKED PATH"

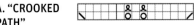

CHART, RIGHT MITTEN

D. RIGHT MITTEN HAND

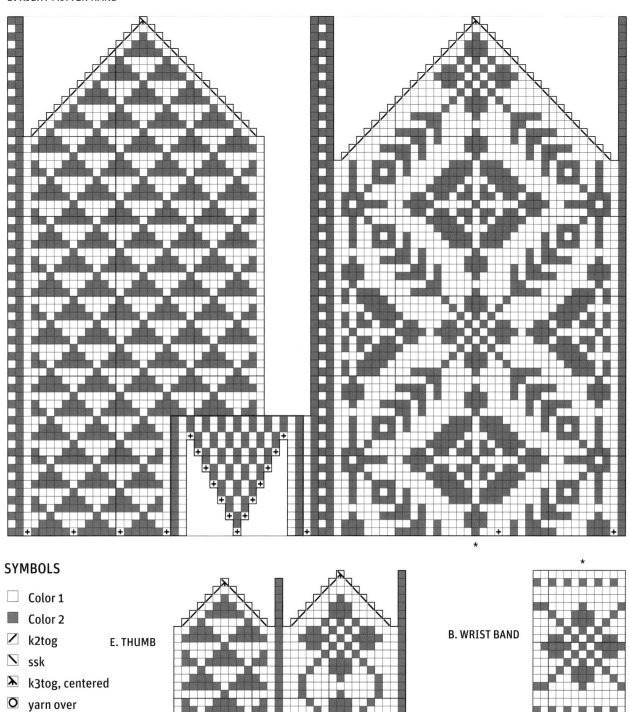

SYMBOLS

☐	Color 1
◼	Color 2
◪	k2tog
◪	ssk
◪	k3tog, centered
⊙	yarn over
◪	k1 tbl
⊞	M1
☐	thumb gore

E. THUMB

B. WRIST BAND

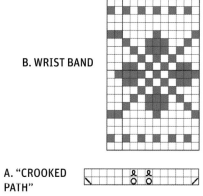

A. "CROOKED PATH"

CABLES AND ENDLESS ROSES: A MITTEN AND A HALF MITT

Chart from *Norwegian Knitting Designs*, figure 8, page 16.

The classic "Endless Roses" motif shows up often on Selbu mittens, and will probably always be popular. In this book, you'll find it on the Kongro Socks/ Weaver Socks (p. 199) and on the Selbu Mittens (p. 231). It's simple to knit, and looks lovely. Here, it's accompanied by a cable pattern on the back of the hand. You might like to knit both the socks and the mittens as a heartwarming gift for a friend.

SKILL LEVEL
Experienced

SIZES
Women's M

FINISHED MEASUREMENTS
Circumference: around hand, above thumbhole, approx. 8 in / 20 cm
Hand Length: above cuff, mitten: approx. 7½ in / 19 cm; half-mitt: approx. 5 in / 13 cm
Thumb Length: mitten: approx. 2½ in /6.5 cm; half-mitt: approx. 1½ in / 4 cm
Cuff Length: approx. 2¾ in / 7 cm

YARN
CYCA #2 (sport, baby) Hifa Ask (100% wool; 344 yd/315 m / 100 g)

YARN AMOUNTS AND COLORS SHOWN
Mitten
Color 1: Gray Heather 316055, 75 g
Color 2: Dark Gray 316051, 10 g
Color 3: Semi-bleached White 316047, 15 g

Half-Mitt
Color 1: Natural White 316057, 50 g
Color 2: Wine Red 316139, 10 g

SUGGESTED NEEDLE SIZES
US 1.5 / 2.5 mm: set of 5 dpn
US 2.5 / 3 mm: set of 5 dpn

GAUGE
24 sts and 32 rnds in stockinette on larger gauge needles = 4 x 4 in / 10 x 10 cm
29 sts (4 pattern reps + 1 st) in cable pattern on larger gauge needles = approx. 8.5-9 cm
Adjust needle size to obtain correct gauge if necessary.

A. Mitten

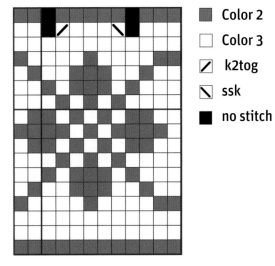

- ■ Color 2
- □ Color 3
- ◪ k2tog
- ◩ ssk
- ■ no stitch

A. Half-mitt

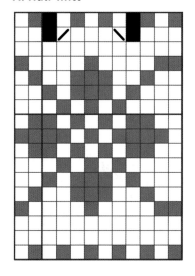

- □ Color 1
- ■ Color 2
- ◪ k2tog
- ◩ ssk
- ■ no stitch

B. Cable pattern

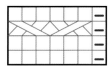

- □ knit
- ⊟ purl
- ⧄ C3B
- ⧅ C3F

INSTRUCTIONS

The mitten and the half-mitt are almost the same, until a little ways after the thumbhole. There are 3 colors on the mitten, and 2 colors on the half-mitt, so the pattern band on the wrist isn't quite the same.

RIBBING

With smaller gauge needles and Color 1, CO 56 sts on 4 needles. Join, being careful not to twist cast-on row. Work around in twisted ribbing (k 1 through back loop, p 1) for 6 rnds.

K 2 rnds; on 2nd rnd, inc 4 sts evenly spaced around = 60 sts.

Mitten: Cut yarn, or catch it up every 4th rnd while knitting the Endless Roses pattern.

WRIST BAND

Join Colors 2 and 3 and knit color pattern following Chart A for mitten or Chart A for half-mitt. The chart reps 5 times widthwise. On next-to-last rnd of chart, dec 10 sts as shown = 50 sts rem. When pattern is complete, cut Colors 2 and 3. Knit 2 rnds with Color 1.

HAND AND THUMB GORE

Switch to larger gauge needles. K 1 rnd and place markers to mark beg of rnd, sides, and thumb gore sts:

Left Mitten/Half-Mitt

Pm (beg of rnd), k 16, pm (beg of thumb gore), k 3, pm (end of thumb gore), k 2, pm (side marker),

k to end of rnd. The first 21 sts are the palm, and the last 29 are the back of the hand.

Right Mitten/Half-Mitt

K 1 and move st end of rnd, pm after it (side marker); k29, pm (side marker), k2, pm (beg of thumb gore), k3, pm (end of thumb gore), k rest of rnd. The first 29 sts are the back of the hand, and the last 21 sts are the palm; beg of rnd has hopped a step (1 st) to the left.

From here, work stockinette on palm (including thumb gore) and work cable pattern following Chart B on back of hand. Make sure the cabling doesn't get too tight.

Left Mitten

K to side marker (palm side), work cable pattern following Chart B—there are 4 cables/repeats—and end with p1 (back of hand).

Right Mitten

Work cable pattern following Chart B—there are 4 cables/repeats—and end with p1 (back of hand), then k to side marker (palm).

Continue as est while, *at the same time*, every 3rd rnd, inc at thumb gore 1 st each side with M1 inside thumb gore markers. After 18 rnds, you have worked 6 inc rnds, and there are 15 sts between thumb gore markers.

Next rnd: The cable pattern continues as est; thread a piece of scrap yarn through the 15 sts of thumb gore. CO 7 sts over thumbhole, and remove thumb gore markers = 54 sts.

For the rest of the project, follow directions for either "Finishing Mitten Hand" or "Finishing Half-Mitt Hand."

FINISHING MITTEN HAND

Continue working around in cables as est until mitten is approx. 6 in / 15 cm long (about 2 in / 5 cm shorter than desired length). End with a full vertical pattern rep. If it can't both end with a full pattern rep and be 6 in / 15 cm long, end instead with a few rnds of stockinette to the desired length.

DECREASE THE MITTEN TIP

This mitten takes a circular dec:
K 4 rnds in stockinette.
Dec Rnd 1: *K4, k2tog. Repeat from * to end of rnd = 45 sts.
K 4 rnds.
Dec Rnd 2: *K3, k2tog. Rep from * to end of rnd = 36 sts.
K 3 rnds.
Dec Rnd 3: *K2, k2tog. Rep from * to end of rnd = 27 sts.
K 2 rnds.
Dec Rnd 4: *K1, k2tog. Rep from * to end of rnd = 18 sts.
K 1 rnd.
Dec Rnd 5: K2tog to end of rnd = 9 sts.

Cut yarn. With tapestry needle, draw tail through rem 9 sts. Tighten firmly to close.

FINISHING HALF-MITT HAND

Continue in pattern as est until there are 9-10 vertical reps of cable chart. Try half-mitt on to see if it is long enough—you are about ¾ in / 2 cm from BO. End with a full vertical rep of Chart B.

Change to smaller gauge needles and k 2 rnds; on 2nd rnd, dec 4 sts evenly spaced around = 50 sts.

Work twisted ribbing (k1 into back loop, p1) for 6 rnds. BO loosely in twisted ribbing.

THUMB

With larger gauge needles, transfer the 15 thumb gore sts to a needle and carefully pick out scrap yarn. Pick up 7 sts on palm side of thumbhole and 1 st in each corner, which will be k tog with a neighboring st = 22 sts. Divide sts onto dpn. For the rest of the thumb, follow the directions for "Thumb on Mitten" or "Thumb on Half-Mitt."

Thumb on Mitten

K around in stockinette until thumb measures 2½ in / 6 cm, or until it covers $^2/_3$ of thumbnail.
Dec Rnd 1: K2tog to end of rnd = 11 sts.
Next rnd: K around.
Dec Rnd 2: K2tog to the last st, k 1 = 6 sts.
Cut yarn and, with tapestry needle, draw end through rem sts. Tighten firmly to close.

Thumb on Half-Mitt

K around until thumb measures approx. ¾ in / 2 cm. On last rnd, dec 4 sts evenly spaced around = 18 sts. Switch to smaller gauge needles and work twisted ribbing (k1 through back loop, p1) for 6 rnds. BO in twisted ribbing.

FINISHING

Weave in all loose ends neatly on WS.

WOMEN ON A MITTEN

Chart from *Norwegian Knitting Designs*, figure 5, page 14.

This mitten is based off a pair of Selbu mittens in *Norwegian Knitting Designs*, but I've made some adjustments to the cuff and thumb gore. Traditionally, mittens were knitted with many, many stitches and a much tighter gauge than is usual today. Mittens knit solidly are warm and strong, and the more stitches you have, the finer and more detailed the patterns can be. If you don't want to knit that tightly, though, you can felt the finished mittens lightly. If you felt by hand, you can watch and control the shrinkage.

SKILL LEVEL
Experienced

SIZES
Women's M/L

FINISHED MEASUREMENTS
Circumference: around mitten hand, above thumbhole, approx. 8¾ in / 22 cm
Hand Length: above cuff, approx. 7½ in / 19 cm
Thumb Length: approx. 2½ in / 6.5 cm
Cuff Length: approx. 4¼ in / 11 cm

YARN
CYCA #2 (sport, baby) Sølje Pelsullgarn (100% wool; 383 yd/350 m / 100 g)

YARN AMOUNTS AND COLORS
Color 1: Red 642132, about 50 g
Color 2: Black 642109, about 50 g

SUGGESTED NEEDLE SIZES
US 0 / 2 mm: set of 5 dpn
Remember, these mittens are worked very tightly and densely. Check your gauge, and choose needles that give you the right number of sts per inch/cm. (Or knit a bit more loosely, and then felt your mittens by hand when they're done. Knit to allow up to 20% shrinkage lengthwise, 10% widthwise, when felting.)

GAUGE
34 sts and 40 rnds in pattern = 4 x 4 in / 10 x 10 cm.
Adjust needle size to obtain correct gauge if necessary.

Tips for knitting men's version: Use Hifa Ask wool yarn, needles US 0 or 1 / 2 or 2.5 mm (approx. 31-32 sts and 25-36 rnds = 4 x 4 in / 10 x 10 cm). Change the cuff to an ordinary ribbed one and swap out the "woman" design for a "man," or use both. Two pairs of these mittens are ideally suited for a wedding present.

INSTRUCTIONS

CUFF

With Color 1, CO 64 sts. Divide the sts onto 4 needles and join, being careful not to twist cast-on row. P 2 rnds.

Work "crooked path" (*krokvekk*) pattern following Chart A. The pattern rep is 16 sts, and reps 4 times around; the 2 rnds rep vertically *at the same time* as you work horizontal stripes:

K 8 rnds Color 1; *1 rnd Color 2; 2 rnds Color 1; 2 rnds Color 2; 2 rnds Color 1; 1 rnd with Color 2;* 6 rnds with Color 1. Rep * to * once, and end with 4 rnds with Color 1 = 34 rnds total.

K 1 rnd stockinette with Color 1. Work wrist band on Chart B. The 4-st chart reps 16 times around and is worked only once vertically.

K 2 rnds with Color 1.

HAND AND THUMB GORE

To position the "crooked path" perfectly on back of mitten, move beg of rnd: On right mitten, move beg of rnd back 3 sts in rnd; on left mitten, move beg of rnd forward 5 sts in rnd. Pm for new beg of rnd (little finger side), and divide sts across needles to fit with pattern.

Knit following Chart C for right mitten and Chart D for left. Make sure one of the points of "crooked path" is lined up with center of Charts C or D.

The thumb gore chart is marked with a red frame. Pm on each side of thumb gore sts. Inc as shown on chart. When thumb gore is complete, there will be 15 sts between markers. On next rnd, thread the 15 thumb gore sts onto scrap yarn, and CO 12 new sts over thumbhole = 75 sts.

Continue to work chart and BO as shown. **Note:** The incs on back of hand beg 3 rnds earlier than on palm.

When decs are complete, cut yarn and, with tapestry needle, draw tail through 9 rem sts. Tighten firmly to close.

THUMB

Left and right thumbs are worked the same way. Slide the 15 thumb gore sts onto a needle and carefully pick out scrap yarn. Pick up 12 sts on palm side of thumbhole, and 2 sts in each corner = 31 sts. Divide sts onto needles, dividing the 2 x 2 corner sts between palm and front needles. Follow Chart E, Thumb. Make sure the pattern is continuous onto the thumb on both palm and front sides.

Dec as indicated on chart. Cut yarn and, with tapestry needle, draw ends through rem 7 sts. Tighten firmly to close.

FINISHING

Weave in all loose ends neatly on WS.

CHART, LEFT MITTEN

D. LEFT MITTEN HAND

SYMBOLS

- ☐ Color 1
- ■ Color 2
- ◪ k2tog
- ◩ ssk
- ⬕ k3tog, centered
- Ⓞ yarn over
- ⊟ purl
- ⊞ M1
- ☐ thumb gore

B. WRIST PATTERN BAND

A. "CROOKED PATH"

E. THUMB

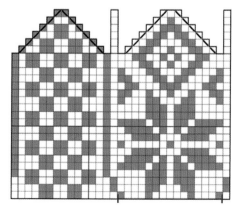

Alternative chart

Replace women in chart with men, or use both!

CHART, RIGHT MITTEN

C. RIGHT MITTEN HAND

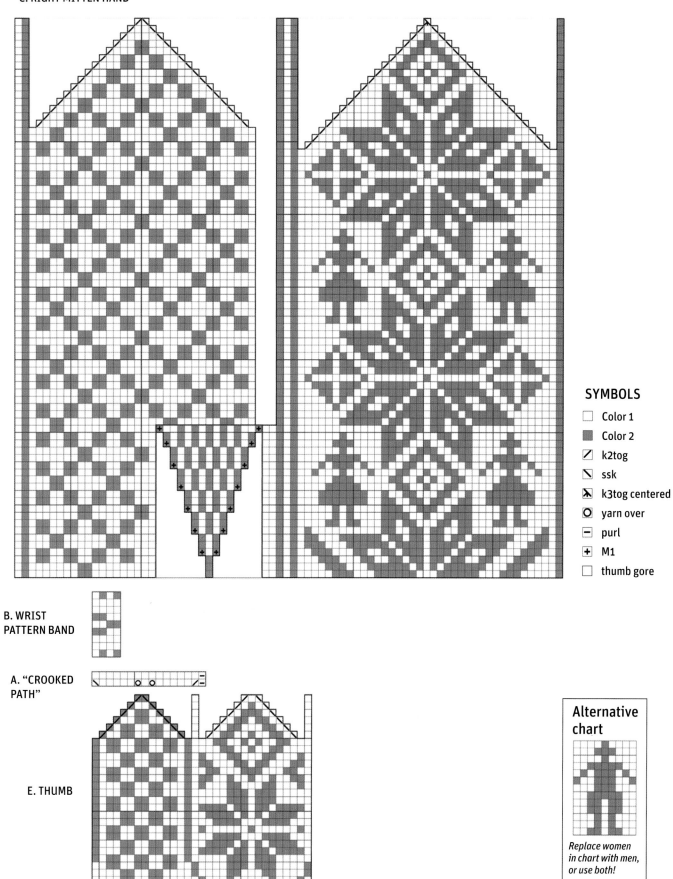

SYMBOLS

- ☐ Color 1
- ■ Color 2
- ◹ k2tog
- ◺ ssk
- ◪ k3tog centered
- Ⓞ yarn over
- − purl
- ＋ M1
- ☐ thumb gore

B. WRIST PATTERN BAND

A. "CROOKED PATH"

E. THUMB

Alternative chart

Replace women in chart with men, or use both!

BUZZING BEES AND FLOWERS
BABY BLANKET

Chart from *Norwegian Knitting Designs*, figure 3, page 12.

This magnificent pattern of birds, bees, flowers, and hearts is so gorgeous that it deserves to be used! Here it is, put together on a large surface just big enough to use as a baby blanket. It's both impractical and challenging to knit with floats as long as those shown in the original chart (which, in fact, is better suited to embroidery). So we've laid the pattern out on a honeycomb background. The birds sit and wait for the bees to finish their pollinating, and for the fruits and berries to grow and ripen, sweet and full, over the summer.

FINISHED MEASUREMENTS

About 23 x 26¾ in / 58 x 68 cm.
The blanket can also be blocked out to a somewhat larger measurement.

YARN

CYCA #2 (sport, baby) Sol Lamullgarn yarn (317
yd/290 m / 100 g)

YARN AMOUNTS

Color 1: 150 g
Color 2: 100 g
Color 3: 100 g

COLORS SHOWN

Brown and White Version
Color 1: Natural White 58400
Color 2: Medium Brown 58403
Color 3 (edging): Light Air Force Blue 58411

Pink and White Version
Color 1: Natural White 58400
Color 2: Old Rose 58407
Color 3 (edging): Red 58406

SUGGESTED NEEDLE SIZES

US 4 / 3.5 mm: 2 32 in / 80 cm circular needles
for BO
US 6 / 4 mm: for central pattern panel

GAUGE

22 sts in stockinette on smaller gauge needles =
4 in / 10 cm
22 sts and 28 rnds in pattern on larger needles =
4 x 4 in / 10 x 10 cm
Adjust needle size to obtain correct gauge if
necessary.

NOTIONS

Optionally, fabric to line the blanket.

INSTRUCTIONS

The blanket is knitted in the round on a circular and cut open. The binding, which is double, is knitted on at the end and hides the cut edges. Optionally, the blanket can be backed with fabric.

With Color 1 and larger gauge needle, CO 109 sts + 5 steek sts. Steek sts are *not* included in st count, and are *not* worked in color pattern. Work steek sts in vertical 1-st stripes (Color 1, Color 2, Color 1, Color 2, Color 1).

Join, being careful not to twist cast-on row. Knit around and pm at each side of steek sts. K 1 rnd stockinette, then beg pattern following chart. Work chart twice vertically. End with 1 rnd stockinette in Color 1. BO.

ASSEMBLY
Machine stitch tight seams on each side of center steek st. Cut open between seams.

BINDING
With smaller gauge circular needles and Color 3, pick up sts around entire edge. With RS facing, beg just after right corner of a long side: *Pick up and k 11 sts per 2 in / 5 cm, in space between pattern and steek sts. At next corner, pick up and k 1 st (corner st). Along short side (CO or BO edge), pick up and k 1 st in each st. At corner, pick up and k 1 st (corner st).* Repeat from * to * once.

Now work stockinette around with 2 incs at each corner:

Inc Rnd: *Knit to corner st, M1R, k1, M1L, rep from * 3 times. Work to end of rnd = 8 sts inc.

Next rnd: K around, knitting M1s from preceding rnd to face right or left.

Repeat these 2 rnds, working inc rnd *every other* rnd, until edging measures 1½ in / 4 cm. End with an inc rnd.

Next rnd: P around, twisting and purling corner M1s to lean right or left = p fold line.

Now knit in stockinette—this will be the back side of the edging—and dec at corner sts:

Dec Rnd: Starting at a corner st, k1, *k2tog, work to 2 sts before next marker, ssk, k1.* Rep from * to * 3 more times this rnd = 8 sts dec.

Next rnd: K around.

Rep these 2 rnds, working dec rnd *every other* rnd, until edging measures 1½ in / 4 cm from purl rnd and there are as many dec rnds on back as inc rnds on front. End with a dec rnd.

BO loosely. Hem edge to the WS.

Weave in loose ends neatly on the WS.

If you wish, the blanket can be lined with fabric. Measure the blanket within the edging. Add ¾ in / 2 cm seam allowance all the way around. Be careful to be generous with the fabric, or else the lining may pull the blanket in. Iron the fabric first, and fold over and iron seam allowances to WS of fabric. Baste or pin the fabric in place, and use invisible stitch edge to edge on back side of edging, right where it was hemmed down to WS of blanket.

Color 1

Color 2

knit twice

BEEHIVE POTHOLDERS

Chart from *Norwegian Knitting Designs*, figure 3, page 12.

If you have to have insects in the kitchen, there's no better place for them than a pattern on your potholders. The bees were selected from the chart for "An Old Handbag," photographed on p. 13 of *Norwegian Knitting Designs*. At first glance, the handbag almost seems embroidered, but it's actually knitted! Which is also a nice reminder that embroidery patterns can be translated into knitting wonderfully—and vice versa. Because the motif is bees, a honeycomb background seemed appropriate, and the pattern isn't just decoration; it reduces long floats on the inside, too. (They're double!)

FINISHED MEASUREMENTS
Approx. 8¼ x 8¼ in / 21 x 21 cm

YARN
CYCA #1 (sock, fingering, baby) Hifa Perle Cotton yarn 12/6 (100% cotton; 366 yd/335 m / 100 g)

YARN AMOUNTS
Color 1: 100 g
Color 2: 50 g
Color 3 (optional): approx. 5-10 g

COLORS SHOWN
Black and White Version:
Color 1: Hifa Perle cotton 12/6, Unbleached 18342
Color 2: Hifa Perle cotton 12/6, Black 18351

Copper and White Version:
Color 1: Hifa Perle cotton 12/6, Unbleached 18342
Color 2: Hifa Perle cotton 12/6, Copper 18339
Color 3 (optional): Hifa Perle cotton 12/6, Black 18351

SUGGESTED NEEDLE SIZES
US 1.5 / 2.5 mm: 16 in / 40 cm circular
US C or D / 2.5 mm: crochet hook (for edging)

GAUGE
30 sts and 36 rnds in color pattern = 4 x 4 in / 10 x 10 cm
Adjust needle size to obtain correct gauge if necessary.

INSTRUCTIONS

The potholders are knitted in the round on a circular. They are double. The edge is crocheted all the way around at the end.

With circular and Color 1, CO 120 sts. Join, being careful not to twist cast-on row. Pm in 1st st and in 60th st (the two side sts). Work around in pattern following chart. The chart is worked 2 times around. Because the potholder is double and the floats are on the inside, they can be a good deal longer than usual; mostly, it's important that they remain somewhat loose, so they don't pull on the work widthwise. Knit entire chart to end. Work a single rnd of stockinette with Color 1. BO.

CROCHETED EDGING
Fold work at side sts. With crochet hook and Color 1, beg in upper corner and crochet layers together all the way around with slip st. First work down left side, and then continue; on sides, crochet 1 sl st into both loops of side sts, 5 sts to every 6 rnds (skip the 6th rnd). Along top and bottom edges, sl st 1 per 1 st. Crochet 3 sl st into every corner. End with a chain st in the first sl st. Change to Color 2 (or 3). Beg by joining yarn with a chain st in corner, and then crochet a loop with 18 chain sts. Crochet 1 sc in every sl st around edge, and sc 3 times into each other corner. End by working single crochet over every chain st in chain loop. Cut yarn and work all loose ends invisibly into potholder.

Color 1
Color 2

ANNICHEN'S "ESKIMO" (GREENLANDER) PULLOVER

The "Eskimo Sweater" is the only project in this book not based on charts from *Norwegian Knitting Designs*. But this pullover is such an important part of Annichen's life's work and Norwegian knitting history that it demands a place here. Besides, it's gorgeous! Annichen designed her "Eskimo" pullover in 1930, naming the pattern for its inspiration: the first Norwegian "talkie" film, also called *Eskimo*, in which the heroine Eukaluk, played by Mona Mårtenson, wore Greenlander Inuit clothing with a beadwork cape over the shoulders. After designer Unn Søiland made another version in 1953, used in the film *Troll i Ord*, this sweater became a trendy garment everyone wanted to knit, and the pattern is still in style today.

The original design has a little band of patterning at the wrist. We opted not to use that here, but if you want to make a completely authentic copy of Annichen's "Eskimo" pullover, we provide a chart for the wrist pattern in these directions.

SKILL LEVEL
Experienced

SIZES
Women's XS (S, M, L, XL, XXL)

FINISHED MEASUREMENTS
Chest: approx. 34½ (36¼, 38½, 41¼, 44, 47¼) in / 87.5 (92, 97.5, 104.5, 112, 120) cm
Total Length: approx. 23¼ (23¾, 24, 24½, 25¼, 25½) in / 59 (60, 61, 62, 64, 65) cm
Sleeve Length: approx. 17¾ (17¾, 18, 18½, 19, 19) in / 45 (45, 46, 47, 48, 48) cm

YARN
Color 1: CYCA #3 (DK, light worsted) Hifa Tinde (100% wool; 284 yd/260 m / 100 g) or CYCA #2 (sport, baby) Hifa Sol Lamullgarn (317 yd/290 m / 100g)
Color 2: CYCA #2 (sport, baby) Hifa Sol Lamull-garn (100% wool; 317 yd/290 m / 100g)

YARN AMOUNTS
Color 1: Tinde pelsull, 400 (400, 400, 450, 500, 550) g or Sol Lamullgarn, 350 (350, 400, 450, 450, 500) g
Color 2: Sol Lamullgarn, 50 (50, 50, 50, 60, 60) g

COLORS SHOWN
Blue Version
Color 1: Tinde Pelsull Medium Blue 652135;
Color 2: Sol Lamull Unbleached White 58400

Black Version
Color 1: Sol Lamull Black 58414;
Color 2: Sol Lamull Unbleached White 58400

SUGGESTED NEEDLE SIZES
US 2.5 / 3 mm: 24 and 32 in / 60 and 80 cm circulars and set of 5 dpn
US 6 / 4 mm: 16, 24, and 32 in / 40, 60, and 80 cm circulars and set of 5 dpn

GAUGE
22 sts in single color stockinette on US 6 / 4 mm needles = 4 in / 10 cm.
Adjust needle size to obtain correct gauge if necessary.

INSTRUCTIONS

This pullover is knitted in the round from the top down. Decide whether you want the neckline higher in back and with or without shaping at the waist.

YOKE

With Color 1 and smaller gauge, shorter circular, CO 112 (112, 120, 120, 128, 128) sts. Join, taking care not to twist cast-on row. Pm at beg of rnd, which will be center of back. Work k1, p1 ribbing for 1½ (1½, 1½ 1¾, 1¾) in / 4 (4, 4, 4.5, 4.5, 4.5) cm. Change to larger gauge circular, and k 1 rnd.

The original "Eskimo" sweater neckline was the same on front and back, but if you would like the back neckline to be a little higher than the front, to give a better fit, you can knit a few short rows before starting the color pattern (see page 23, "German Short Rows," if you're new to this.)

Short rows (optional):
Row 1 (RS): K 24 (24, 26, 26, 28, 28) sts, turn and DS.
Row 2 (WS): P 47 (47, 51, 51, 55, 55) sts, turn and DS.
Row 3 (RS): K to previous turn, k DS as one st, k 8 st, turn and DS.
Row 4 (WS): P to previous turn, p DS as one st, p 8 sts, turn and DS.
Rep Rows 3 and 4 once more.

Next row (RS): K to beg of rnd (center back).

There are now 6 more rows at back of neck, making it about ¾ in / 2 cm higher than front. K 1 rnd, working last DS as a single st as you pass it.

Whether you choose to work short rows or not, start Chart A at point indicated for desired size. The pattern repeats around 14 (14, 15, 15, 16, 16) times. Inc as indicated on chart, and be aware that various inc methods are used. Change to a longer circular when sts become crowded. This color pattern has long gaps—and therefore long floats—between color changes. Catch floats on WS when there are more than 3 or 4 sts between color changes: K 1 over floating yarn, then k 1 under floating yarn. Take care not to stack these vertically from rnd to rnd, as that will show on RS. Work to end of Chart A = 308 (322, 330, 345, 352, 368) sts. Cut Color 2.

Continue in stockinette with Color 1, and work 1 rnd. On next rnd, inc in sizes L to XXL:

L: Inc 1, k to end = 1 st inc.
XL: K 11, M1, then (k 22, M1) 15 times, k 11 = 16 sts inc.
XXL: K 11, M1, (k 23, M1) 15 times, k 12 = 16 sts inc.

You should now have 308 (322, 330, 346, 368, 384) sts total. Continue in plain stockinette until work below neck band measures 8 (8¼, 8¼, 8¾, 9, 9½) in / 20 (21, 21, 22, 23, 24) cm, measured at center front.

Now, divide work as follows: K 43 (46, 47, 50, 54, 56) sts, place the next 68 (70, 72, 74, 77, 80) sts on a holder (right sleeve), CO 5 (5, 7, 8, 8, 10) sts, pm (right underarm "seam" and new beg of rnd); CO 5 (5, 7, 8, 8, 10) sts, k 86 (91, 93, 99, 107, 112) sts (front); place next 68 (70, 72, 74, 77, 80) sts on a holder (left sleeve), CO 5 (5, 7, 8, 8, 10) sts, pm (left side "seam"); CO 5 (5, 7, 8, 8, 10) sts, work to new beg of rnd, and remove old beg-of-rnd marker in passing.

BODY

There are now 192 (202, 214, 230, 246, 264) sts on the needle. Continue working stockinette until body measures 2 in / 5 cm from BO at underarm. The waist shaping starts here with some decs and incs. Skip over this if you prefer a straight body.

Dec Rnd: *K 1, k2tog, k to 3 sts before side marker ssk, k1. Rep from * once = 4 sts dec.

Work dec rnd twice more, with approx. 1½ in / 4 cm between dec rnds = 180 (190, 202, 218, 234, 252) sts. Then k around for approx. 1½ 4 (2, 2, 2, 2) in / (4, 5, 5, 5, 5) cm.

Inc Rnd: *K 1, M1, work to 1 st before side marker, M1, k 1. Rep from * once = 4 sts inc.

Work inc rnd twice more, with approx. 1½ in / 4 cm between inc rnds = 192 (202, 214, 230, 246, 264) sts.

Continue working stockinette in Color 1 until body measures 13 (13, 13¾, 13¾, 13¾, 13¾) in / 34 (34, 35, 35, 35, 35) cm to underarm, or until it is 2 (2, 2, 2, 2½, 2½) in / 5 (5, 5, 5, 6, 6) cm shorter than desired full length. Change to smaller gauge circular needle and work k1, p1 ribbing for 2 (2, 2, 2, 2½, 2½) in / 5 (5, 5, 5, 6, 6) cm. BO in ribbing.

SLEEVES

Transfer one set of sleeve sts onto large gauge, shorter circular (or dpn). With Color 1, start in the middle of sts CO for armhole, and pick up and k 5 (5, 7, 8, 8, 10) sts; then k the 68 (70, 72, 74, 77, 80) sleeve sts; then pick up and k the remaining 5 (5, 7, 8, 7, 10) sts of armhole CO. Pm for beg of rnd = 78 (80, 86, 90, 92, 100) sts. Work around in stockinette until sleeve measures 1½ (1½, 2, 1½, 1½, 2) in / 4 (4, 5, 4, 4, 5) cm from underarm join.

Dec Rnd: K 1, k2tog, knit to 3 sts before marker, ssk, k 1 = 2 sts dec.

Rep dec rnd every 1¼ (1¼, 1, 1, 1, ¾) in / 3 (3, 2.5, 2.5, 2.5, 2) cm a total of 12 (12, 14, 15, 15, 18) times = 54 (56, 58, 60, 62, 64) sts rem.

Note: If you want the band of pattern on the wrist, as in the original design, work Chart B when sleeve is 13 (13, 13½, 13¾, 13¾, 13¾) in / 33 (33, 34, 35, 35, 35) cm long. Count back from center st of sleeve and chart to find starting point on Chart B. The decs continue as est, as long as decs rem to be worked.

Then, continue without decs until sleeve measures 15¾ (15¾, 16½, 16½, 16½) in / 40 (40, 41, 42, 42, 42) cm, or until the sleeve is 2 (2, 2, 2, 2½, 2½) in / 5 (5, 5, 5, 6, 6) cm shorter than desired length. Change to smaller gauge dpn and work k1, p1 ribbing for 2 (2, 2, 2, 2½, 2½) in / 5 (5, 5, 5, 6, 6) cm. BO in ribbing.

FINISHING

Weave in all loose ends on WS.

Chart A, sizes XS, M, and XL

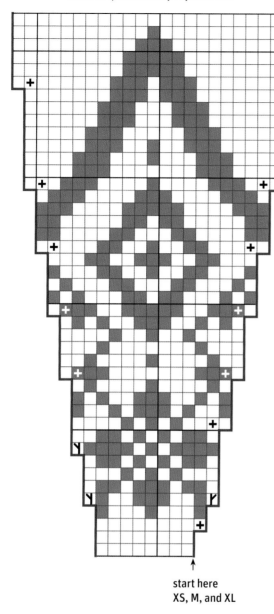

start here
XS, M, and XL

Chart A, sizes S, L, and XXL

start here
S, L, and XXL

Chart B, optional band for sleeve

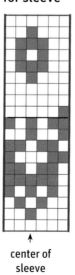

center of sleeve

☐ Color 1

■ Color 2

➕ / ➕ Inc 1 st by picking up loop between sts from previous rnd and k into back (w Color 1 / Color 2)

ꓘ Inc 1 st by k 1 st in the st under the last st on the right needle.

ꓗ Inc 1 st by k into the st in rnd under the first st on the left needle.

| | Repeat

Dette var det som gav støtet til at jeg utgav "Norske Strikkemønstre", og at jeg har fortsatt med å lave mønstre og farver for strikningen. Men de håndstrikkede ting blir dessverre så dyre, at kun et fåtall ser sig istand til å anskaffe dem til bruksgjen- stande. Flertallet tyr hen til de maskinstrikkede ting som er bil- ligere, men disse er desverre sjelden hvad farver og mønster angår, utvalgt med den smag man kunde ønske.

Det er synd at økon... intetgjøre smagen, for e... dreverdige ting

... skal kunde få lov til å til- ... i blir vandt til å se min- ...den.

...felt ligger åpent, vi må ...skin også - så smaken ikke

...slog det mig at denne ...t det her måtte være en ri ...husflid og industri. ...så langt at der ad ...som hvad kvalitet og ...t beste utlandet byr

...de i mønstre og far- ...gått foran og det ...rbeidet sig så

...kre. Vi må bare ...er maskinens ...kape liv i møn- ...marbeide mellem ...nsul P. Chris- ...ere tid er ...fabrikkens ...g nu surrer

...nd- og ma- ...rforbundet ...rt ...lt hvad ...l stor

Husflid og Industri.

De som så vår første norske talefilm "Eskimo", kunde umulig undgå å legge merke til Mona Mortenson's bedårende drakt, som i sin gjennemførte faste komposisjon fremhevet filmens kvinnelige hovedperson på en så iøinefallende og smukk måte.

Iallfall gjorde den et dypt inntrykk på mig, og da spe- sielt draktens overstykke. Jeg grep ideen og komponerte en genser til oss selv over det samme motiv. En typisk damegenser, med den mørke linning rundt hals og håndledd som er så flaterende, et strikket skul- derstykke, som en bred krave, men ellers ganske enkel. Det er nettop det plagg vi skal ha, hvad enten til sport eller annet bruk, sommer som vinter, i tynne og tykke kvaliteter.

Resultatet er da genseren "Eskimo" som jeg har den gle- de å få vise frem.

Det er min tanke å motta bestillinger på denne og på andre strikkede gensere, luer, votter o.s.v. og herved skaffe folk en bifortjeneste ved strikning, et arbeide som ved siden av å være nyttig også er hyggelig. Kan der av dette opnåes at interessen for håndstrikning og sansen for mønstre og farver vinder almindelig ut- bredelse i vårt land, således at ikke bare nogen enkelte, men også alle våre husmødre og døtre optar strikningen som en del av det dag- lige arbeide, har jeg ikke anstrengt mig forgjeves.

Det som fikk mig til å ta fatt få strikketøiet det var dette at alt hvad vi hadde av gode, hjemlige mønstre holdt på å gli ut. Vi holdt på å tape sansen for den rikdom vi eiet i gamle mønstre. En herlig fantasi og en sikker formsans har i fullt monn preget også denne gren av vår gamle husflidskultur, og så lenge vi ikke selv her- hjemme eller utenfra kan skape no bedre - gjør vi rett i å holde på og utvikle den videre. En opgave som efter min mening først og fremst bør har sitt utspring i skolen, og derfra gå videre til hjemmene.
• Vi er jo kommet så langt at vi fort vekk ser tyske Selbuvätter og lig- nende uhyrligheter frembudt på vårt norske marked. Og den som har en aldri så liten interesse for å sette sig inn i hvad vi selv eier på dette område, kan ikke være annet enn enig med mig i at nu gjelder det at vi holder hånd over det som er vårt, og ikke tillater at det for- fuskes med mmere eller mindre gode plagiater.

Annichen Sibbern Bøhn's private notes on the "Eskimo" pullover for an article series she wrote for Morgenbladet *in the 1930s. (Private ownership)*

Still photos from the Norwegian "talkie" film Eskimo *(1930).*
The Greenlander beadwork cape worn by the actress was the
inspiration for Annichen Sibbern Bøhn's "Eskimo" pullover.
(Loaned by Det Danske Filminstitut)

ACKNOWLEDGMENTS

Thanks to Annichen Sibbern Bøhn, who by collecting old knitting patterns and preserving them has inspired knitters for almost 100 years. Many stitches and meters of yarn have been knitted in the course of those years. Because of her work, the pleasure of knitting, the science of knitting, and a culture of handwork lives on today in the best of health, and will be passed forward to coming generations.

Thanks to Editor Silje Iversen Hammersland and my Norwegian publisher, Font Publishing, for choosing me for this book project!

Thanks to photographer Sara Johannessen for the great photos, and your good humor.

Thanks to all who helped knit samples for this book: Anne Cathrine Johansen, Liv Marie Fostervold, Siri Eikrem Skotland, Kathe Beatrix Andreasen, Mette Berg, Anne Birte Monsen Sigtbakken, Gunvor Bakke, Kari Øvland, Gro L'Orsa, Margrethe Norum, Hilde Marie Rødølen, Airin Hansen, Mona Janne Johansen, Inger-Lise Rokstad, Hege B Torvik, Ruth Iris Kold Gabrielsen, Rie Norum, Myrna Haukebø, and Orla Dahn. You have put forth a magnificent effort!

Thanks to all you super folks and dogs who were our photo models. Patient, happy and brave children: Aksel, Jenny, Theodor, Hedda, Kian, Johanna, Maja, Amalie, Noa, Nikolai, Edvard, and Herman. Wonderful and handsome adults: Stella Visnes, Maria Härter Christiansen, Nashia Søraune, Jens Kristian Berg, Jarle Johannessen, and Jeanette Amundsen, who posed with the charming dogs Wilma and Link. Thanks to all who lent us themselves and their time for this book—and for all the great photos that resulted!

Thanks to Annichen Sibbern Bøhn's descendents, who gave us permission to reprint *Norske Strikkemønstre—Norwegian Knitting Designs*—and thanks to the Nasjonalbibliotek (the Norwegian National Library) and the Norsk Folkemuseum, which helped us with materials.

Thanks to Hifa Ullvarefabrikk for all the yarn they contributed to the book.

Thanks to Bjarne Hjelmtvedt Sytilbehør AS for all the fine pewter buttons.

And finally, thanks to my Erik, who understands how important it is for me to use and develop my creative faculties.

Wenche Roald

YARN INFORMATION

Some Hillesvåg/Hifa yarns may be purchased (with international shipping charges) from:

Knit with Attitude

knitwithattitude.com

However, some varieties may be difficult to find. Additional and substitute yarns are available from:

Webs—America's Yarn Store

75 Service Center Road

Northampton, MA 01060

800-367-9327

yarn.com

LoveKnitting.com

loveknitting.com/us

If you are unable to obtain any of the yarn used in this book, it can be replaced with a yarn of a similar weight and composition. Please note, however, the finished projects may vary slightly from those shown, depending on the yarn used. Try www.yarnsub.com for suggestions.

For more information on selecting or substituting yarn, contact your local yarn shop or an online store; they are familiar with all types of yarns and would be happy to help you. Additionally, the online knitting community at Ravelry.com has forums where you can post questions about specific yarns. Yarns come and go so quickly these days and there are so many beautiful yarns available.

NORWEGIAN
KNITTING DESIGNS

NORWEGIAN KNITTING DESIGNS

ANNICHEN SIBBERN

A facsimile edition

GRØNDAHL & SØNS FORLAG   OSLO

GRØNDAHL & SØN, OSLO 1929

FOREWORD

The Norwegian farm woman and her *binding*–a rural word for knitting–have been faithfully bound together through the ages, for many hundreds of years, and they continue to be so today.

In the long, dark winter evenings, knitting was an accepted part of rural home industry, for reasons of both practical utility and pleasure; and in the long, light summer evenings, many stockings and mittens were knitted in the mountain pastures to pass the time, and for amusement during lonely hours.

Our Norwegian national temperament and our imaginative design and color sense soon demanded their place in knitting as well. Over time, we have developed a unique artisanry, worth preserving and developing further by inviting it into a thousand homes.

I've therefore set myself the goal of collecting and developing a portion of the patterns I find prettiest and most typical of various districts in our country. I believe that this little book will broaden their area of use.

Here, then, is a new printing of *Norske Strikkemønstre*, for several reasons:
- The first printing has sold out.
- The book has been so well received.
- The publisher has continued to receive daily requests for the book.
I hope and believe that these patterns will always be used and preserved, no matter the comings and goings of fashion, because they are good Norwegian craftsmanship.

Annichen Sibbern Bøhn
From the original foreword to the second printing

GUIDELINES

Knitting in patterns can be used for many things. Especially clothing, but handbags, pillows, blankets, and more can be made by combining different borders and motifs in new ways. But there are, of course, certain things—hats, mittens, gloves, pullovers, stockings, and scarves—that some color patterns are particularly well suited for.

To make these different patterns accessible, I've drawn them out on charts: each square is one stitch. Most of our traditional Norwegian patterns are worked in black and white, the two most fundamental colors. But there is nothing preventing you from choosing your own colors, if there's another combination you like better. If you're uncertain about trying other combinations, though, you can always stay on the safe side and stick to classic black and white.

To determine how many stitches to cast on to make the color pattern fit, remember that the number of cast-on stitches must be divisible by the total number of stitches in the charted pattern. For example: if a pattern element has a repeat of 8 stitches, the number of cast-on stitches must be some multiple of 8–56, perhaps, or 64, or 72, or whichever greater multiple is necessary to achieve the desired width. This rule holds for all patterns.

The photographs in figures 72 through 77 show various mittens, and one stocking design, with no accompanying charts. They are all rich and imaginative in their colorwork, and at the same time elegant and of excellent overall quality.

Each square in a chart corresponds to a knitted stitch. The pattern will often—but not always—be marked by black squares. For example, the process of knitting the pattern shown at the bottom of the next page (at least if you are working in the round on a circular, and not back and forth on straight needles) will be:

Rnd 1: Working in stockinette, knit side facing, you will start at the bottom right corner–k 3 sts black, 4 sts white, 1 st black, 4 sts white, 3 sts black, 4 sts white, 1 st black, and so on across all the squares.

Rnd 2: Begin at the right side again. K 3 white, 1 black, 2 white, 3 black, 2 white, 1 black, 3 white, 1 black, 2 white, and so forth.

Rnd 3: K 4 white, 1 black, 1 white, 3 black, 1 white, 1 black, 5 white, 1 black, 1 white, and so forth.

Rnd 4: K 5 white, 1 black, 1 white, 1 black, 1 white, 1 black, 7 white, 1 black, 1 white, and so forth.

Rnd 5: K 3 white, 2 black, 1 white, 1 black, 1 white, 1 black, 1 white, 2 black, 3 white, 2 black, 1 white, 1 black, and so forth.

Rnd 6: K 1 black, 1 white, 4 black, 1 white, 1 black, 1 white, 4 black, 1 white, 4 black, 1 white, and so forth.

Continue this way as shown on the chart.

If you wish to knit a scarf, however, or any other pattern better worked back and forth than in the round, then you progress this way:

Row 1: Working in stockinette, knit side facing, you will start at the bottom right corner–k 3 sts black, 4 sts white, 1 st black, 4 sts white, 3 sts black, 4 sts white, 1 st black, and so on across all the squares.

Row 2: Turn the work. This row will be a purl row, and you will read the chart from left to right, not right to left: starting at the left edge of the last pattern repeat (not shown below, but this pattern is symmetrical), you will purl 3 white, 1 black, 2 white, 3 black, 2 white, 1 black, 3 white, 1 black, 2 white, and so forth.

Row 3: Turn the work. This row will be a knit row, and you will go back to reading the chart from right to left. K 4 white, 1 black, 1 white, 3 black, 1 white, 1 black, 5 white, 1 black, 1 white, and so forth.

Row 4: Turn the work. This row will be a purl row, and read off the chart in the same manner as for Row 2. Rows will alternate knit and purl.

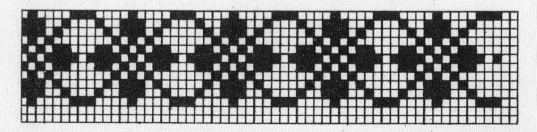

DESIGNS

Back of
mitten →

Fig. 1. Pattern chart for the accompanying fig. 2.

Fig. 2
MEN'S MITTENS FROM SELBU
See fig. 1 for pattern chart.

Fig. 3. Pattern chart for the accompanying fig. 4.

Fig. 4. Design for handbag. Sample worked in lavender background with brown design.

Design pattern
for the thumb

Fig. 5. Pattern chart for the accompanying figs. 6 and 7.
75 stitches were cast on for this mitten.

Fig. 6. Back.   Fig. 7. Palm.

MITTEN FROM SELBU
See fig. 5 for the pattern chart.

Fig. 8. Pattern chart for the accompanying figs. 9 and 10.
The repeat for the *kongro*/endless roses at bottom is 12 stitches.

Fig. 9. Palm.   Fig. 10. Back.

MITTEN FROM SELBU
See fig. 8 for the pattern chart.

Fig. 11. Pattern chart for the accompanying fig. 12.

Fig. 12. MITTEN FROM SELBU
See fig. 11 for the pattern chart.

Fig. 13. Pattern chart for the accompanying fig. 14.
The pattern repeat is 8 stitches.

Fig. 14 CHILDREN'S MITTEN FROM HALLINGDAL
See fig. 13 for the pattern chart.

Fig. 15. Pattern chart for the accompanying fig. 16.
Stjerne (star) border is worked across a multiple of 12.
The calf was 102 stitches in the medium men's stocking in fig. 16.

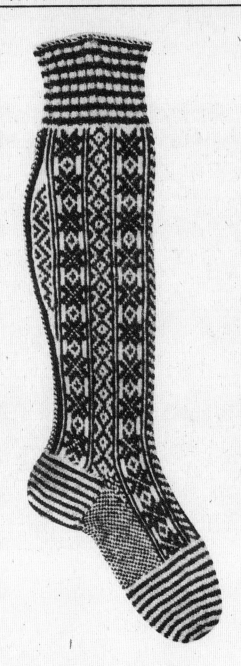

Fig. 16 STOCKING FROM HALLINGDAL
See fig. 15 for the pattern chart.

Fig. 17. Pattern chart for the accompanying fig. 18.
The pattern repeat is 22 stitches.

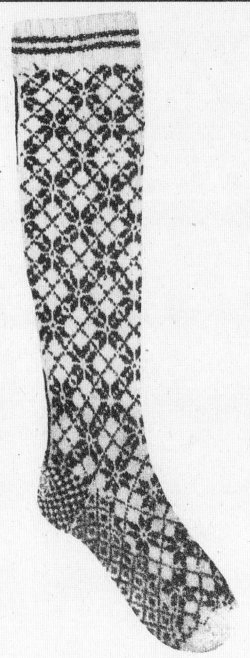

Fig. 18 STOCKING FROM SELBU
See fig. 17 for the pattern chart.

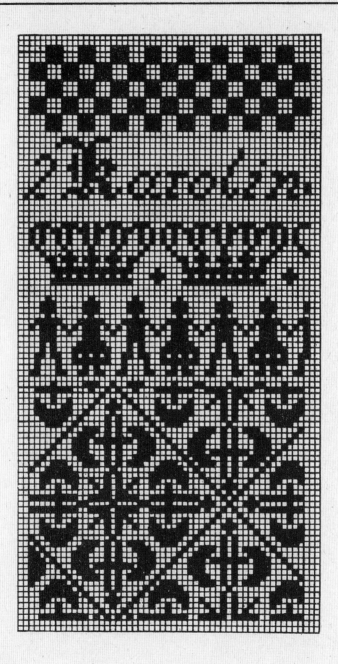

Fig. 19. Pattern chart for the accompanying fig. 20.

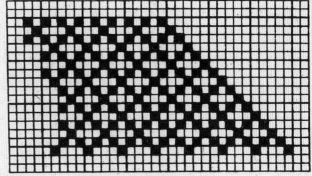

Fig. 21. Sole of the foot.

Fig. 20 STOCKING FROM SELBU
See figs. 19 and 21 for the pattern charts.

Fig. 22. Pattern chart for the accompanying fig. 23.
The pattern repeat is 29 stitches.

Fig. 23 STOCKING FROM TELEMARK
in blue and white.
See fig. 22 for the pattern chart.

Fig. 24. Pattern chart for the accompanying fig. 25.
The pattern repeat is 25 stitches.

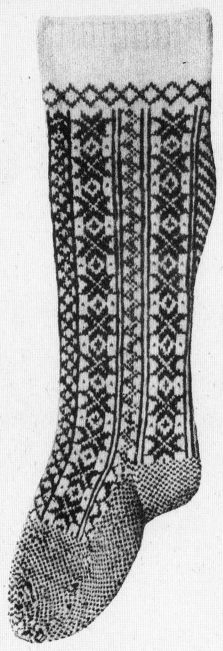

Fig. 25 STOCKING
See fig. 24 for the pattern chart.

Fig. 26. Pattern chart for the cuff shown in fig. 28.

Fig. 27. Pattern chart for the sock leg shown in fig. 28.

Fig. 28 STOCKING FROM SELBU
See figs. 26 and 27 for the pattern charts.

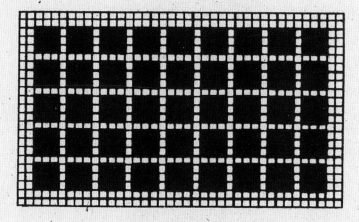

Fig. 29. Pattern chart for the accompanying fig. 30.
The pattern repeat is 4 stitches.

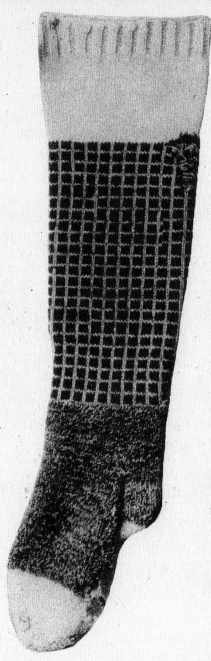

Fig. 30 STOCKING
See fig. 29 for the pattern chart.

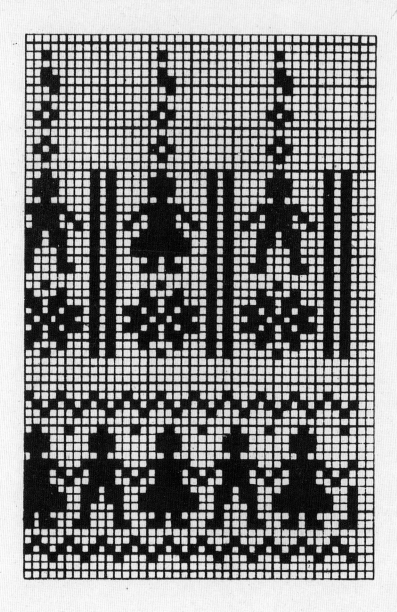

Fig. 31. Pattern chart for the accompanying fig. 32.

Fig. 32 HAT FROM SELBU
See fig. 31 for the pattern chart.

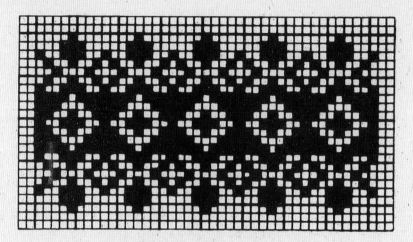

Fig. 33. Pattern chart for the accompanying fig. 35.

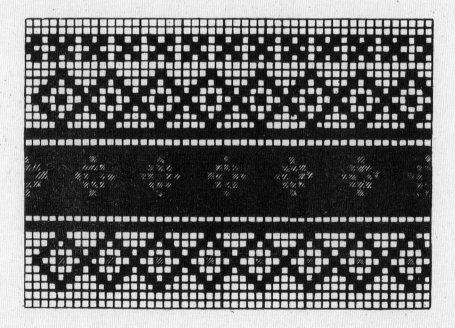

Fig. 34. Pattern chart for the accompanying fig. 35.

Fig. 35 STOCKING CAP
See figs. 33 and 34 for the pattern charts.

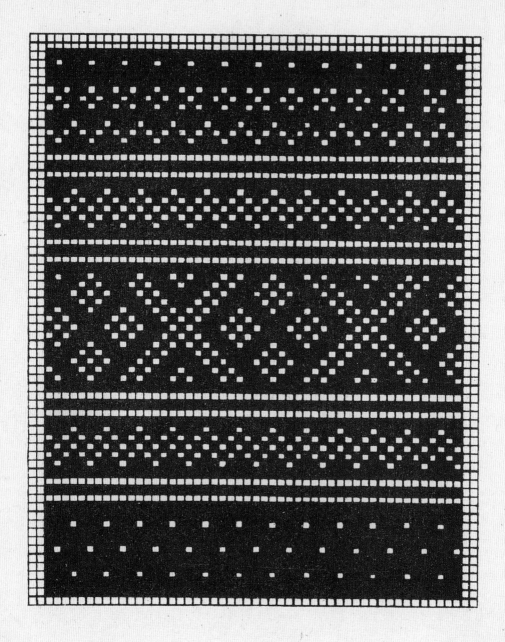

Fig. 36. Pattern chart for the accompanying fig. 37.

Fig. 37. LICE SWEATER (*LUSEKOFTE*) FROM SETESDALEN
See figs. 36, 38, and 39 for pattern charts.

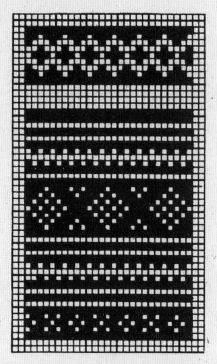

Fig. 38. Pattern chart for fig. 37.

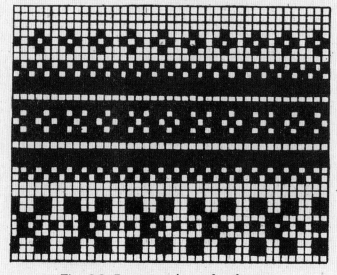

Fig. 39. Pattern chart for fig. 37.

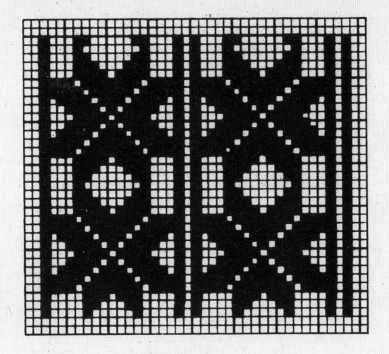

Fig. 40 DESIGN FROM HALLINGDAL
The pattern repeat is 18 stitches.

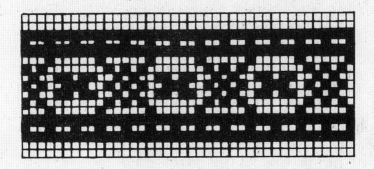

Fig. 41 BORDER DESIGN
The pattern repeat is 12 stitches.

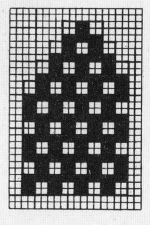

Fig. 42
MITTEN
FROM JÆREN

Fig. 43
STAR
FROM SELBU

The pattern repeat is 31 stitches.

Fig. 44
MOTIF
FROM SELBU

The pattern repeat is 29 stitches.

Fig. 45.
MITTEN FROM SELBU

Fig. 46. The thumb pattern for the Selbu mitten in fig. 45.

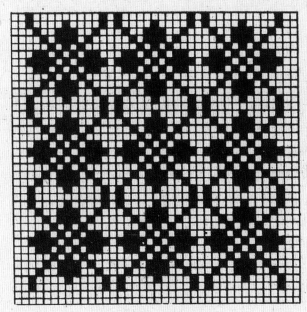

Fig. 47.
SCARF DESIGN
Knit to the desired length and attach fringe to the ends.

Fig. 48. Ornament used with the border below. It may be placed by a low-cut neck, or down by the border design.

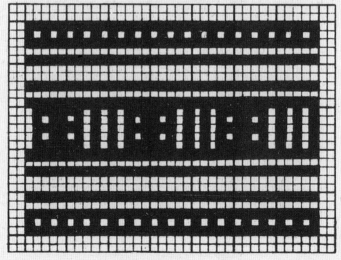

Fig. 49. BORDER DESIGN FOR A CHILDREN'S SWEATER
The pattern repeat is 11 stitches.

Fig. 50. BORDER
The pattern repeat is 20 stitches.

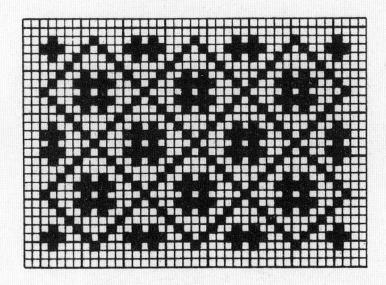

Fig. 51. BACKGROUND DESIGN
The pattern repeat is 12 stitches.

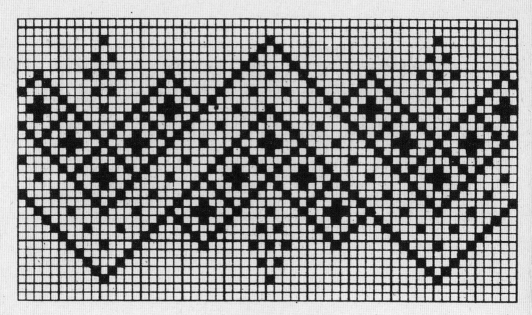

Fig. 52. BORDER
The pattern repeat is 40 stitches.

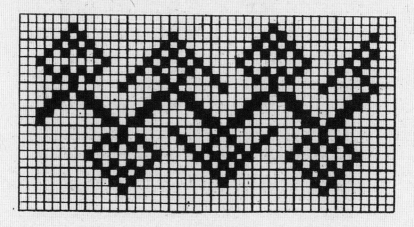

Fig. 53. BORDER
The pattern repeat is 24 stitches.

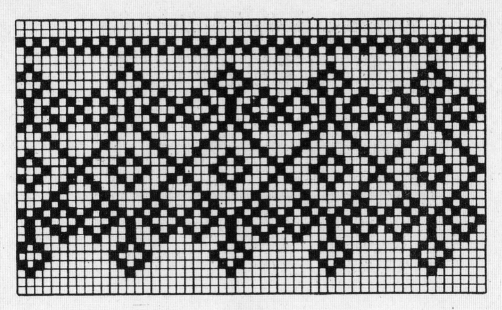

Fig. 54. BORDER
The pattern repeat is 12 stitches.

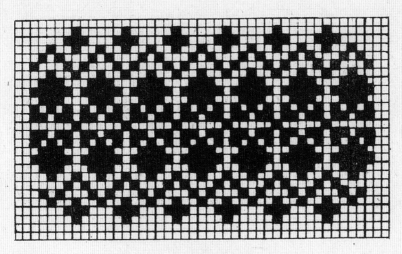

Fig. 55. BORDER

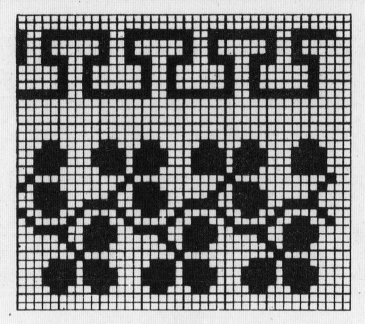

Fig. 56. DESIGN FROM NORDENFJELSKE
Originally worked in white on a red background.
The pattern repeat is 12 stitches.

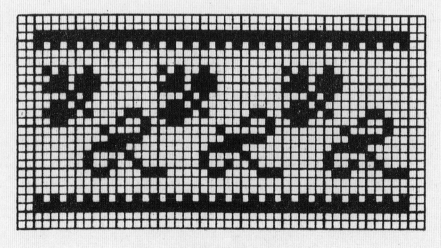

Fig. 57. SELBU BORDER
The pattern repeat is 15 stitches.

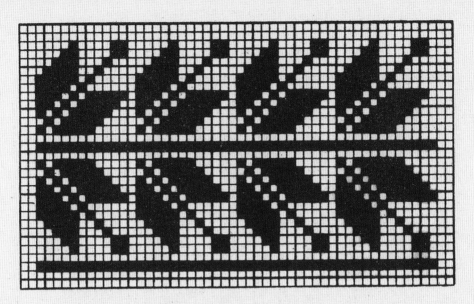

Fig. 58. HALLING BORDER
The pattern repeat is 11 stitches.

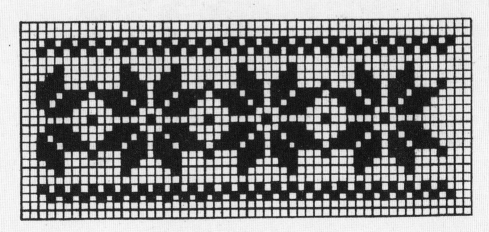

Fig. 59. SELBU STAR BORDER
The pattern repeat is 14 stitches.

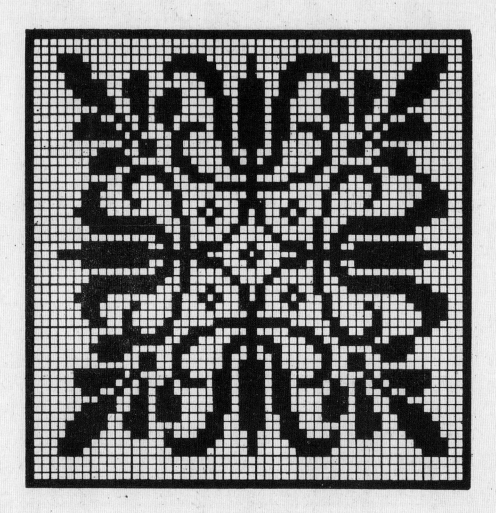

Fig. 60. ORNAMENT
The pattern repeat is 54 stitches.

Fig. 61. HALLINGDAL MITTEN
Back of the hand and background pattern (see fig. 77).

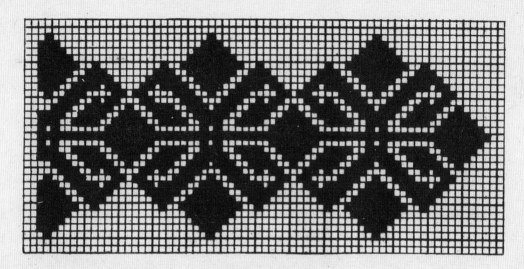

Fig. 62. BORDER
The pattern repeat is 24 stitches.

Fig. 63. BORDER
The pattern repeat is 27 stitches.

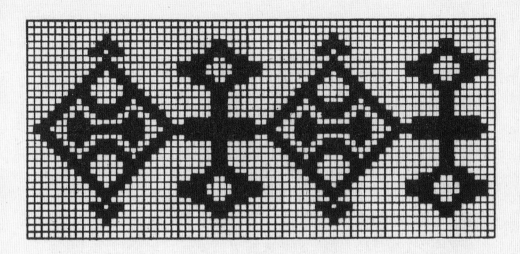

Fig. 64. BORDER
The pattern repeat is 33 stitches.

Fig. 65. BORDER
The pattern repeat is 14 stitches.

Fig. 66. ORNAMENT
The pattern repeat is 52 stitches.

Fig. 67
BORDER

Fig. 68
SELBU STAR

The pattern repeat for fig. 67 is 31 stitches.
The pattern repeat for fig. 68 is 32 stitches.

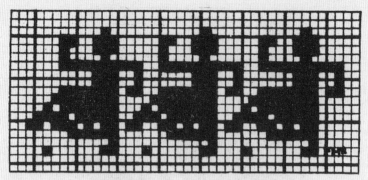

Fig. 69. SIMPLE KJERRING BORDER

Fig. 70. DANCE BORDER

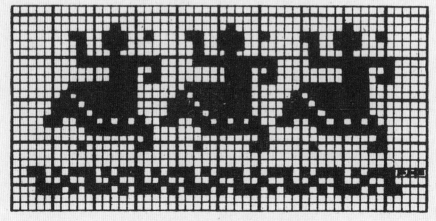

Fig. 71. KJERRING BORDER

Fig. 72.

Fig. 73.

HALLINGDAL MITTENS
The cuffs shown are worked in k2, p2 ribbing, before
knitting begins in color pattern.

Fig. 74.
HALLINGDAL MITTEN
The cuff shown is
worked in k2, p2 ribbing,
before knitting begins in
color pattern.

Fig. 75.
GAMMEL STOCKING
The cuff shown is worked with a few
alternating rounds of knit and purl, and
then a fairly long knit section, before
knitting begins in color pattern.

Fig. 76.
HALLINGDAL MITTEN
The cuff shown is worked in k2,
p2 ribbing: 5 rounds in white, two
rounds in black, repeated until
there are 5 black stripes total.

Fig. 77.
HALLINGDAL MITTEN
The cuff shown is worked in k2,
p2 ribbing, to the desired length.